P9-ARK-033

Business and Industry

EDITORS

William R. Childs
Scott B. Martin
Wanda Stitt-Gohdes

VOLUME 1

ACCOUNTING AND BOOKKEEPING to BURNETT, LEO

MARSHALL CAVENDISH
NEW YORK • TORONTO • LONDON • SYDNEY

Marshall Cavendish
99 White Plains Road
Tarrytown, New York 10591-9001

www.marshallcavendish.com

Library of Congress Cataloging-in-Publication Data

Business and industry / editors, William R. Childs, Scott B. Martin, Wanda Stitt-Gohdes.
p. cm.
Includes bibliographical reference and index.
Contents: v. 1. Accounting and Bookkeeping to Burnett, Leo--v. 2. Business Cycles to Copyright--v. 3. Corporate Governance to Entrepreneurship--v. 4. Environmentalism to Graham, Katharine--v. 5. Great Depression to Internship--v. 6. Inventory to Merrill Lynch--v. 7. Microeconomics to Philip Morris Companies--v. 8. Price Controls to Sarnoff, David--v. 9. Savings and Investment Options to Telecommuting--v. 10. Temporary Workers to Yamaha--v. 11. Index volume
ISBN 0-7614-7430-7 (set)--ISBN 0-7614-7431-5 (v. 1)
1. Business--Encyclopedias. 2. Industries--Encyclopedias. I. Childs, William R., 1951-II. Martin, Scott B., 1961-III. Stitt-Gohdes, Wanda.

HF1001 .B796 2003
338'.003--dc21 2002035156

Printed in Italy

06 05 04 03 5 4 3 2 1

MARSHALL CAVENDISH
Editorial Director Paul Bernabeo
Production Manager Alan Tsai

Produced by The Moschovitis Group, Inc.

THE MOSCHOVITIS GROUP
President, Publishing Division Valerie Tomaselli
Executive Editor Hilary W. Poole
Associate Editor Sonja Matanovic
Design and Layout Annemarie Redmond
Illustrator Richard Garratt
Assistant Illustrator Zahiyya Abdul-Karim
Photo Research Gillian Speeth
Production Associates K. Nura Abdul-Karim, Rashida Allen
Editorial Assistants Christina Campbell, Nicole Cohen, Jessica Rosin
Copyediting Carole Campbell
Proofreading Paul Scaramazza
Indexing AEIOU, Inc.

Directory of Editors and Contributors

Editors

William R. Childs
Ohio State University

Scott B. Martin
Columbia University

Wanda Stitt-Gohdes
University of Georgia

Editorial Consultants

Judith Olson-Sutton
Madison Area Technical College

Don Wentworth
Pacific Lutheran University

Contributors

Carol Ann Alaimo
Arizona Daily Star

Peter Alles
National Fluid Power Association

Richard Alm
Dallas Morning News

Curt Anderson
University of Minnesota–Duluth

Karen Ayres
Freelance writer

Gary Baughn
Waukesha South High School, Wisconsin

Jonathan Bean
Southern Illinois University

Lynne Bernstein
Freelance writer

Michael Bernstein
Benetar, Bernstein, Schair, and Stein

Karen Boehme
National Fluid Power Association

Scarlet Bolden
Wilmington College

Robert Bradley
Institute for Energy Research

J. Isaac Brannon
Office of Management and Budget

Stephen Buckles
Vanderbilt University

Stephanie Buckwalter
Freelance writer

Douglas Bradshaw Bynum
University of North Carolina–Chapel Hill

Jean Caldwell
Freelance writer

Christina Campbell
Freelance writer

Kay J. Carr
Southern Illinois University

Barbara Coyner
Freelance writer

Thomas H. Davies
Carpenter Bros., Inc.

Denise Davis
Freelance writer

Dawn Dicker
Freelance writer

Will Drago
University of Wisconsin–Whitewater

Karen Ehrle
University of Wisconsin–Milwaukee

John D. Emory, Jr.
Emory Business Valuation, LLC

Walter C. Farrell, Jr.
University of North Carolina–Chapel Hill

Don Fersh
Freelance writer

Ken Friedman
Norwegian School of Management, Sandvika

Barbara Gerber
Freelance writer

Donald W. Gribben
Southern Illinois University

Peter Grosvenor
Pacific Lutheran University

Joseph Gustaitis
Freelance writer

Carl Haacke
Skylight Consulting

Stephen Haessler
Marquette University High School

Alexander Halavais
State University of New York–Buffalo

Guilbert C. Hentschke
University of Southern California

Bradley Hobbs
Florida Gulf Coast University

Tracy Hofer
University of Wisconsin–Stevens Point

Blake Hurst
Hurst Greenery

John Keckhaver
University of Wisconsin–Madison

Reneé Sartin Kirby
University of Wisconsin–Parkside

Andréa Korb
Union High School, New Jersey

David Korb
Ernst & Young, LLP

Mikhail Kouliavtsev
Temple University

Beth Kraig
Pacific Lutheran University

William Kritek
University of Wisconsin–Milwaukee

Anil Kumar
Central Michigan University

Angeline M. Lavin
University of South Dakota

Marilyn Lavin
University of Wisconsin–Whitewater

David Long
International Baccalaureate Program
Rufus King High School, Wisconsin

Rich MacDonald
St. Cloud State University

Lisa Magloff
Freelance writer

David Mason
Young Harris College

Rich McHugh
Freelance writer

Mary Ann McLennon
Freelance writer

Donna Ozolins Miller
Freelance writer

Andrew Morriss
Case Western Reserve University School of Law

Alan Murray
Wall Street Journal

Samuel L. Myers, Jr.
Humphrey Institute, University of Minnesota

Theresa Gavin Overbey
Freelance writer

Carl Pacini
Florida Gulf Coast University

Donna Pasternak
University of Wisconsin–Milwaukee

Ty Priest
History International, LLC

Sheri Rehwoldt
Freelance writer

Peter K. Reinhart
Freelance editor

John Riddle
Freelance writer

Russell Roberts
Washington University

Solveig Robinson
Pacific Lutheran University

Michael Schlappi
Marquette University

Mark Schug
University of Wisconsin–Milwaukee

G. Edward Schuh
University of Minnesota

James K. Self
Indiana University–Bloomington

Jane Shaw
Political Economy Research Center

Mary Sisson
Crain's New York Business

Lois Smith
University of Wisconsin–Whitewater

Dean Starkman
Wall Street Journal

Colleen Sullivan
Freelance writer

William Z. Tan
Transcendent International

Andrea Troyer
University of California–Irvine

John Troyer
Carlson School of Management
University of Minnesota

Connie Tuttle
Freelance writer

Phillip J. VanFossen
Purdue University

Randall Waldron
University of South Dakota

John Washbush
University of Wisconsin–Whitewater

Shelton Weeks
Florida Gulf Coast University

Donald R. Wentworth
Pacific Lutheran University

David Wessel
Wall Street Journal

John Western
Administrative Resource Options

Linda Western
National Fluid Power Association

Chris Woodford
Freelance writer

McGee Young
University of South Florida

Alphabetical Table of Contents

Volume 5

Volume 6

Volume 7

Volume 8

Volume 9

Volume 10

Thematic Outline of Contents

This outline organizes the encyclopedia articles into the following nine categories:

Finance

Labor

Economic Concepts

Law and Public Policy

Institutions and Associations

Industrial and Economic Sectors

Company Profiles

Biographies

Introduction

Business and industry affect people's lives every day, whether they are directly aware of the influences or not. The creation of one piece of clothing, for one example, involves exchanges within several industries, including agriculture (growing cotton, raising sheep for wool), manufacturing (spinning the cotton into thread, weaving the thread into cloth, tailoring the cloth into suits and dresses), advertising (in magazines and on television), distribution (on ships and trucks), and retail (in department stores or through catalogs).

Money is exchanged at every step—from banks lending funds to farmers, manufacturers, and retail establishments, to companies issuing paychecks and credit card companies financing purchases. Technology undergirds the process as well; new technologies increase the efficiency of firms, from improving agricultural output to creating manufacturing techniques that increase quality and efficiency to more efficient distribution methods.

Governments also have important roles to play in the commercial process; in the United States the legal system has been structured deliberately to encourage business and industry. Furthermore, producers and consumers frequently pay tax on goods and services, for example, property, sales, and income taxes, that help build and maintain transport networks over which raw materials and finished products move, and that help educate workers and managers who create the products and the salespeople who sell them. Taxes also pay for government agencies that protect against dangerous, unfair, or illegal trade practices.

Business and industry have existed for thousands of years. Most of the topics in this encyclopedia, however, focus on the last two centuries of economic development, with a primary—but not exclusive—focus on the United States. As such, the articles in this work collectively present an overview of how capitalism works. Capitalism is a form of market-based economics that is in some ways similar to but in many more ways different from competing economic systems like mercantilism, socialism, and communism (which are all also covered in this work).

Individuals have been important to the evolution of capitalism, accordingly, this encyclopedia includes entries on people—entrepreneurs, managers, workers, consumers—living and working within the range of organizations that make up industries and markets, including: business firms, banks, stock markets, unions, and schools. Although no reference work could include every person who has been important to the history of business and industry, the 60 or so people profiled here represent a wide variety of enterprises and perspectives, from classic entrepreneurs like Henry Ford to contemporary business leaders like venture capitalist Jim Clark. This work also covers economists such as Adam Smith and John Maynard Keynes, as well as critics of capitalism like Karl Marx and critics of industry like Ralph Nader. Not everyone sets out deliberately to be a businessperson, and we have attempted to cover some of the more unusual paths to business success, those taken by Oprah Winfrey and Jim Henson, for example. Labor leaders like A. Philip Randolph and Cesar Chavez are also included, as are mold-breaking women such as makeup entrepreneur Mary Kay Ash and eBay CEO Margaret Whitman.

Many entries in this encyclopedia focus on individual companies and industries. The editors selected a heterogeneous group designed to represent as many business sectors as possible. This encyclopedia contains entries on small-scale firms (Ben & Jerry's Homemade) and enormous multinationals (Coca-Cola) as well as manufacturing firms (General Motors) and service firms (Southwest Airlines). Standard-bearers of the old economy, for example, General Electric, are represented, as are new economy firms like Internet portal Yahoo!

The editors hope that readers will not only learn about business and industry by becoming familiar with the histories of particular companies and the men and women who created and run them but will be inspired to participate in business and industry themselves. To that end, many entries discuss how a company operates; these include articles on accounting and bookkeeping, advertising, downsizing, management theory, overhead, and partnerships, among others. The editors have also endeavored to reflect ongoing concerns about the relationship of industry to society, with substantive articles on corporate governance, business ethics, and corporate social responsibility. Students of business and industry, as well as business managers, often study topics related to economic thought to help them understand the evolution of capitalism. Such topics covered in this work include comparative advantage, competition, division of labor, economies of scale, macroeconomics and microeconomics, overhead, profit and loss, and recession.

Other entries focus on workers—those who craft the products or deliver services. Management–labor relations are a key aspect of any business, and to reflect this importance, the encyclopedia includes entries on unions, union leaders, and labor-related legislation. Additional entries relating to workers cover child labor, collective bargaining, equal employment opportunity, pay equity, sexual harassment, and working conditions.

A large number of entries focus on business and government relationships. The following partial list of topics indicates the pervasiveness of government involvement in business and industry that is reflected in the encyclopedia: bankruptcy, Better Business Bureau, deregulation, federal budget, fiscal and monetary policies, minimum wage, monetary policy, Securities and Exchange Commission, and taxation. Other entries are devoted to key pieces of legislation, including the Americans with Disabilities Act and the National Labor Relations Act.

The increasingly global nature of business and industry has also not been overlooked. Non-U.S. firms like British Airways and Volkswagen are included as are many U.S.-based multinationals. The encyclopedia also features entries on globalization and some of the agreements and organizations that have supported and resulted from it, including the General Agreement on Tariffs and Trade, the International Monetary Fund, and the World Trade Organization.

The impact of technology on industry should not be underestimated. Entries that reflect its importance in the history of business include genetic engineering, the Internet, reverse engineering, and telecommuting. Technology companies are also well represented—Cisco, IBM, Intel, and Microsoft, to name a few.

How to Use This Encyclopedia

Most articles in this encyclopedia touch on more than one theme. For example, the entry "Corporate Governance" relates not only to how a firm functions but also to the place of business in society and to business–government relations. "Assembly Line" embraces firm management, technology, and labor relations. Cross-references are included with each article to guide readers to related entries. Readers are also encouraged to make use of the Thematic Outline of Contents in Volume 1, which is an excellent tool for locating specific material within broad areas of interest. The indexes, which are included at the back of each volume and, in greater detail, in Volume 11, will help the researcher locate material on specific topics.

Every entry contains suggestions for further reading; Volume 11 amplifies these suggestions with an extensive, thematically organized bibliography and a separate section on resources available on the World Wide Web. Volume 11 also features general statistical information on topics like employment and contains extensive excerpts of important laws described within entries in the body of the encyclopedia.

Many articles include special features like quotes from important figures and text extracts of relevant documents. Other articles include sidebars highlighting particularly interesting aspects of the topic, for example, a sidebar on sustainable industrial design accompanies "Environmentalism." The entry on the AFL-CIO features a short biography of union leader John Lewis, while "Cultural Difference" features a sidebar on the tragedy caused by cultural insensitivity in the marketing of baby formula in Africa. Entries on business sectors all contain short sidebars about careers; for example, "Sports Industry" suggests career options for sports fans who are not athletic superstars, while the "Agriculture Industry" sidebar explains that agriculture involves more than riding a plow. The names of the authors of sidebars are listed in the sidebar only when the author of the sidebar differs from the author of the article.

—*William Ralph Childs*

PHOTO CREDITS:

Asian Development Bank (file photos): 78, 80
Associated Press: 28, 37, 42, 49, 50, 53, 55, 56, 71, 72, 77, 79, 95, 102, 113, 115, 126
Corbis: AFP/CORBIS 65, 105; Bettmann/CORBIS 35, 39, 40, 51, 67, 112; John B. Boykin/CORBIS 135; Duomo/CORBIS 117; Brownie Harris/CORBIS 85; John Henley/CORBIS 32; Hulton-Deutsch Collection/CORBIS 87; Howard Jacqueline/Corbis Sygma 30; Lester Lefkowitz/CORBIS 104; Lawrence Manning/CORBIS 90; Richard T. Nowitz/CORBIS 107; Jose Luis Pelaez, Inc./CORBIS 130; Reuters NewMedia Inc./CORBIS 95, 122, 123; Tony Roberts/CORBIS 92; Charles E. Rotkin/CORBIS 88; Royalty-Free/CORBIS 131; Chuck Savage/CORBIS 116; Richard Hamilton Smith/CORBIS 46, 82; Joseph Sohm, ChromoSohm Inc./CORBIS 48; Vince Streano/CORBIS 110; Bill Varie/CORBIS 119; Tom Wagner/CORBIS SABA 118; Keith Wood/CORBIS 83
Getty Creative: 137
Hulton Getty: 26, 68, 125
Leo Burnett Company: 140
Library of Congress: 23, 31, 38, 43, 81
Mary Kay, Inc.: 76
Walt Disney/Photofest: 75

Accounting and Bookkeeping

Businesses use accounting and bookkeeping to identify, measure, record, and communicate information about their financial activities. Information provided through accounting and bookkeeping helps people—those working within a firm and those with whom the firm does business—make informed decisions about business operations and strategy.

Accounting as it is practiced today can be described as a cycle including the following steps:

1. Collect data.
2. Analyze data.
3. Enter data into journals.
4. Post to ledger accounts.
5. Prepare a trial balance.
6. Calculate adjustments and record adjusting entries.
7. Prepare adjusted trial balance.
8. Compile financial statements.
9. Close appropriate accounts and prepare post-closing trial balance.

In this cycle, the first five steps fall into the realm of bookkeeping; the final four steps, into accounting.

Bookkeeping Functions

For as long as people have been engaged in commerce or trade, they have needed to do some form of bookkeeping. Before computers, records of business transactions were kept in journals or books (hence the term bookkeeping). Although the term has evolved to reflect technological advances (such data recording is now often referred to as record keeping or data processing), its purpose has remained the same: to document and preserve information about financial activity, thus providing information to be used in financial decision making.

Bookkeeping begins with a collection of data. Many events affect a business every day; however, only those activities that affect it financially qualify as sources of data for bookkeeping. Such activities are called transactions. Examples of transactions include purchases or sale of inventory or equipment, loans taken out or paid, and payment of employees' salaries. Documentation is gathered representing these transactions in the form of receipts, bank statements, invoices, and so on. Activities that cannot be documented in dollar amounts, such as the hiring and training of new employees or a competitor lowering its prices, do not qualify as transactions, even though they do affect the business.

After data are collected, they must be analyzed. The analysis involves business accounts in five main categories: assets, liabilities, owner's equity, revenue, and expenses. Revenue and expenses are considered part of owner's equity. The amount of money in each category, or the balance of each account, is recorded on an ongoing basis, and an analysis is done to determine the effect of each transaction on the accounts. For example, if a business uses $500 cash to purchase goods to sell, the analysis would show that, as the bill was paid in cash, the amount of cash (an asset) held by the business has decreased by $500. At the same time, the business gained goods to sell, increasing the amount of inventory (also an asset) by $500.

Once data are collected and analyzed, they must be recorded, or entered, in a journal. This is the third step of the

See also:
Amortization and Depreciation; Assets and Liabilities; Balance Sheet; Capital; Income Statement.

In 1943, an accountant totals the returns at the seed dealers, W. Atlee Burpee Company in Philadelphia.

accounting cycle. This third step reflects the basic accounting equation:

Assets = Liabilities + Owner's Equity

Every transaction is entered chronologically into a journal using the double-entry accounting system. This system reflects the fact that every transaction affects two accounts, which keeps the accounting equation balanced. For example, one entry can increase assets and another entry can decrease assets by the same amount; or assets can be increased and liabilities can be increased by the same amount. Both examples preserve the accounting equation.

Activity in each of the three types of account of the basic accounting equation is divided into debits and credits, representing increases and decreases. A debit is an increase in an asset account or a decrease in a liability or equity account. A credit is the opposite—a decrease in an asset account or an increase in a liability or equity account. Each transaction, following the double-entry accounting system, is entered twice: in one account as a debit, and in another as a credit.

Steps in bookkeeping: (1) collecting data; (2) analyzing data; (3) entering data into journals; (4) posting to ledger accounts; and (5) preparing a trial balance.

Because the basic accounting equation must balance, the debit and credit for each transaction must be equal. If a business purchases supplies for $500 cash, a journal entry is made as a debit on the inventory account and a credit on the cash account, both in the amount of $500.

Once a transaction is recorded in the journal, it is transferred into the company's ledgers. This process, called posting, is the fourth step in the accounting cycle. A company typically uses a general ledger and a subledger. The general ledger shows each debit and credit from the journal—listed for each account on a single page of a book, with debits appearing on the left and credits on the right. The general ledger is usually maintained by computer; a subledger is maintained if more detail is required for a specific account than the general ledger provides.

The final bookkeeping responsibility, preparing a trial balance, is typically done every month. The trial balance is a report summarizing the general ledger; it lists all accounts in the general ledger with their corresponding

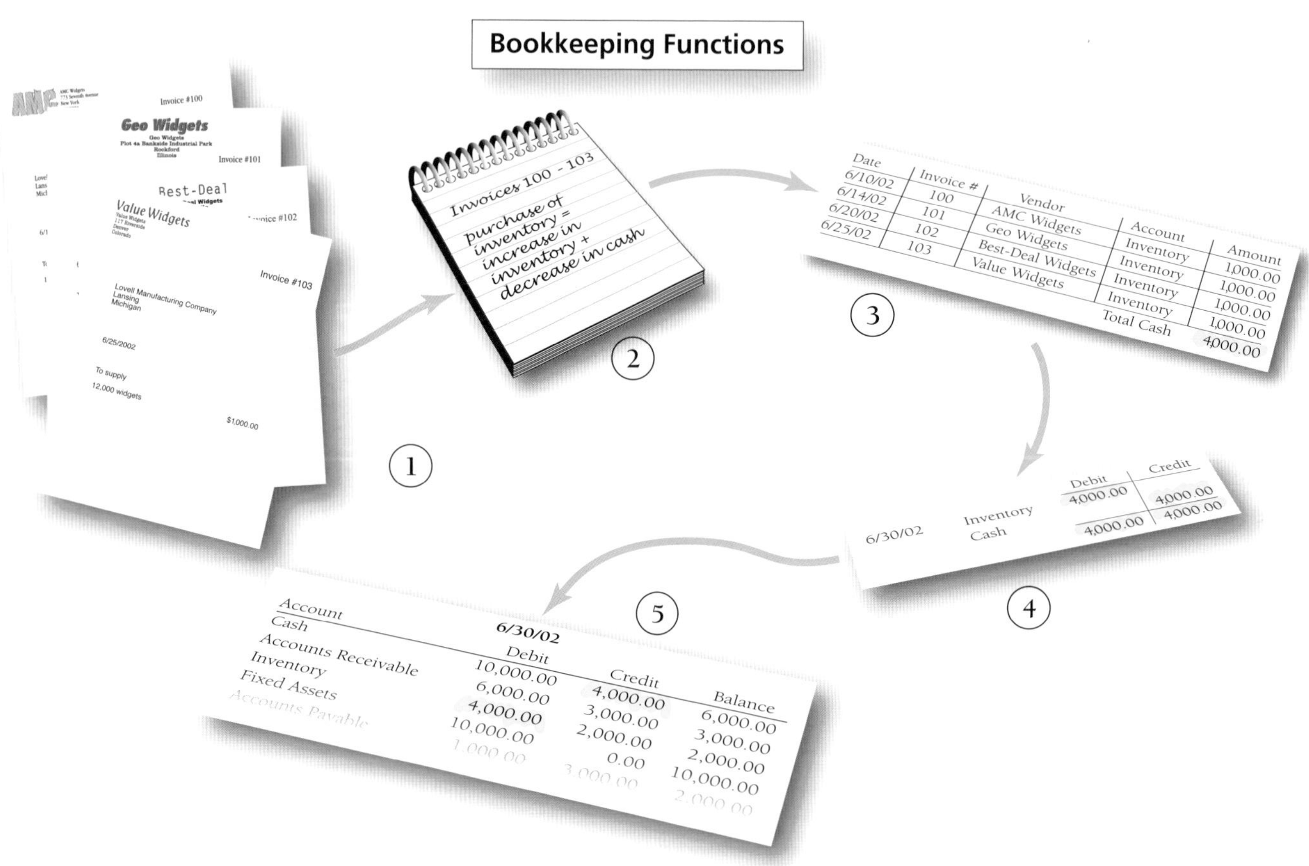

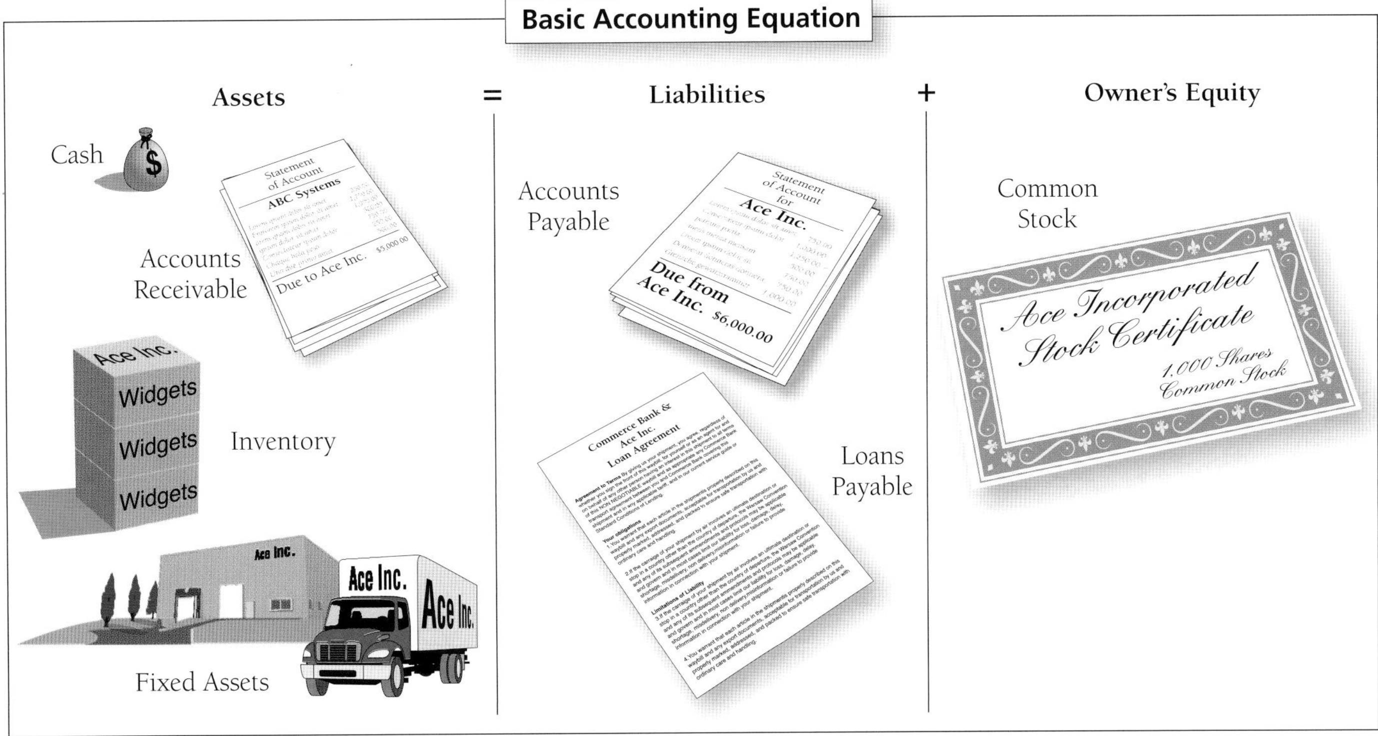

The basic accounting equation.

debit or credit balances, as well as the total amount of debits and credits. The trial balance is critical because it ensures that journal entries have been posted correctly. The total dollar debit amount must equal the total dollar credit amount; if it does not, the bookkeeper must go back through the previous four steps in the accounting cycle to find where the error was made. Once the trial balance is correct, the bookkeeper's work is done.

Accounting Functions

The general purpose of accounting is to use the bookkeeper's data to create reports that can be used internally (management reporting) and externally (financial reporting). Management reporting provides members of the company's management with information to help them understand the company's performance and to make decisions for improving it. Financial reporting enables people outside the company to understand how well or poorly the company is operating. To successfully create these reports, the accountant must complete the final four steps of the accounting cycle.

The accounting functions begin with the completed trial balance. Although the trial balance summarizes the important financial transactions that have taken place, it does not include other information such as interest earned but not yet received or prepaid expenses not yet recorded by bookkeepers that may have a significant economic impact on the company. Economic events like these must be calculated and adjusted in the sixth step of the accounting cycle.

After all adjusting entries are made, the accountant must prepare the adjusted trial balance. The adjusted trial balance is the same as the trial balance produced in the bookkeeping process, but it includes all of the accountant's adjusting entries. Again, the total dollar amounts of the debits and credits must be equal; if they are not, the accountant must review the adjusting entries for errors and correct them.

Once the adjusted trial balance is established, it can be used in the creation of financial statements, which is the eighth step of the accounting cycle. Four primary financial statements are used to convey account information: the income statement, statement of changes in retained earnings, balance sheet, and cash flow statement.

Computers play a key role in accounting.

Income Statement. The income statement reports the profitability of the company for a specific period. It uses all of the revenue and expense accounts from the trial balance and summarizes them. For example, the company may have many expense accounts, but on the income statement they are reported on one line called "Other Expenses." The result is a net income figure (revenues minus expenses).

Statement of Changes in Retained Earnings. This report shows all transactions that affect retained earnings during the period. The report is created using the previous period's retained earnings, the net income from the income statement, and anything that decreases the retained earnings. The result is the current period's retained earnings.

Balance Sheet. The balance sheet shows the company's financial position at a single point in time. It uses all asset and liability accounts from the trial balance and summarizes them. For example, a company may have one account for office supplies, another account for cleaning products, and so on. These accounts may be reported in one line item called "Other Assets." The goal is to summarize the company's financial position clearly so people inside and outside the company can make informed decisions.

Cash Flow Statement. The cash flow statement summarizes the inflows and outflows of cash during a given period. The report is typically broken out into cash flows from operating activities, investing activities, and financing activities. The cash balance at the beginning of the period plus or minus the cash flows from these three activities equals the current cash balance in the trial balance and on the balance sheet.

When the financial statements are completed, the accountant must close the appropriate accounts and prepare the post-closing trial balance. This is the final step in the accounting cycle. Revenue and expense accounts are not cumulated over time. In each accounting period, revenues and expenses must start at zero to correctly generate the income statement for the next period. Therefore, the accountant must enter reversing entries to transfer revenue and expense account balances into owner's equity. For example, if interest expense had a debit balance of $500, an entry to credit interest expense and debit owner's equity must be made. Once all closing balances are made, a post-closing trial balance is generated to ensure that the debits still equal the credits.

In the same way that individuals need money to survive, so does every business organization. From local schools and hospitals to the largest, richest corporations, all institutions base their daily decisions on their financial status. Can they afford to buy the new equipment they need? Will a decline in revenue force them to lay off employees? The decisions institutions make determine their success, and accounting and bookkeeping inform those decisions.

Further Reading

Godin, Seth, and Paul Lim. *If You're Clueless about Accounting and Finance and Want to Know More.* Chicago: Dearborn Financial Publishing, 1998.

Jacquet, Jay L., and William C. Miller, Jr. *The Accounting Cycle: A Practical Guide to Accounting Basics.* Menlo Park, Calif.: Crisp Publications, 1992.

Mullis, Darrell, and Judith Handler Orloff. *The Accounting Game: Basic Accounting Fresh from the Lemonade Stand.* Naperville, Ill.: Sourcebooks Trade, 1998.

Tracy, John A. *Accounting for Dummies.* Hoboken, N.J.: John Wiley & Sons, 2001.

—*Andréa Korb and David Korb*

Advertising, Business Practice

See also:
Advertising Industry; Demographics; Market Research; Public Relations and Marketing, Business Practice.

Every business with a product or service to sell uses advertising in one form or another. The purpose of advertising is twofold: first, to create awareness of the company's product in the mind of the consumer, and second, to create desire to possess that product. To accomplish these purposes, companies place advertisements in various media: newspapers and magazines, radio, television, and the Internet. Advertising can also take the form of direct mailings, billboards, promotional giveaways, and contests. This article will examine the reasons why companies advertise and how ads are made.

Why Advertise?

Advertising is one of the most necessary components of any business plan. When a new product is released into the marketplace, advertising alerts consumers who might find the product useful. Truly innovative advertising often attempts to persuade consumers that a product serves a need they were not aware they had. For instance, in the 1920s Listerine mouthwash was advertised as a method of getting rid of halitosis, an obscure medical term for bad breath. Before Listerine, bad breath was not considered socially unacceptable; today, hundreds of products—mints, sprays, gums, mouthwashes, and toothpastes—advertise their ability to cure this advertising-created social problem.

Once a product is established in the marketplace, advertising can be used to improve sales by increasing market share—the percent of total dollars spent on one kind of product that is received by a specific company. Increasing a company's market share necessarily decreases the market share of its competitors. Advertising designed to increase market share often highlights an advantage of the company's product over its competitors or exposes a disadvantage of the competitor's product.

Another purpose of advertising is customer retention—keeping the company's customers loyal to a company's product. This may include highlighting the advantages of the company's product but may also include direct mailings and special offers or discounts on the company's future products.

How an Ad Campaign Is Planned

The first question of an advertising agency or department in planning a campaign is: "What is to be accomplished?" Does the client want to create awareness of its product? Increase market share? Retain customers? Some or all of these goals? Which is most important? Once the purpose of the campaign is known, these goals are translated into concrete sales goals through market research.

The second question an ad agency often asks its client is: "What is your budget?" A large multinational corporation may be able to allocate hundreds of millions of dollars to its advertising campaigns; a local business or regional chain may only have thousands.

Market research has evolved to help advertisers find out as much as possible about their audiences. The agency uses market research to discover the product's demographics, psychographics, and geographics. Demographics are the external

Subliminal Advertising

How much impact does advertising have on our minds without our even realizing it? The average individual sees dozens, even hundreds, of ads a day; yet when a national advertising survey asked consumers what the most memorable ads were they had seen in the past year, 40 percent of respondents could not recall one.

Advertisers have long realized that much of advertising's effect is unconscious. Researchers attempted to take advantage of this fact through subliminal advertising, including ads inserted into a single frame of a feature film or played at low volume underneath music in a store. The hope was that the viewer would absorb the message without ever realizing he had seen or heard an ad. After a 1957 experiment in which subliminal advertising seemed to increase movie concession stand sales, hundreds of retailers adopted the practice.

Many consumers were distressed, fearing that this powerful new technique could be abused. In 1974, the Federal Communications Commission banned all forms of subliminal advertising from the airwaves. Unnoticed in the controversy was the fact that the researcher involved in the 1957 experiment confessed to falsifying the results. No subsequent studies have been able to reproduce the effect.

qualities of the product's buyers—age, gender, income, and so on. Psychographics are the buyers' personalities and attitudes—are they adventurous? Conservative? Sentimental? Sarcastic? Geographics are the consumers' location—does the product sell better in the South or the Northeast?

Once these qualities are determined, the advertisers begin the creative work of the campaign, designing ads that will appeal to the target consumers. Ads can be humorous or hip, classy or crude, reassuring or radical, depending on whom the client hopes to reach. Advertising professionals may suggest to their clients using slogans or jingles ("Good to the last drop"), hiring a celebrity spokesperson (Derek Jeter for Gatorade), or creating a distinctive icon or logo to embody the product (Aunt Jemima, the Nike swoosh).

Humor is a key tool in advertising, as in this ad for the Washington Cherry Growers, which associates their product with the famous smile of the Mona Lisa.

Advertisers strive to establish a unique selling position (USP) for their product—a claim or quality associated with that product and none other. The USP need not be a quality that is actually unique to that product. Presumably, all kinds of soda are refreshing, but if one particular brand of soda is able to establish a USP as "the Refresher," competitors will be reluctant to use the word "refreshing" in campaigns for fear of confusing consumers.

Once the style and target of the campaign have been decided upon, the advertiser decides on the form of media that the campaign will use. Budget is often a big factor in this decision—most small businesses simply cannot afford to buy advertising time during prime-time network television, for instance—but the campaign's targets and goals are equally important. If an advertiser desires to create widespread awareness of a product, he or she will likely choose media that offer the largest and most varied audiences, such as newspapers, network television, or highway billboards. If the product has appeal for only a small segment of the population, the advertiser may choose a magazine read solely by that group (Clearasil in *Seventeen*) or a cable television station with specialized programming (gourmet coffee on *The Food Network*). As most forms of media rely on advertising income for support, magazines, newspapers, radio, and television stations often conduct market research to help attract advertisers who want to reach a certain demographic. Advertisers working with a limited budget may attempt more specialized and varied appeals for their messages, such as direct mailings, promotional giveaways, or local ads.

Effect of Advertising on the Consumer

Good advertising seeks to carve out a niche in the public mind so that when consumers prepare to act on a need, they recall the company's product. Good advertising must be as memorable as it is persuasive. In the first half of the twentieth century, for instance, many advertisers relied upon jingles, that is, ad copy set to music. Advertising jingles often linger far longer than printed or spoken words. People can recall jingles long after the products they advertised have been taken off the market or switched to new slogans.

One of the most important concepts in modern advertising is the idea of the brand, that is, the qualities associated with a particular product in the mind of the consumer. Symbols like the product's logo or mascot, combined with the reputation of its manufacturer and customers, work to help create a brand's image. Companies attempt to manipulate their brands to attract different consumers. For instance, a car company selling minivans to families might design its ads to emphasize qualities like safety, reliability, convenience, and flexibility. In contrast, a company selling cars to young, single, first-time buyers might choose to emphasize speed, adventure, and stylishness.

Successful cultivation of a brand can create brand loyalty, establishing a preference for a particular product over its competitors in the mind of the consumer. Brand loyalty is a valuable asset for any company; if brand loyalty is strong, consumers will often choose to pay more for a familiar product rather than buy a near-identical product unknown to them. The ingredients in and effects of Bayer aspirin and drugstore-brand aspirin are precisely the same, yet consumers often choose the more expensive Bayer over its generic competitors.

Judging the effectiveness of advertising campaigns upon the consumer can be difficult. Factors other than advertising can cause the sales of a product to increase or decrease—if the economy as a whole is doing poorly, sales of luxury goods usually decrease regardless of how well targeted and persuasive the ad campaigns are.

The Death of Commercials?

Coming soon to a living room near you: the end of television as we know it, in the form of a digital video recorder (DVR). Sold under such names as Tivo and Replay, DVRs are devices that may be attached to a television to record programs, much like a VCR. However, DVRs come with hard drives installed that hold 30 or more hours of programming—a week's worth of shows. Moreover, they can be easily programmed to record only the programs the viewer enjoys and to skip the commercials.

The prospect of commercial-free television is something advertisers and television executives have worried about since the invention of the VCR enabled viewers to fast-forward past advertisements. Advertising dollars are wasted if viewers are not watching the ads, and, without advertising dollars, the networks have no money to make shows. DVRs promise something more extreme—the total elimination of commercials. A consortium of media and advertising producers has sued DVR manufacturers, hoping that the courts will declare the ad-skipping feature an illegal infringement on their product. Should they lose the case—and many experts believe they will—it may change the nature of TV forever. Commercials may be replaced entirely by product placement (real products featured as part of the set, props, and plots of TV shows) or viewers might have to start paying a fee for every show they record.

Future of Advertising

The Internet represents a new frontier for advertising. It is a medium somewhat distinct from others because an Internet advertiser can expect an immediate and direct response to his or her ads—clicking on an Internet ad usually loads the advertiser's Web page, and the consumer may buy the product immediately. This advantage makes the Internet very appealing to advertisers. However, attention instantaneously won may be instantaneously lost as well. Internet advertisers sometimes have difficulty determining whether their ads are effective. Methods of grabbing and holding the attention of Web surfers have grown ever more intrusive, with innovations such as the pop-up and pop-under ads drawing the ire of consumers.

As the number of ads and the prevalence of advertising have increased, consumers have become more and more inured to individual ads and their messages. As a result, advertising has grown ever more sophisticated, and its messages more subtle. Budweiser's "True" campaign featured the popular beer only incidentally,

Companies spend millions of dollars every year to get their products into films and movies; here a subtle plug for Dunkin' Donuts has been worked into the 2001 movie Anywhere but Here.

in the background of the action; instead of extolling the beer's qualities, the ads focus on humorous incidents whose moral centers around a "truth" about young men's attitude toward women or toward their friends. The campaign is meant primarily to entertain, while implying consumers who are amused by the ads have values in common with other Budweiser drinkers and would also enjoy Budweiser.

Such advertising, which revolves completely around establishing a favorable brand image in the mind of the consumer while ignoring entirely the qualities and purposes of the product itself, is likely to increase in the future. Combined with the trend toward product placement and other subtle forms of advertising in movies and television (even books—the 2001 romance novel *The Bulgari Connection* by Fay Weldon was sponsored by the diamond merchant Bulgari), the line between advertising and entertainment is likely to grow more and more blurred in the twenty-first century.

Further Reading

Aitchison, Jim. *Cutting Edge Advertising: How to Create the World's Best Print for Brands in the 21st Century.* New York: Prentice Hall, 1999.

Kupferman, Theodore R., ed. *Advertising and Commercial Speech.* Westport, Conn.: Meckler, 1990.

Lewis, Herschell Gordon, and Carol Nelson. *Advertising Age Handbook of Advertising.* Lincolnwood, Ill.: NTC Business Books, 1999.

Minsky, Laurence, and Emily Thornton Calvo. *How to Succeed in Advertising When All You Have Is Talent.* Lincolnwood, Ill.: NTC Business Books, 1994.

Percy, Larry, and Arch G. Woodside, eds. *Advertising and Consumer Psychology.* Lexington, Mass.: Lexington Books, 1983.

Tipper, Harry, ed. *Advertising: Its Principles and Practice.* New York: Garland Pub., 1986.

Twitchell, James B. *Twenty Ads That Shook the World.* New York: Crown Publishers, 2000.

—*Colleen Sullivan*

Advertising Industry

See also: Advertising, Business Practice; Demographics; Market Research.

The advertising industry is a multibillion-dollar operation that drives the public's perceptions about goods, services, and even social policies throughout the United States and abroad. Private companies, public programs, and even political candidates spend billions of dollars every year to convey a specific message to the public through a variety of media.

Industry experts define advertising very simply: It is a message designed to promote a product, an idea, or a service; the message can take a variety of forms and can appear in multiple ways. The industry is so massive that many people may not realize how much they are inundated with advertising in their daily lives.

Advertising most likely started in 3000 B.C.E., when the Babylonians began to use signs to promote their stores. Most people could not read, so merchants used symbols to advertise their wares; for example, a picture of food might advertise a market. In ancient Egypt, merchants hired town criers to travel city streets and yell information about incoming ships and cargo. The criers, who are better known for having conveyed the news in the same fashion, were commonplace in Europe by 900 C.E.

Advertising's key component was not available until 1440, when Johannes Gutenberg invented movable type in Germany. Eventually, the invention led to the first printed advertisements. The first newspaper advertisement on American soil appeared in a Boston newspaper in 1704. Magazines had adopted advertising by the 1800s.

Advertising agencies also started to evolve in the 1800s. During the late nineteenth century, most advertisements did little more than state the existence of the products they represented; the primary function of an advertising agency at the time was to place advertisements in various publications. Albert Lasker, often considered the father of modern advertising, introduced the idea that advertising copy should actively and imaginatively promote products rather than just politely inform readers of their existence. One of his most successful campaigns, mounted in the 1920s on behalf of the California Fruit Growers Exchange (later Sunkist, Inc.), promoted drinking orange juice as part of a healthful daily routine.

Radio stations offered a new avenue for advertisers in the 1920s, and the advertising industry boomed when television became commonplace in the 1950s. The advertising business has continued to expand in the twenty-first century as the number of media outlets has soared.

Some companies send their messages through the mail, a practice called direct

Albert Lasker's highly successful campaign for the California Fruit Growers Exchange emphasized nutrition information.

Advertising executives review a proposed campaign, 1999.

mail. Others display their company's name on large billboards that have proliferated along the nation's highways; meanwhile, transit advertising reaches millions of urban commuters through signs on trains and buses. However, the most popular means of conveying an advertising message is through the media: magazines, newspapers, television, and the Internet. On average, about 60 percent of a newspaper consists of advertising. The advertising industry entirely supports television and radio stations. Without the revenue from advertising, those stations would be forced to charge consumers for their services, as is done with ad-free cable television.

Advertisers aim to reach their target audience, the group of people they believe would be interested in their product or message. Extensive research is conducted about the personal and financial habits of the target audience. Stanley Resor, an advertiser in the early 1900s, was one of the first professionals to hire economists and statisticians to perform market research. Advertisers place advertisements in media they believe their target audience will see. For example, children's television shows feature commercials for children's toys, not retirement plans. Those in the industry must be constantly aware of new television and radio programs because they offer opportunities for specific advertising.

To be successful, an advertiser needs to carefully pick the type of message he or she wishes to send about a particular product and needs to convey it in a way that attracts the consumer. In short, an advertiser needs to create a brand image to show the product's personality. Advertisers also keep a close eye on their own industry to make sure their images are unique. Slogans are created with the intention of having a message remain in a consumer's mind. Fictional characters—for example, the popular Energizer bunny used in battery commercials—are developed to symbolize the product. Sometimes celebrities are hired to attest to the product's benefits; in the 1920s Lasker's agency hired a singer from the Metropolitan Opera to promote cigarettes.

Thousands of advertising agencies in the United States earn money every year by charging clients for developing a message and then conveying it to the public. Agencies no longer sell ad space. They drive the creative process of developing an ad and executing it. Big corporations often have their own advertising departments.

Debates over the ethics of advertising have persisted since its inception, and many efforts have been made to control the industry. Federal and state laws attempt to regulate the type of advertising; for example, cigarette ads are not allowed on television. The Federal Trade Commission often asks advertisers to prove their claims in an attempt to minimize false advertising (the practice of presenting incorrect information to consumers). Many public advocacy groups, including the Better Business Bureau, are devoted to fighting false advertising and making sure advertising does not present damaging messages to children.

Advertising provides vital financial support to many newspapers and magazines. However, those two forms of media also strive to present balanced and fair reporting of the news, and publishers should take care that editorial content is separate from advertising. For example, most people believe that a newspaper publishing a story

Careers in Advertising

The advertising industry employs people to do research, manage accounts, and develop creative ideas to market products.

Researchers, who often have a college degree in psychology or statistics, are responsible for completing unbiased studies on an advertiser's target audience. In some cases, the study may require interviews with people who fall into a certain demographic. Account executives, who may have business degrees, are responsible for keeping the client and the agency connected. Ultimately, the client makes the decision to approve or reject an ad; thus an agency must make sure its workers are clear on the client's wishes.

The creative side of advertising offers many employment opportunities. Copywriters are responsible for developing written material for an ad. They must be creative and in some cases humorous to convey the appropriate message to the consumer. Art directors use written prose to create a picture. Experience in film, layout, and photography is often required of an art director. Creative directors bring all the work together.

Advertising: Estimated Expenditures by Medium 1990 to 2000
(in millions of dollars)

Medium	*1990*	*1992*	*1994*	*1995*	*1996*	*1998*	*2000*
Newspapers							
National	3,867	3,602	3,906	3,996	4,400	5,402	7,184
Local	28,414	27,135	30,450	32,321	34,002	38,890	42,062
Total	32,281	30,737	34,356	36,317	38,402	44,292	49,246
Broadcast TV							
TV networks	9,863	10,249	10,942	11,600	13,081	13,736	15,706
Syndication	1,109	1,370	1,734	2,016	2,218	2,609	3,128
Spot (National)	7,788	7,551	8,993	9,119	9,803	10,659	11,970
Spot (Local)	7,856	8,079	9,464	9,985	10,944	12,169	13,631
Total	26,616	27,249	31,133	32,720	36,046	39,173	44,438
Cable TV							
Cable TV networks	1,860	2,227	3,052	3,535	4,472	5,827	9,000
Spot (Local)	597	974	1,250	1,573	1,966	2,474	3,364
Total	2,457	3,201	4,302	5,108	6,438	8,301	12,364
Radio							
Network	482	424	463	480	523	622	850
Spot (National)	1,635	1,505	1,902	1,959	2,135	2,823	3,822
Spot (Local)	6,609	6,725	8,164	8,899	9,611	11,628	14,913
Total	8,726	8,654	10,529	11,338	12,269	15,073	19,585
Magazines	6,803	7,000	7,916	8,580	9,010	10,518	12,348
Yellow Pages	8,926	9,320	9,825	10,236	10,849	11,990	13,367
Direct mail	23,370	25,392	29,638	32,866	34,509	39,620	44,715
Business papers	2,875	3,090	3,358	3,559	3,808	4,232	4,700
Billboards	1,084	1,030	1,167	1,263	1,339	1,576	1,870
Internet	NA	NA	NA	NA	NA	1,050	3,200
Miscellaneous	16,452	16,977	19,456	20,943	22,560	25,769	30,502
All Advertising							
National	73,380	76,710	88,250	95,360	103,040	118,966	142,742
Local	56,210	55,940	63,430	67,570	72,190	82,628	93,590
Total	129,590	132,650	151,680	162,930	175,230	201,594	236,332

NA = not available.
Source: Crain Communications, Inc.

This chart shows an overall increase in advertising expenditures from 1990 to 2000, particularly in newer media, like cable TV and the Internet.

about an advertiser's company for no reason except its financial contribution to the newspaper is inappropriate. Nevertheless, the practice occurs regularly.

The advertising industry plays a part in everyone's daily lives. The industry incorporates everything from small ads for cars in the newspaper to massive campaigns on television. It has a profound influence on how people dress, what they drive, and what they eat. The industry, which continues to grow as more forms of media are created, drives the U.S. economy and shapes American opinions.

Further Readng

Meyers, William. *The Image Makers—Power and Persuasion on Madison Avenue*. New York: Times Books, 1984.

Ogilvy, David. *Ogilvy on Advertising*. New York: Crown Publishers, 1983.

Schudson, Michael. *Advertising, The Uneasy Persuasion—Its Dubious Impact on American Society*. New York: Basic Books, 1984.

—*Karen Ayres*

See also:
Business Law; Civil Rights Legislation; Equal Employment Opportunity Commission; Women in the Workforce.

Affirmative Action

Affirmative action is a set of policies designed to overcome the effects of past discrimination against members of minority groups. Affirmative action is sometimes mandated by legislation; at other times, as with corporate employment practices or university admissions, its extent and the way in which it is administered may vary.

In the United States the key minority classifications include age, race, religion, national origin, physical disability, sex, and status as a Vietnam War veteran. Although the majority of the U.S. population is female, women are normally classified as a minority; sometimes the phrase "minorities and women" is used in discussions of affirmative action. Despite affirmative action's range and the fact that women have arguably benefited more than any other group from it, as a matter of public policy and as a subject of contention, affirmative action has regularly been, especially in recent times, considered primarily a racial issue, or, even more narrowly, as a matter most pertinent to African Americans.

It is important to distinguish between antidiscrimination legislation and policies and affirmative action. Although the Civil Rights Act of 1964 prohibited discrimination of all kinds, that ban did not necessarily imply the active recruitment of minorities or the establishment of formal goals for minority representation. Those processes developed later and came to be called affirmative action. In this sense, affirmative action can be defined as an initiative aimed at actively increasing opportunities for minorities and promoting diversity in workplaces and classrooms.

What would come to be known as affirmative action was first championed by the civil rights movement. The first recorded reference to affirmative action occurred in March 1961 when President John F. Kennedy issued Executive Order 10925, which mandated that projects financed with federal money "take affirmative action" to ensure that employment practices are racially nondiscriminatory. The term itself is credited to

Affirmative Action in U.S. Law

- **Equal Pay Act of 1963**: Requires employers to give equal pay to men and women for work of comparable skill and responsibility.
- **Civil Rights Act of 1964, Title VII**: Prohibits discrimination on the basis of race, religion, sex, or national origin and covers businesses with 15 or more employees in matters of hiring, training, placement, promotion, layoff, and termination. Title VII was amended in 1972 to allow the EEOC to enforce it through court action.
- **Executive Order 11246 (amended by Executive Order 11375)**: Requires an affirmative action plan, to be monitored by the Department of Labor, from all federal contractors and subcontractors.
- **Age Discrimination Act of 1967** and **Age Discrimination Act of 1975**: Prohibits an employer of 20 or more people or any employer receiving federal money from discriminating against persons over age 40.
- **Rehabilitation Act of 1973**: Prohibits discrimination against people on the basis of handicaps, both visible and invisible, and mandates that firms seek opportunities to hire such people and, as necessary, modify their facilities to accommodate them. In addition to physical disabilities, handicapped people are defined as those with a record of mental impairment, alcoholism, and illnesses such as diabetes, asthma, and epilepsy.
- **Vietnam Era Veterans Act of 1974**: Requires contractors with federal contracts of $10,000 or more to take affirmative action in hiring Vietnam era veterans.
- **Pregnancy Discrimination Act of 1978**: Bans discrimination on the basis of pregnancy and mandates equal medical coverage and leave policies for pregnancy.

Some of the more notable federal laws and executive orders that relate to affirmative action.

Hobart Taylor, Jr., a black attorney employed by the Kennedy administration. In 1964, President Lyndon Johnson signed the Civil Rights Act, which prohibited discrimination on the basis of race, religion, or national origin and created the Equal Employment Opportunity Commission (EEOC), the agency charged with preventing workplace discrimination.

In June 1965 Johnson described affirmative action as "the next and more profound stage of the battle for civil rights. We seek not just freedom but opportunity." Three months later, he issued Executive Order 11246, which for the first time made affirmative action a federal mandate. It did so by requiring government contractors to take specific measures to deliberately seek out minority employees (this order covered only race; gender was added in 1971). It was left to a Republican president, however, to initiate what amounted to employment quotas. In 1969 Richard Nixon implemented the "Philadelphia Plan," which imposed quotas on building contractors in five counties in eastern Pennsylvania that had been selected as a test case because federal officials viewed hiring practices there as flagrantly discriminatory. The plan's impact, however, went beyond Philadelphia as it also required contractors on all federally funded projects exceeding $500,000 to make "good-faith efforts" to hire predetermined percentages of black workers.

In the area of business and corporate hiring and promotion, an overlap exists between legislation designed to prevent discrimination and to encourage the active recruitment and promotion of minorities. Various bills and executive orders over the past 35 years have had a powerful effect on the workplace by attempting to render personnel decisions bias-free (see box). In addition to these federal policies, employers also need to be aware of state or municipal regulations dealing with affirmative action and discrimination.

Despite affirmative action's good intentions, a backlash began to emerge, especially in regard to what was called "reverse discrimination," the argument being that if certain individuals are favored in matters of admission and employment, others must necessarily be discriminated against. So far, the most important Supreme Court case in this area has been *Regents of the University of California v. Bakke* (1978), which concerned Allan Bakke, a white applicant to medical school who had been passed over in favor of minority applicants with lower test scores. The Court ruled against the medical school because the school had used a quota system in which a precise number of positions were

Freedom is the right to share, share fully and equally, in American society—to vote, to hold a job, to enter a public place, to go to school. It is the right to be treated in every part of our national life as a person equal in dignity and promise to all others.

But freedom is not enough. You do not wipe away the scars of centuries by saying: Now you are free to go where you want, and do as you desire, and choose the leaders you please.

You do not take a person who, for years, has been hobbled by chains and liberate him, bring him up to the starting line of a race and then say, "you are free to compete with all the others," and still justly believe that you have been completely fair.

Thus it is not enough just to open the gates of opportunity. All our citizens must have the ability to walk through those gates.

This is the next and the more profound stage of the battle for civil rights. We seek not just freedom but opportunity. We seek not just legal equity but human ability, not just equality as a right and a theory but equality as a fact and equality as a result.

—Lyndon Johnson, speaking at Howard University, June 4, 1965

In 1978 Allan Bakke sued the University of California–Davis, arguing that his medical school application had been unfairly rejected because of affirmative action.

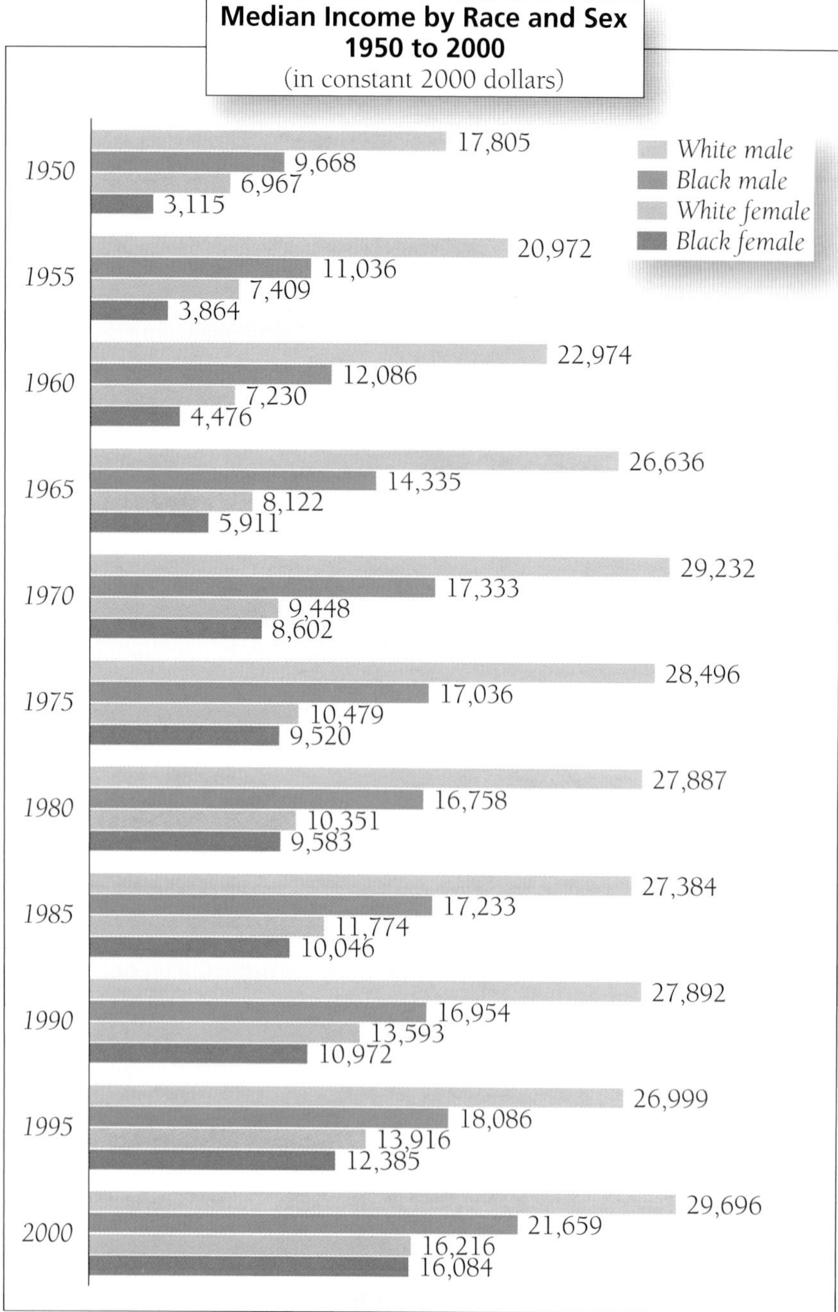

Note: Sufficient data not available for other races.
Source: Current Population Survey, U.S. Census Bureau.

Activists and politicians study statistics like these to try to determine if affirmative action policies have helped minority groups work toward economic parity.

set aside for minorities. Although the Court thus effectively outlawed quotas, it still maintained that race could be rated a positive factor in admissions.

In a more recent case, *Adarand Constructors v. Pena* (1995), the Court ruled that the federal government had to apply "strict scrutiny" to show that an affirmative action policy was "narrowly tailored" and fulfilled a "compelling governmental interest." The Court's ruling was hailed by opponents of affirmative action, and it prompted the Clinton administration to reassess its affirmative action programs, ordering that such programs could exist only if specific past discrimination could be demonstrated. Clinton endorsed the concept of affirmative action but issued an executive order asking for the abolishment or reform of any program that established quotas, that favored unqualified persons or created reverse discrimination, or that had outlived its usefulness. "Mend it, but don't end it" was his slogan.

One of the most highly publicized reactions against affirmative action was California's Proposition 209, which was approved by state voters in 1998. The proposition barred the state government from relying on race-based or gender-based preferences in school admissions, public hiring, and contracting. Affirmative action also came under attack in several other states. For example, in 1999 Governor Jeb Bush of Florida unveiled a plan to end race-based preferences at state universities, and in 2001 a court of appeals ruled unanimously that the race-based admissions policy of the University of Georgia violated the equal-protection clause of the U.S. Constitution.

Despite the controversy affirmative action policies cause, they have had success. For example, in 1980 there were five times as many black high school dropouts as there were employed black college graduates; by 2000 the size of these two groups was about the same. In 1980 white women occupied 27.1 percent of middle- and upper-level managerial positions in business, while black women accounted for 3.2 percent. A decade later, the corresponding percentages were 35.3 percent and 6.9 percent. Nevertheless, advocates of affirmative action point to remaining disparities. For example, 95 percent of top management jobs are held by white males, and for every $100 earned by a white household, a black household earns $63.

Although voters, legislators, and the Supreme Court appear to be rethinking affirmative action, in the area of private business it continues to flourish and many

In 1999 Jesse Jackson, right, and Martin Luther King III, left, led a march protesting the affirmative action policies of Governor Jeb Bush of Florida.

firms consider a diverse workforce a business asset. The U.S. Department of Labor actively encourages workplace diversity and annually bestows awards on companies with outstanding records of aiding minorities. One of the most notable of these honors is the Opportunity 2000 Award, whose recipients have included Procter & Gamble, Pacific Gas & Electric, and Xerox. In one survey of 140 corporate executives, 95 percent responded that federal requirements had prompted them to institute affirmative action programs. Seventy-three percent, however, added they would continue such efforts even without federal regulations.

Further Reading

Beckwith, Francis J., and Jones, Todd E., eds. *Affirmative Action: Social Justice or Reverse Discrimination?* Amherst, N.Y.: Prometheus Books, 1997.

Bowen, William, and Derek Bok. *The Shape of the River.* Princeton, N.J.: Princeton University Press, 1998.

Curry, George E., and Cornel West, eds. *The Affirmative Action Debate.* Cambridge, Mass.: Perseus Press, 1996.

Post, Robert, and Michael Rogin, eds. *Race and Representation.* Cambridge, Mass.: MIT Press, 1998.

Thernstrom, Stephan, and Abigail Thernstrom. *America in Black and White: One Nation, Indivisible.* New York: Simon & Schuster, 1997.

—Joseph Gustaitis

AFL-CIO

See also:
Fair Labor Standards Act; Labor Union; National Labor Relations Act; New Deal; Taft–Hartley Act; Teamsters Union; United Automobile Workers of America; Women in the Workforce.

With approximately 13 million members representing a wide spectrum of the nation's workforce, the American Federation of Labor–Congress of Industrial Organizations (AFL-CIO) is one of the most influential labor unions in the United States. Its history dates to the nineteenth century, a time marked by tension between an emerging capitalist nation, with its tycoons and industries, and a nascent labor union movement.

The Birth of the AFL

Before the AFL was formed, an organization known as the Knights of Labor was founded in Philadelphia, Pennsylvania, in 1869. Unlike most of the unions of the time, the Knights of Labor was open to all workers, including African Americans and women. The Knights of Labor, like the later Industrial Workers of the World (IWW; founded in 1905), believed that all workers in an industry, regardless of skill level or specific job, should be eligible for union membership. This approach is known as industrial unionism and was popularized by the IWW as "one big union."

The AFL organized workers according to craft. Craft unionism, unlike the inclusive industrial unionism, organized workers according to the specific job performed. Organizing on the basis of craft allowed unions to represent only certain workers within any given company or work site. Critics of craft unionism argue that it divides the working class and weakens union solidarity. Craft unionism may have been appealing in the early years of industrialization because of its similarity to the centuries-old tradition of workers organizing into guilds according to what they produced. Whatever the reason, under the direction of Samuel Gompers, a cigar maker who migrated to the United States as a young child, the AFL became a key voice for American workers.

Samuel Gompers testifies to the Federal Commission on Industrial Relations, 1915.

The AFL was formed in 1886 in Columbus, Ohio, with Gompers as its first president. Unlike some other unions of the time, the AFL rejected the idea of deep-seated economic reform, the creation of a political party consisting of workers—for example, the Workingman's Party—and the socialist ideas percolating among other labor organizations and the working class. Under Gompers's leadership, the AFL accepted the capitalist economic system and sought a greater share of the material wealth generated by the system for its members.

Gompers, who consistently prevailed in setting the tone for the AFL, succeeded in keeping the union essentially nonpartisan,

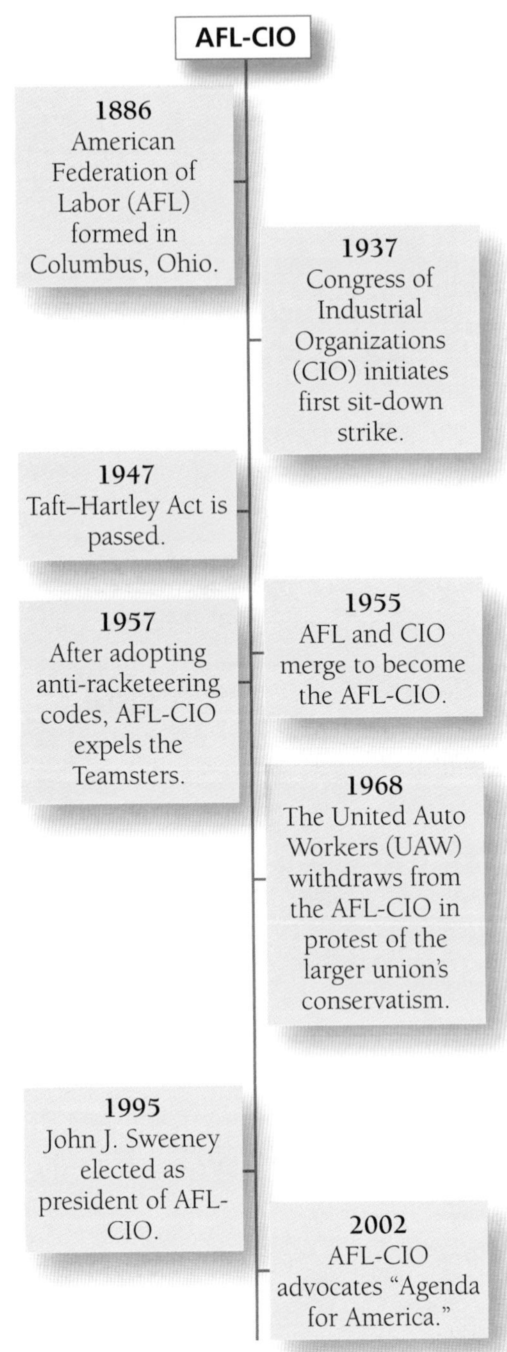

giving notice to the major political parties that the union would support candidates who were friends of labor regardless of party affiliation. Rather than promoting a change in the economic system or any fundamental reforms, the AFL focused its efforts on wages, working conditions, and the relationship between labor and management.

Traditionally, Gompers and the AFL did not welcome women in the union for several reasons. They believed that women would take jobs away from men, would work for lower wages, and were less able to negotiate with employers as forcefully as men. Most fundamentally, Gompers believed that women belonged at home, not in the workforce. Many women were employed outside the home but were significantly underrepresented as union members. Nevertheless, the AFL announced its support for women's suffrage at its first annual convention; at a subsequent convention in 1903, the formation of the National Women's Trade Union League was announced.

John L. Lewis

John L. Lewis (1880–1969), the son of Welsh immigrants, was one of the most controversial and powerful American labor leaders of the twentieth century. Born in Iowa, he worked as a miner with other family members but his real vocation was organizing coal miners and mass production workers in America's factories.

In 1909 he started working for the American Federation of Labor (AFL) as a union organizer but returned to the United Mine Workers (UMW) to become its president in 1920. During the 1930s Lewis's genius as an organizer and negotiator gained national attention.

A supporter of Franklin D. Roosevelt's New Deal programs, Lewis worked with the administration to strengthen the UMW and successfully organize coal mining regions that lacked union representation. Lewis's leadership of the Committee for Industrial Organization (CIO) helped the CIO win union recognition and an agreement for collective bargaining from two of the nation's then-largest companies: General Motors and U.S. Steel.

During World War II, when the AFL and the CIO had agreed to refrain from strikes to show their support for the war effort, Lewis earned the enmity of many Americans when he led several strikes by coal miners during the "no-strike" period. In 1948, when Lewis refused to end a long coal strike, a federal court ordered him to pay a large fine for contempt. In 1960 Lewis resigned the presidency of the UMW, and in 1964 was awarded the Presidential Medal of Freedom by President Lyndon Johnson.

John L. Lewis addresses 10,000 textile workers in Lawrence, Massachusetts, on May 24, 1937.

The Rise of Industrial Unionism

In 1924 William Green succeeded Gompers as the new president of the organization. Under his leadership the AFL remained committed to the idea of organizing skilled workers based on craft. However, with the introduction of technological changes and the growth of mass production, industrial America required a growing number of unskilled or semiskilled workers. As a result, the craft union idea was again challenged by the concept of industrial unionism.

Industrial unionism is based on the premise that all workers in a given industry, automaking for example, should be members of one labor organization regardless of their level of skill or the work they perform. Because the new technologies did not require advanced skill levels, the majority of workers in the United States were unskilled or semiskilled and consequently ineligible for AFL membership.

These workers found a voice in John L. Lewis, the leader of the United Mine Workers (UMW). At first he tried to integrate industrial unions into the AFL as the Committee for Industrial Organization. Dissension led to the formation of a separate organization: in 1936 the AFL ousted Lewis and the industrial unions he represented. Lewis named the now-independent group the Congress of Industrial Organizations (CIO). The AFL and CIO were to remain separate entities until they reunited as the AFL-CIO 20 years later.

The separation of the AFL and CIO no doubt weakened the labor movement at a crucial moment. Rather than being able to negotiate with management from a position of solidarity, the labor movement was internally divided, often distrustful of immigrants, women, and people of color, and, some believe, committed to a conservative agenda. However, the formation of the CIO, with its more inclusive approach, opened the door to union membership to many workers who had been left out, including women and African Americans.

The CIO went about the business of organizing workers in mass production industries like automaking, steel, textiles, and rubber, among others. Under Lewis's direction, some of the most powerful unions in U.S. labor history were formed, including the United Steelworkers of America, the United Auto Workers (UAW), and the Communication Workers of America.

Some consider tactics used by the CIO to be more militant than those of the AFL; for example, the CIO inaugurated the sit-down strike in 1937. Nevertheless both organizations agreed to suspend strike activity for the duration of World War II.

Traditionally the CIO urged its members to more political action than did the AFL. However, as the cold war was beginning to heat up, the CIO expelled several of its affiliated unions on the grounds that they were influenced by communists. The International Ladies Garment Workers Union and the UMW withdrew from the CIO in 1938 and 1942, respectively. Some argue that the labor legislation enacted during the Depression undermined the cohesion of the labor movement and inspired smaller unions to withdraw over political or philosophical differences.

George Meany, left, and Walter Reuther, right, announce the merger of the American Federation of Labor with the Congress of Industrial Organizations in 1955.

The Postwar Era

Following World War II, despite the estimated 12 million members of the AFL and CIO, the reforms instituted during the New Deal, and a flurry of strike activity immediately after the war, the power of labor diminished. An increasing number of states were passing laws to hamper labor's traditional tactics—strikes, boycotts, picketing. With the passage of the Taft–Hartley Act of 1947, these strictures were extended to the federal level.

In 1955, at the time the AFL and CIO merged to become the AFL-CIO with George Meany serving as the first president of the organization, its combined membership was approximately 15 million, making it the largest and most powerful labor union in the nation. In 1957, after adopting antiracketeering codes, the union expelled the Teamsters.

Strikes, demonstrations, boycotts, and picket lines, labor's traditional arsenal, were slowly replaced by arbitration and negotiation. As the number of strikes declined, the number of negotiated settlements increased. If negotiation failed to produce a labor contract, arbitration between labor and management might avert a last-minute labor walkout.

In 1968 the UAW, under the direction of Walter Reuther, withdrew from the AFL-CIO in protest against its conservative stance on civil rights and social welfare. Reuther had had numerous disagreements with Meany. For example, while Reuther supported the 1963 March on Washington led by Martin Luther King, Jr., the executive board of the AFL-CIO, headed by Meany,

U.S. Membership in AFL-CIO Affiliated Unions 1979 to 1998
(in thousands)

Labor Organization	1979	1985	1995	1998
Actors and artists	75	100	76	69
Automobile, aerospace, and agriculture workers	NA	974	760	742
Bakery, confectionery, and tobacco workers	131	115	95	105
Boilermakers	129	110	43	40
Bricklayers	106	95	84	62
Carpenters and joiners	626	609	354	324
Communications workers	485	524	490	511
Electrical workers	825	791	673	659
Electronic, electrical, and salaried workers	243	198	137	115
Firefighters	150	142	151	171
Flight attendants	NA	NA	31	39
Food and commercial workers	1,123	989	1,010	1,123
Garment workers	314	210	NA	NA
Glass molders, pottery and plastics workers	50	72	69	61
Government employees	236	199	157	181
Graphic communications employees	171	141	96	86
Hotel and restaurant employees	373	327	232	230
Ironworkers	146	140	80	83
Laborers	475	383	331	299
Letter carriers	151	186	210	210
Longshoreman's association	63	65	61	62
Machinists and aerospace workers	688	520	432	456
Mineworkers	NA	NA	75	75
Needletrades, industrial and textile employees	308	228	245	205
Office and professional employees	83	90	83	81
Operating engineers	313	330	296	289
Oil, chemical, and atomic workers	146	108	82	NA
Painters	160	133	90	97
Paper, chemical, and energy workers	262	232	235	290
Plumbers and pipefitters	228	226	220	220
Postal workers	245	232	266	281
Retail, wholesale, department store employees	122	106	73	NA
Rubber, cork, linoleum, and plastics workers	158	106	NA	NA
Seafarers	84	80	80	77
Service employees	537	688	1,078	1,144
Sheet metal workers	120	108	103	93
Stage employees, moving-picture machine operators	50	50	51	49
State, county, municipal employees	889	997	1,211	1,247
Steelworkers	964	572	517	468
Teachers	423	470	632	787
Teamsters	NA	NA	1,286	1,231
Transit union employees	94	94	96	104
Transport workers	85	85	75	75
Total [1]	**11,792**	**11,305**	**11,666**	**12,500**

NA = Not available. [1]Includes other AFL-CIO affiliated unions, not shown separately.
Note: Figures represent labor organizations as constituted in 1989 and reflect past merger activity. Membership figures reflect only actively employed members. Not all unions shown.
Source: American Federation of Labor and Congress of Industrial Organizations, *Report of the AFL-CIO Executive Council* (annual).

The AFL-CIO represents millions of workers in a wide variety of professions.

John Sweeney, AFL-CIO president, leads an anti-sweatshop rally in New York's garment district on October 26, 1995.

would extend only sympathy rather than support for the civil rights marchers.

When Lane Kirkland was elected president in 1979, the influence of organized labor was in decline and some believed the death knell for unionism had sounded. By the mid-1990s, however, union activity was on the rise. As jobs traditionally held by union workers were lost in the wake of globalization, and multinationals exported jobs to low-wage developing nations, labor leaders in the United States formed alliances with the emerging labor movements in those nations.

While industrial jobs were being exported, the service industry in the United States became the fastest growing sector of the economy. The election of John J. Sweeney as AFL-CIO president in 1995 was an indication of the extent of the transformation in labor politics. Sweeney started his career with the Service Employees International Union (SEIU). The SEIU, which began as a union for some of the most underrepresented workers in the nation, now represents workers as varied as janitors, doctors, taxi drivers, engineers, and graduate students. In 1998 the SEIU became the second largest AFL-CIO affiliate and by 2001 represented approximately 1.5 million members.

In a historic shift reflecting the AFL-CIO's recognition of the significant changes in global economic conditions, the union's new leadership has actively focused on organizing many different kinds of workers, as well as reaching out to students, intellectuals, feminists, and other politically progressive groups, while continuing to endorse political candidates, regardless of political affiliation, who support specific labor issues. In 1999 the union passed a resolution recognizing the role of African Americans and immigrants in building the economy of the United States and calling for immigration reform.

In spring 2002, the AFL-CIO advocated an "Agenda for America." Faced with a federal administration that the union considered unsympathetic to working families, the AFL-CIO called for an investment of tax dollars in schools, infrastructure, and job training; reforming trade rules; and more worker protection. While the future of the AFL-CIO in a global marketplace is unclear, one thing is certain: Unions will be forced to adopt new tactics and look beyond the nation's borders to remain an effective voice for workers.

Further Reading

Filippelli, Ronald L. *Labor in the USA: A History.* New York: Alfred A. Knopf, 1984.

Fine, Sidney. *Sit-Down: The General Motors Strike of 1936–1937.* Ann Arbor: University of Michigan Press, 1969.

Foner, Philip. *A History of the Labor Movement in the United States.* 4 vols. New York: International Publishers, 1947–1965.

Kimeldorf, Howard. *Battling for American Labor: Wobblies, Craft Workers, and the Making of the Union Movement.* Berkeley: University of California Press, 1999.

Yellen, Samuel. *American Labor Struggles, 1877–1934.* New York: Pathfinder, 1974.

Zinn, Howard. *A People's History of the United States, 1492–Present.* New York: HarperCollins, 1999.

—*Connie Tuttle*

Agriculture Industry

Agriculture, the production of food and fiber, is the most basic of human endeavors, dating back nearly 12,000 years. Preagricultural societies depended upon hunting and gathering. Their nomadic lifestyle has generally been supplanted throughout the world by settled communities dependent upon farming.

Early gains in efficiency were produced when farmers began to save seed from their highest-yielding plants and breed animals from among those with the most desirable traits. As farm productivity increased, trade in farm products became possible, and increased yields allowed farmers to look beyond basic production of food to improvements in tools, housing, and clothing for their families. Today, U.S. consumers reap the benefits of a complicated, technologically advanced agricultural system that supplies food in abundance while employing less than 2 percent of the population.

Modern Agriculture in the United States

Agriculture in the United States can be described in part by the changes it has undergone since the early days of the republic. It has been marked by a movement of farms and farmers from the eastern seaboard to midwestern and western regions. It has been transformed by a shift from dependence upon human labor to the use of animal and mechanical labor. Agriculture has grown away from self-contained farming, in which farm families raised and made most of the inputs (supplies and equipment, for example) they used on their farms, to an industry that depends upon inputs, such as chemicals, produced elsewhere. As a result, the average U.S. farm today is larger, more specialized, and many times more efficient than its predecessor of 300 years ago.

In 1900 the average yield of corn, the most widely planted crop in the United States, was 28 bushels per acre. By 1940, yield had risen to only 28.9 bushels per acre. Soon after, however, the introduction and adoption of hybrid seed corn sparked a half century of productivity increases. By 1950, corn yields had increased to 38 bushels per acre. The 1950s and 1960s also saw a 50 percent increase in the use of commercial fertilizer; by 1970, corn yields had increased to 73 bushels per acre. Ongoing improvements in hybrid seeds, together with other practices—including careful use of fertilizers and weed and pest-control strategies—have increased average corn yields to nearly 140 bushels per acre. Corn is not the only crop by which such growth can be measured. In the half-century from 1950 to 2000, total agriculture productivity more than doubled in the United States.

In 2000 there were more than two million farms in the United States. These farms generated about $200 billion annually from the sale of agricultural products, split evenly between crops and livestock. Corn is grown on a half-million farms, accounting for 70 million acres of total production. Soybeans are planted on about 66 million acres; wheat is grown on 59 million acres. Corn, soybean, and wheat farming are concentrated in the center of the United States. Cotton and rice are grown mostly in the South. Other crops

See also:
Chicago Board of Trade; Commodities; Deere, John; Environmentalism; Genetic Engineering; Subsidy.

This 1859 print by Currier & Ives, A Glimpse of the Homestead, *depicts the traditional, somewhat romanticized image of a farm.*

U.S. Principal Crops 1990 to 2000

Crop and Year	*Planted (in million acres)*	*Harvested (in million acres)*	*Yield per Acre*	*Farm Price*[1]
Corn for grain				
1990	74.2	67.0	119 bu.	$2.28/bu.
1995	71.5	65.2	114 bu.	$3.24/bu.
2000	79.5	72.7	137 bu.	$1.85/bu.
Soybeans				
1990	57.8	56.5	34.1 bu.	$5.74/bu.
1995	62.5	61.5	35.3 bu.	$6.72/bu.
2000	74.5	72.7	38.1 bu.	$4.75/bu.
Hay				
1990	NA	61.0	2.40 tons	$80.60[2]
1995	NA	59.8	2.58 tons	$82.20[2]
2000	NA	59.9	2.54 tons	$80.00[2]
Wheat				
1990	77.0	69.1	39.5 bu.	$2.61/bu.
1995	69.0	61.0	35.8 bu.	$4.55/bu.
2000	62.5	53.0	41.9 bu.	$2.65/bu.
Cotton				
1990	12.3	11.7	634 lb.	$0.68/lb.
1995	16.9	16.0	537 lb.	$0.77/lb.
2000	15.5	13.1	631 lb.	$0.58/lb.
Potatoes				
1990	1.4	1.4	293 cwt.	$6.08/cwt.
1995	1.4	1.4	323 cwt.	$6.77/cwt.
2000	1.4	1.4	382 cwt.	$4.95/cwt.
Tobacco				
1990	NA	0.7	2,218 lb.	$1.74/lb.
1995	NA	0.7	1,914 lb.	$1.82/lb.
2000	NA	0.5	2,264 lb.	$1.87/lb.
Rice, rough				
1990	2.9	2.8	5,529 lb.	$6.68/cwt.
1995	3.1	3.1	5,621 lb.	$9.15/cwt.
2000	3.1	3.0	6,278 lb.	$5.75/cwt.
Sorghum for grain				
1990	10.5	9.1	63.1 bu.	$2.12/bu.
1995	9.4	8.3	55.6 bu.	$3.19/bu.
2000	9.2	7.7	60.9 bu.	$1.75/bu.
Barley				
1990	8.2	7.5	56.1 bu.	$2.14/bu.
1995	6.7	6.3	57.2 bu.	$2.89/bu.
2000	5.8	5.2	61.1 bu.	$2.15/bu.

NA = Not available; bu. = bushels; cwt. = hundredweight (100 lbs). [1] Average price. [2] Prices are for hay sold baled.
Sources: U.S. Dept. of Agriculture, National Agricultural Statistics Service. In *Crop Production*, annual; and *CropValues*, annual.

This chart shows the U.S. principal crops and increasing productivity gains over the course of the 1990s.

include fruit, vegetables, ornamental horticulture, tobacco, and peanuts.

California leads the nation in agricultural production. It accounts for only 4 percent of the nation's farms, but it yields 13 percent of total agricultural receipts, with sales twice those of Texas, the second-largest producer. The leading farm product in California is milk; grapes and wine are second. California also produces more than half of the U.S. supply of fruits and vegetables. Much of this output is heavily dependent on irrigation, and water is always in short supply. Demands to protect endangered species, continued urban growth, and Native American tribes seeking to reestablish their traditional fishing areas have intensified an increasingly contentious fight over scarce water supplies in the state.

What becomes of U.S. farm crops? Fifty-eight percent of the U.S. corn crop is fed to livestock; 22 percent is exported; 6 percent is used for producing high-fructose corn syrup; and 6 percent is used for the creation of ethanol, a substance with a wide variety of uses, including as a solvent, a gasoline additive, and an ingredient in alcoholic beverages. Soybeans are processed to produce meal and oil. (Meal is the solid part of the soybean after processing, resembling corn meal, and more granular than flour.) Most of the meal is fed to poultry, pigs, and cattle. Soybean oil is used mostly for human consumption—in salad oil and cooking oil, for example. About 40 percent of the U.S. soybean crop is exported. Most of the wheat—six different grades of wheat are grown in the United States, with special varieties for producing bread and pasta—is used for human consumption.

Livestock and Other Farm Products

Cattle are usually owned by more than one farmer or rancher before they reach the market. Most cattle are born on ranches in the West or on Midwest farms, where they are kept for about six months to a year, feeding on grass. Then they are sold to feedlots, where they are fattened for slaughter. Cattle feeding is now concentrated in Texas, Nebraska, Kansas, and Colorado. The Western states are well suited for feedlots because they provide an ample supply of irrigated corn, the main ingredient in cattle-feeding rations, and they offer a dry climate, ideal for fattening cattle in feedlots.

Swine production has changed rapidly in the 1990s. It was once spread among many family farms; grain raised on these farms was fed to pigs and the pigs were brought to market. Swine production has now been concentrated in a few large companies, some owning their own slaughtering and packing facilities. These large companies typically own the pig from farrowing, or birth, to the grocery meat counter. In 1900, 76 percent of U.S. farms had pigs, but by 1997, only 6 percent were still raising them. The decline in the number of farms with cattle has been much less severe, with 55 percent of U.S. farmers still raising cattle in 1997.

The changes in swine production were foreshadowed by the changes in poultry production. In 1950 almost all poultry producers were independent, selling their broilers (chickens raised for meat and slaughtered at a young age, in contrast to chickens kept for eggs) on the open market. By 1955, only 10 percent of poultry producers sold their birds on the open market, with the rest of

Careers in Agriculture

A typical modern farm is operated by a single proprietor or two or more family members. Most beginning farmers join an existing family operation. Because capital requirements are high (to purchase expensive equipment, for example), getting started in farming is difficult, although not impossible, without help. The Farm Service Agency, part of the U.S. Department of Agriculture, provides financial help to beginning farmers.

Many other career paths are available in agriculture; consolidation of the modern agriculture industry has been difficult for family farms but has also led to a diversification of employment. Most farm managers are salaried employees whose job often includes traditional duties like soil treatment and livestock maintenance but may also involve hiring and supervising farm workers. Managers may also help determine the farm's financial success by deciding which crops to plant and how to market them, and perhaps even managing a portfolio of stocks and futures that hedge against the farm's potential losses.

A corporation overseeing thousands of acres requires far more than a roadside stand to market products. Such companies rely on marketers, advertisers, and financial analysts to help appeal to the public and determine where, when, and how to sell the product. These businesses also employ agricultural scientists who research further methods of increasing crop yields. Genetic engineers have become particularly important to agriculture as their work promises to increase the resistance of crops to diseases and insects, improve yields, and even make crops more nutritious. Because these techniques have many potential drawbacks, the need for ethicists and lawyers specializing in agricultural issues has arisen.

Many opportunities lie outside corporate agribusiness. For example, horticulture and aquaculture provide promising avenues for success. Horticulture, the raising of ornamental plants and fruits, generally requires fewer acres and less equipment to provide a profitable yield, and is thus ideal for small-scale operations. Aquaculture, the farming of fish and shellfish, is a growing industry whose importance will only increase as the world's population continues to grow.

—Colleen Sullivan

Cowboys, circa 1990s, herd cattle in Lubbock, Texas.

their production controlled under contract arrangements. The poultry industry experienced rapid gains in productivity and large increases in consumption after 1955. In 1990 a ton of poultry feed could produce 43 percent more poultry meat than in 1955. Broiler production increased by a factor of 25 from 1946 through 1997.

Increased consolidation in the livestock industry has generated controversy in rural areas. In 1987 only 37 percent of the hogs sold in the United States came from farms raising 1,000 hogs or more, but by 1997, 71 percent of hogs came from farms with more than 1,000 animals. Large hog farms have provoked complaints from neighbors concerned about the smell and disposal of animal waste, and from small-farm advocates concerned about the decline in diversified family farms. Despite economic incentives to foster consolidation, environmental pressures may halt or slow consolidation of the pork industry, at least within U.S. borders.

A bright spot in agriculture has been the growth in sales of floriculture and environmental horticulture (trees, turf, and ground covers). Total sales in this category increased about 25 percent from 1992 to 1997, and the sales of bedding and garden plants doubled. In contrast to the trend elsewhere in agriculture, the number of firms involved in ornamental horticulture increased in the 1990s.

Distribution of Farm Products

When agricultural products leave the farm, they are funneled into a sophisticated food processing and distribution system. The most basic farm marketing involves direct sale to consumers through farmers' markets and roadside stands. Farmers sell their grain to neighboring livestock producers, local grain elevators, and terminal elevators that gather grain for export. Trading in futures markets, the largest being the Chicago Board of Trade, sets prices for grains.

Livestock is sold in auction barns to meatpackers, and directly from the farm to slaughtering plants. In the past, most livestock prices were set in open markets, but meat production is now often governed by contracts entered into before the production process begins. Livestock processors sell directly to supermarkets or to brokers for supermarket chains and restaurants.

The food processing chain, from farmer to consumer, accounts for some 13 percent of the U.S. gross domestic product, and 17 percent of the civilian workforce is involved in the production, processing, packaging, and shipping of agricultural goods. About one-third of all agricultural products grown in the United States are exported, with total exports reaching more than $50 billion a year.

Policy Issues Related to Agriculture

The U.S. government has been more involved in agriculture than in most other industries. By enacting the Homestead Act in the nineteenth century, by establishing land grant colleges for agricultural research, and by developing farm subsidy programs, the government has variously aided, controlled, encouraged, and discouraged farm production.

Much of the productivity growth in U.S. agriculture can be credited to publicly funded research because, historically, farms have tended to be small economic entities unsuited for carrying out private research. Farm subsidy programs emerged alongside other government programs during the Roosevelt administration's New Deal, as agriculture had preceded other sectors of the economy into the Great Depression. Farm programs since the 1930s have attempted to raise farm income by controlling production and encouraging exports, and by direct cash payments to farmers. In 2000 direct government payments to farmers reached record levels—about $32 billion.

Farmers' incomes vary because the demand for farm products is relatively unresponsive to changes in the price level. A substantial price decline is needed to increase consumption of agricultural products; thus, when farmers produce more than the market demands, prices can fall to very low levels. Farmers have little control over their levels of

In 2000 the United States had more than two million farms; this map shows the state-by-state distribution and the average acreage per farm. The greatest number of farms are in the Midwest and West.

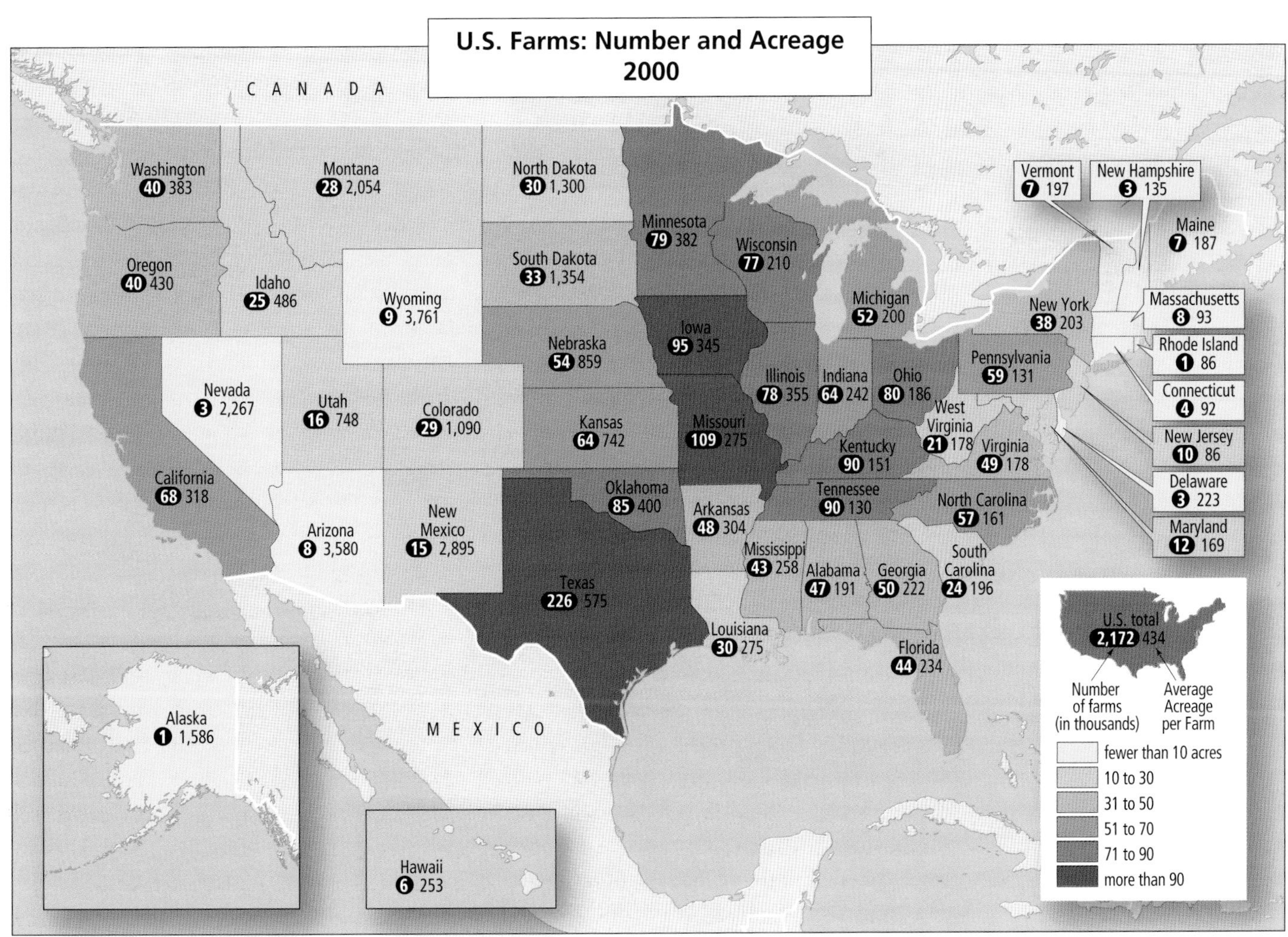

Source: U.S. Department of Agriculture.

An aquacultural research tank at the Environmental Research Lab of the University of Arizona at Tucson, in May 1987.

production because yields are dependent upon the weather. A series of excellent crop years in the middle to late 1990s, coupled with economic problems affecting some of the best export customers, led to a sustained period of low prices and continued aid to farmers from the U.S. government.

Most nonurban land in the United States is involved in agricultural production. Consequently, the increased environmental awareness that arose in the late twentieth century intensified pressure on farmers to raise crops in a manner acceptable to the general population. Critics of modern agriculture voice concerns about chemical means of controlling insects and weeds, ground and surface water contamination, erosion, the protection of endangered species, and the odors, noise, and dust that accompany the production of food and fiber.

Agriculturalists have developed cropping methods that do not disturb the soil, for example, by protecting the land from wind and water erosion and protecting water supplies from contamination. Site-specific farming, which involves the use of global positioning satellites to map farm fields, allows farmers to apply inputs precisely, avoiding the overapplication of herbicides, insecticides, and fertilizer. Although genetically altered seeds remain controversial, their development has decreased farmers' use of herbicides and pesticides.

U.S. agriculture is productive, efficient, and technologically advanced, providing a nutritious, safe, and economical food supply for consumers. That efficiency has not come without a price: Improvements in productivity have forced many farmers to leave agriculture, with small towns and rural areas suffering as a result. The real cost of food (the cost adjusted for changes in earning power) has declined. U.S. consumers today spend 10 percent of their disposable income on food. No other country feeds its population for less than 15 percent of disposable income. At the same time, the percentage of the consumer's food dollar spent on marketing, preparation, and packaging of food has increased, leaving a smaller and smaller share of total revenues for farmers.

Further Reading

Economic Research Service/USDA. *Floriculture and Environmental Horticulture—Summary.* Washington, D.C.: Government Printing Office, 1999.

House Committee on Agriculture. *Today's Agriculture: Farm Facts from the House Agriculture Committee.* http://www.agriculture.house.gov/factseco.html (March 2002).

Kauffman, Kyle D., ed. *Advances in Agricultural Economic History.* Stamford, Conn.: JAI Press, 2000.

United Soybean Board. 2000 Soy Stats. http://www.unitedsoybean.org (March 2002).

Zinn, Jeffrey A. *IB96030: Soil and Water Conservation Issues.* Washington, D.C.: Congressional Research Service, Issue Brief for Congress, May 30, 2001.

—*Blake Hurst*

Amazon.com

Amazon.com is a leading online retailer with company headquarters in Seattle, Washington. Originally strictly a bookseller, the company now offers a wide array of products including music, videos, electronics, kitchen- and housewares, tools and hardware, magazine subscriptions, toys, baby products, cameras, and computers. The company was incorporated on July 5, 1994, and launched its Web site a year later (July 16, 1995).

Amazon.com is inextricably linked with its founder, Jeffrey Preston Bezos, who was born in New Mexico on January 12, 1964, and grew up in Texas and Florida. A 1986 graduate of Princeton University, he became a successful computer systems analyst in New York, first at Fiftel, a financial telecommunications company, and then at Bankers Trust Co. and D. E. Shaw & Co. While working for Shaw, Bezos was asked to look into the business potential of an exciting new medium—the Internet. An often cited episode in Bezos's biography concerns his discovery that usage of the World Wide Web was growing at a rate of 2,300 percent a year.

After some investigation, Bezos concluded that books were the ideal product to sell over the Web for several reasons: A book is the kind of product that a buyer does not necessarily have to examine in person. Also, a vast number of books are in print—more than any real-world bookstore can keep on its shelves. While "bricks and mortar" bookstores can provide only a small number of the books in print at any given time, an online store could provide access to the entire list, without many of the overhead costs of traditional bookselling. For instance, to grow significantly, a traditional chain of booksellers needs to open new stores. This involves acquiring the land, building the stores, training and hiring employees, and maintaining sufficent inventory. An Internet bookstore can grow simply by attracting more users to its site and adjusting its inventory accordingly.

Bezos presented his idea to employers at Shaw but they were unconvinced, so Bezos decided to leave his well-paying job and start his own company. From the beginning, Bezos wanted to be more than a bookseller. He named the company after the South American river because that waterway is enormous—just what he wanted his firm to be. Amazon.com was not the first online bookseller—Computer Literacy had begun selling books over the Internet as early as 1991.

Amazon.com literally began life in a garage, staffed by Bezos and two employees. The first hurdle was developing the software that would enable the firm to master its huge database of inventory and customers and to create an easy-to-use interface. Once that was done and the company's Web site was up and running, growth was extraordinary. Amazon.com's net sales in 1996 were 3,000 percent higher than in 1995; by the fourth quarter of 1998 its revenues were $250 million.

See also:
Computer Industry; E-Business; Information Technology; Internet; Nasdaq.

Jeff Bezos reads his favorite children's book as part of the Read Across America event, in 2001.

The company offered stock on Nasdaq in May 1997 at $18 per share; by April 1999, an original share was worth more than $500. The firm expanded operations into Europe and Japan and by mid-1999 had greatly diversified its offerings, moving beyond books to a wide variety of merchandise. As Bezos put it, "We want to build a place where people can come to find and discover anything they might want to buy online." Corporate analysts were impressed, and *Time* magazine named Bezos its 1999 "Man of the Year."

Amazon.com, as personified by Bezos, became the symbol for the e-commerce boom of the late 1990s. It also became a testing ground for labor organizing in the so-called new economy. Arguing that their wages were too low for the cost of living in Seattle and dissatisfied with their available benefits (which included flagging stock options), a group of employees affiliated with the Communications Workers of America began organizing a union in fall 2000. Because of Amazon's already high visibility, the union campaign attracted a great deal of attention in the press.

Despite its fame, Amazon was losing money at a phenomenal rate. By 2002 it had lost a total of $3 billion. When the so-called dot-com bubble burst, Amazon's stock dropped to a low of $5.51 a share in late 2001. Bezos, however, kept his focus, and Amazon.com reported its first profit at the end of the fourth quarter of 2001. Investors were encouraged, and by spring 2002, Amazon.com stock had risen to around $20 per share. Bezos insisted that the potential of the Internet was still in its infancy. As he put it, "Most people never have the opportunity, even in a small way, to make history, which Amazon.com is trying to do. It's work hard, have fun, make history. That's what we're trying to do."

Amazon.com

1994 Jeff Bezos incorporates Amazon.com.

1995 Amazon.com launches its Web site.

1997 Amazon.com holds initial public offering of stock at $18 per share.

1999 Amazon.com diversifies its offerings to include a wide variety of merchandise.

1999 Original shares of Amazon.com are worth $500.

2001 In the last quarter, Amazon.com posts its first profit.

2001 Shares of Amazon.com drop to $5.51.

2002 Shares of Amazon.com rise to $20.

Workers fill Christmas orders at Amazon's Seattle warehouse in 1999.

Further Reading

Reid, Robert. *Architects of the Web: 1,000 Days That Built the Future of Business.* New York: Wiley, 1997.

Spector, Robert. *Amazon.com: Get Big Fast.* New York: HarperCollins, 2000.

Wolinsky, Art. *The History of the Internet and the World Wide Web.* Berkeley Heights, N.J.: Enslow, 1999.

—Joseph Gustaitis

American Express Company

Founded as a freight company more than 150 years ago, the American Express Company (AmEx) is best known for its flagship charge card and travelers' check products. Since the advent of the credit card, American Express has been locked in a battle with other card issuers for control of the credit card market.

From Transport to Financial Services

On March 18, 1850, the American Express Company was created from the consolidation of three separate express freight transport companies: Livingston, Fargo & Company, founded in 1845 by Henry Wells (1805–1878) and William G. Fargo (1818–1881), later of Wells Fargo fame; Wells & Co., cofounded by Wells in 1846; and Butterfield & Wasson. The company grew quickly and, by the end of the Civil War, had 900 offices in 10 states. In 1866, after a bitter battle for dominance with rival transport company Merchants Union Express, the two companies merged to form Merchants Union Express Company, with Fargo as president. Merchants Union was renamed American Express Company in 1873.

When Fargo died in 1881, his younger brother, James Congdell Fargo (1829–1915), became president; he ran the company for 33 years. James Fargo introduced the American Express Money Order (1882) and the American Express Travelers Cheque (1891). In 1895 he opened the first American Express European office in Paris to handle the overseas banking of American travelers . This service eventually proved so popular that AmEx opened a separate travel department in 1915.

In 1918, with involvement in World War I mounting, the U.S. government nationalized the freight express industry and consolidated all domestic express operations (the industry would be denationalized in 1929). With the loss of its freight express business, AmEx focused on its travel and banking operations. In the 1950s, AmEx's banking business was given a huge boost by the advent of a new type of credit card.

The First Credit Cards

In 1950 Diners Club introduced the first credit card that could be used at a variety of businesses. The company charged cardholders an annual fee and billed them monthly. In 1951 New York's Franklin National Bank issued the first bank credit card. The bank issued the credit card and credited the account of the merchant as sales slips were received. The cardholder was billed for purchases each month and paid the bank in

See also:
Credit Cards and Debit Cards; Wells Fargo.

An American Express deliveryman with a shipment, 1922.

monthly installments. Banks made money off this kind of credit card by extending the repayment time and charging interest on the unpaid balance. Overnight, a new source of profit was created for the banks and they began issuing the cards to almost anyone who asked. To reduce risk, banks imposed relatively low credit limits on cardholders.

American Express began issuing credit cards in 1958 with a different corporate goal in mind. Rather than issue cards to all applicants, AmEx issued cards only to preferred customers. Instead of a credit limit, users could charge almost any amount. The amount paid off by the following month was not charged interest, while any amount not paid off was charged a very high interest rate. American Express also made money by charging a high annual fee to the cardholder and by charging retailers a fee for each transaction using the card.

AmEx became a prestige card. Not having a limit also made the AmEx card useful in emergencies, as emphasized by the company's slogan, "Don't leave home without it." By 2000 the credit card division accounted for 72 percent of the company's profits.

The Competition

Competition between credit card systems was fierce. They raced to sign member banks to issue cards and to enroll merchants. Credit card companies forbade banks and merchants that offered or accepted one card from offering or accepting others. In 1978, with competition stifling business, the MasterCard and Visa organizations signed an agreement allowing banks and merchants to honor and issue both credit cards.

The Visa-MasterCard agreement included bylaws that prevented member banks from issuing American Express cards. Beginning in 1981, Visa-MasterCard also began chipping away at American Express's prestige image by issuing the MasterCard Gold and Visa Gold cards, carrying a minimum credit line of $5,000. Many consumers also began balking at paying American Express's high annual fees, and merchants were unhappy with the high processing fees charged by American Express.

In the 1990s the company's chief executive, James Robinson, led American Express on a series of costly and ill-considered forays into brokerage and investment banking services that left the company weakened and its workforce demoralized. Moreover, American Express's market share of the card business was severely eroded by other, more creative and competitive companies that issued credit and charge cards under the Visa and MasterCard umbrella.

Antitrust Trouble

In 1997 the U.S. Justice Department began investigating charges that the Visa-Mastercard

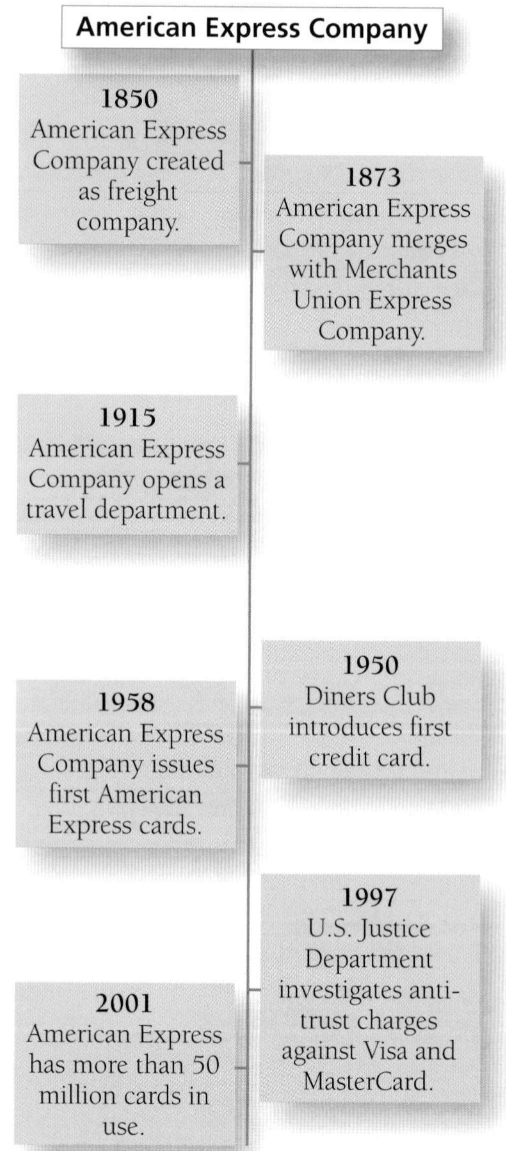

A man looks at an advertisement for American Express in Shanghai in 2001.

bylaws created an illegal cartel. The chain stores Wal-Mart and The Limited then filed an antitrust lawsuit against Visa and MasterCard, alleging that the companies coerced merchants into accepting their debit cards at the same fees as their credit cards. Retailers argued that the debit card fees were so expensive to consumers and retailers that they were competitive only because retailers were forced to accept them. In October 2001, the U.S. District Court ruled against Visa and MasterCard, and forced them to amend the bylaws to allow competition.

Following the antitrust case, many banks began issuing American Express cards. American Express also began making up for lost time by focusing on the growth of its travel related services (TRS) division. The TRS division introduced several new revolving credit card products that focused on specific groups of customers.

By 2001, American Express had more than 50 million cards in force, up 12 percent from the previous year. AmEx also focused on expanding its financial services division, which brought in about 26 percent of the company's profits. American Express is still seen as a prestige brand, and its expansion into other areas, insurance and education among them, will likely keep the company strong for some time to come.

Further Reading

Burrough, Bryan. *Vendetta: American Express and the Smearing of Edmond Safra.* London: HarperCollins, 1992.

Carrington, Timothy. *The Year They Sold Wall Street.* Boston: Houghton Mifflin, 1985.

Friedman, Jon, and John Meehan. *House of Cards: Inside the Troubled Empire of American Express.* New York: Putnam, 1992.

Grossman, Peter Z. *American Express:The Unofficial History of the People Who Built the Great Financial Empire.* New York: Crown Publishers, 1987.

Lipartito, Kenneth, and Carol Heher Peters. *Investing for Middle America: John Elliott Tappan and the Origins of American Express Financial Advisors.* New York: Palgrave for St. Martin's Press, 2001.

Wiersema, Fred, ed. *Customer Service: Extraordinary Results at Southwest Airlines, Charles Schwab, Lands' End, American Express, Staples, and USAA.* New York: HarperBusiness, 1998.

—Lisa Magloff

See also:
Nasdaq; New York Stock Exchange; Savings and Investment Options; Stocks and Bonds.

American Stock Exchange

The American Stock Exchange (Amex) is the second-largest floor-based exchange in the United States. Previously known as the New York Curb Agency, the New York Curb Market, and the New York Curb Exchange, it received its present name in 1953. Coming from a tradition of trading company stocks out-of-doors, the Curb did not have an indoor trading floor until 1921. In 1998 the Amex merged with the National Association of Securities Dealers (NASD), which also operates the Nasdaq stock market, but the Amex has continued to operate independently. In 2000 NASD members voted to restructure the organization, creating a for-profit, shareholder-owned company. Press reports in 2002 indicated that the New York Stock Exchange (NYSE; also called the Big Board) was considering buying the Amex from the NASD.

American Stock Exchange

1890s New York Curb Agency trades on Broad Street in Manhattan.

1921 Curb moves trading floor indoors.

1953 Curb changes name to American Stock Exchange (the Amex).

1962 The Amex receives a new constitution.

1998 The Amex merges with the National Association of Securities Dealers (NASD).

2000 Creation of International Securities Exchange challenges the Amex.

The Amex was traditionally second to the NYSE in prominence until the Nasdaq emerged. Nasdaq was created in 1971 and by the 1990s had grown to surpass the Amex. The Amex and the Nasdaq generally trade shares of companies that are smaller and less established than those traded by the NYSE.

Buying and selling of securities on the Amex is conducted by specialists, that is, traders who work with the securities of specific companies or groups of companies. Common stocks, bonds, and options are traded both through computer-delivered orders and on the floor, with most of the trading done electronically. A popular innovation is index-linked equities based on the Standard & Poor's 500 stock index. More than 800 Amex members use current technology to maintain efficient, reliable, and fair markets.

The trading of stocks in New York City can be traced back as far as the 1790s. As in major European cities, people who wanted to buy and sell shares would meet in a particular place, such as Exchange Alley in London. As trading in New York moved indoors during the nineteenth century, smaller and less respectable traders were left out on the street, literally, and bought and sold stocks in companies that were too small or insignificant to be of interest to the established exchanges. Such traders were sometimes involved in running "bucket shops," a term that implied shady or dishonest practices.

The establishment, represented primarily by the New York Stock Exchange (or its precursor, the Stock and Exchange Board), found specializing in larger and more secure companies more profitable, and left the more marginal issues to those men known as curbstone brokers. These brokers were often able to make substantial profits in dynamic new industries. This market provided opportunities to people like Irish or Eastern European Jewish immigrants, whose ethnic background made it unlikely that they would be granted access to the Big Board.

From the 1890s until 1921 the Curb operated on Broad Street in lower Manhattan, not far from the NYSE. Many brokers had offices in a nearby building, from which their clerks would communicate with them by hand signals, with the brokers wearing brightly colored hats or other distinctive clothing to make them stand out in the noisy, milling crowd. During this period the Consolidated Stock Exchange was the second-most-important stock exchange, the position that the Amex later held through much of the twentieth century.

During the 1920s the Amex thrived in an unregulated, freewheeling atmosphere that allowed practices that would be unacceptable today. During the Depression of the 1930s and World War II, the Amex suffered a decline in its fortunes, and more than one scandal marked this period as state and federal intervention, most notably the creation of the Securities and Exchange Commission, brought increased regulation. A reform movement led to the creation of a new constitution for the Amex in 1962, as well as improving its reputation and bringing new prestige. These changes are reflected in the price of a seat on the Amex, which went, for example, from a high of $254,000 in 1929, to a low of $650 in 1942, and then to a high of $350,000 in 1969.

As the twenty-first century began, questions of improper practices continued to be raised from time to time, and the Amex and other options markets were challenged by competition from the International Securities Exchange (ISE), created in 2000, the first purely electronic options market. The value of seats on the traditional exchanges fell. Increased competition from exchanges in other cities also presented a challenge.

An Amex-Nasdaq flag hangs at the American Stock Exchange, 1998. The Amex and Nasdaq are both operated by the National Association of Securities Dealers.

Further Reading

Sobel, Robert. *Amex: A History of the American Stock Exchange, 1921–1971.* New York: Weybright and Talley, 1972.

———. *The Curbstone Brokers: The Origins of the American Stock Exchange.* New York: Macmillan, 1970.

Weiss, Gary. "The American Stock Exchange: Scandal on Wall Street." *Business Week,* April 26, 1999, 96–100.

———. "Commentary: Has the Curb Market Moved into the Gutter?" *Business Week,* September 11, 2000, 136–138.

—*Peter K. Reinhart*

See also:
Civil Rights Legislation; Cost; Equal Employment Opportunity Commission; Human Resources; Regulation of Business and Industry.

Americans with Disabilities Act

The Americans with Disabilities Act (ADA) was enacted by the U.S Congress in 1990 to open the doors of employment to millions of qualified people with disabilities. The act created new federal rights to protect people with disabilities from discrimination in hiring, employment, and access to places of public accommodation.

Congressional studies in the 1980s had shown that 66 percent of working-age people with disabilities in the United States were not employed. The cost to the nation was estimated at $300 billion per year, including welfare payments and lost taxes and productivity. Congress sought to ensure that people with disabilities could participate in society as members of the workforce.

Civil Rights Legislation

The ADA was enacted near the end of a four-decade period during which the U.S. government undertook new measures to address and eliminate discriminatory practices that had excluded groups of people from participation in civic affairs, work, and education. The Civil Rights Act of 1964 and the Voting Rights Act of 1965 provided federal protection against various forms of discrimination based on race, religion, or national origin. In 1968 Congress passed the Architectural Barriers Act, requiring improved means of access to federal buildings (through ramps and electric doors, for example) for people with physical disabilities. The Rehabilitation Act of 1973 expanded opportunities for qualified workers with disabilities to gain employment in federal government jobs and in work funded by federal government contracts. In 1975 Congress passed the Education for All Handicapped Children Act, a far-reaching measure intended to ensure that handicapped children would receive "a free appropriate public education...designed to meet their unique needs."

Against this background of initiatives, people with disabilities and their supporters in Congress began in the 1980s to argue for a federal law that would bolster employment rights. The Paralyzed Veterans of America and other disability organizations lobbied Congress, and several reports concluded that a new federal law was urgently needed. Late in 1987 Robert L. Burgdorf, Jr., a law professor at the University of the District of Columbia, wrote the original draft of the ADA for the National Council on Disability. Congress first addressed the issue in 1988,

George H. W. Bush signs the Americans with Disabilities Act in 1990.

The Americans with Disabilities Act of 1990
(Excerpt)

FINDINGS AND PURPOSES.

(a) Findings. The Congress finds that—

(1) some 43,000,000 Americans have one or more physical or mental disabilities, and this number is increasing as the population as a whole is growing older;
(2) historically, society has tended to isolate and segregate individuals with disabilities, and, despite some improvements, such forms of discrimination against individuals with disabilities continue to be a serious and pervasive social problem;
(3) discrimination against individuals with disabilities persists in such critical areas as employment, housing, public accommodations, education, transportation, communication, recreation, institutionalization, health services, voting, and access to public services;
(4) unlike individuals who have experienced discrimination on the basis of race, color, sex, national origin, religion, or age, individuals who have experienced discrimination on the basis of disability have often had no legal recourse to redress such discrimination;
(5) individuals with disabilities continually encounter various forms of discrimination, including outright intentional exclusion, the discriminatory effects of architectural, transportation, and communication barriers, overprotective rules and policies, failure to make modifications to existing facilities and practices, exclusionary qualification standards and criteria, segregation, and relegation to lesser services, programs, activities, benefits, jobs, or other opportunities;
(6) census data, national polls, and other studies have documented that people with disabilities, as a group, occupy an inferior status in our society, and are severely disadvantaged socially, vocationally, economically, and educationally;
(7) individuals with disabilities are a discrete and insular minority who have been faced with restrictions and limitations, subjected to a history of purposeful unequal treatment, and relegated to a position of political powerlessness in our society, based on characteristics that are beyond the control of such individuals and resulting from stereotypic assumptions not truly indicative of the individual ability of such individuals to participate in, and contribute to, society;
(8) the Nation's proper goals regarding individuals with disabilities are to assure equality of opportunity, full participation, independent living, and economic self-sufficiency for such individuals; and
(9) the continuing existence of unfair and unnecessary discrimination and prejudice denies people with disabilities the opportunity to compete on an equal basis and to pursue those opportunities for which our free society is justifiably famous, and costs the United States billions of dollars in unnecessary expenses resulting from dependency and nonproductivity.

(b) Purpose. It is the purpose of this Act—
(1) to provide a clear and comprehensive national mandate for the elimination of discrimination against individuals with disabilities;
(2) to provide clear, strong, consistent, enforceable standards addressing discrimination against individuals with disabilities;
(3) to ensure that the Federal Government plays a central role in enforcing the standards established in this Act on behalf of individuals with disabilities; and
(4) to invoke the sweep of congressional authority, including the power to enforce the fourteenth amendment and to regulate commerce, in order to address the major areas of discrimination faced day-to-day by people with disabilities.

focusing on legislation sponsored by Senator Tom Harkin (D–Iowa) and several others. A two-year legislative effort ensued, culminating in passage of the ADA by a landslide vote in July 1990.

Upon its passage, the ADA was described by many as a landmark civil rights statute. "Today," said Senator Harkin at the time, "our nation says 'no' to second-class citizenship for people with disabilities. Today, our nation says 'yes' to dignity and respect for people with disabilities."

What Is a Disability?

Precisely what qualifies for protection under the ADA is not always obvious. The ADA defines a disability as a "physical or mental impairment that substantially limits one or more of the major life activities of such individual; a record of such an impairment; or being regarded as having such an impairment." This broad definition is not based on a list of specific disorders, such as cerebral palsy or the loss of a leg. It is based instead on an individual's ability to perform major life activities, such as "caring for oneself" and "performing manual tasks."

In three cases decided between 1998 and 1999, the U.S. Supreme Court ruled that the determination of disability must also take into consideration whether the person is substantially limited in a major life activity *when using a mitigating measure* such as medication or a hearing aid. These rulings emphasized that effective use of a mitigating measure would not automatically exclude a person from a disability classification. In the aftermath of the rulings, determination of whether a person has a disability has increasingly become a matter of a case-by-case evaluation. The unfixed nature of what constitutes a disability has led to several controversies, such as the lawsuit brought by professional golfer Casey Martin (see box).

Casey Martin and the Americans with Disabilities Act

Since the enactment of the ADA, judicial circles have debated about how broadly its provisions should be applied. Public attention was drawn to this dispute by a 2001 U.S. Supreme Court decision. Casey Martin, a professional golfer, suffers from Klippel-Trenaunay-Weber Syndrome, a rare circulatory disease that causes him great pain when he walks. In light of this disability, Martin asked the Professional Golfer's Association (PGA) Tour to let him use a golf cart during tournaments. The PGA refused, arguing it would give him an unfair advantage over the other players, and Martin sued. In May 2001 the Supreme Court decided in Martin's favor by a 7–2 margin.

The majority's decision rested on whether allowing Martin to use a cart "fundamentally altered the nature" of the contest. They maintained that golf is a game of skill wherein success depends upon the placement of shots, rather than the physical stamina necessary to walk the course, and so allowing Martin his cart did not fundamentally alter the competition.

The minority opinion, written by Justice Antonin Scalia, objected to applying the ADA to Martin's case at all, because Martin was not an employee of the PGA, but rather a voluntary competitor in a privately run contest. Scalia argued that the purpose of a sports competition is to discriminate between the physical abilities of the contestants and that it was not for the Court to decide which rules do and do not fundamentally alter the nature of golf.

The victory was bittersweet for Martin; he was not immediately able to take advantage of the ruling because he failed to qualify for the PGA Tour in 2001. The ruling also received a mixed reaction in the sports world: some lauded it as a victory for disabled athletes, while other commentators worried that sport's governing bodies would feel compelled to make increasingly unreasonable accommodations for certain players rather than risk costly court battles. The Court's decision may have brought one man justice, but it will likely encourage more lawsuits, and even further refinement of the ADA's application.

—Colleen Sullivan

What the ADA Requires

The Americans with Disabilities Act is divided into five sections, or titles. Most experts agree that Title I, which requires equal employment opportunity and nondiscrimination in employment, is the most important section. Businesses that employ 15 or more people must comply with special regulations, overseen by the U.S. Equal Employment Opportunity Commission (EEOC). These regulations cover a range of hiring practices, including help wanted ads and job interview procedures. If a job applicant or worker with a disability believes he or she has been discriminated against by an employer or potential employer, the applicant or worker may file a complaint with the EEOC.

Title II of the ADA requires nondiscrimination in access to the services of state and local governments and to public transportation. For example, it is a violation of the ADA if a person in a wheelchair is unable to use the services of a public library. It is also a violation if a person in a wheelchair is unable to use national or commuter railroads or city buses.

Title III requires access to "places of public accommodation." Places of public accommodation include businesses and other facilities—retail stores, restaurants, parks, grocery stores, banks, drug stores, and college campuses. Title III also requires provisions for access to the professional offices of doctors, dentists, lawyers, and accountants.

Title IV mandates establishment of a national telephone relay service, providing a person who is deaf in Boston, for example, with the ability to communicate over telephone lines to a hearing person in San Francisco. This telephone relay service is now being used by about 26 million Americans. It employs telephone telecommunication devices (TDD). A TDD is a small device that can be hooked up to a personal computer. A deaf person can send text from a TDD directly to a relay service operator. The operator in turn reads the message to a hearing person on the phone and sends back messages to the deaf person on a TDD. The service is available 24 hours a day.

Title V adapts the enforcement mechanisms that appear in the Civil Rights Act of 1964 to cases of discrimination against people with disabilities. Title V gives individuals who have been discriminated against on the basis of a disability a wide range of remedies, including hiring, reinstatement in a job, promotion, back pay, and compensation for attorney's fees and other court costs incurred in the case of a successful complaint. The ADA does not cover employees of the federal government.

Implementation of the ADA

As businesses have implemented the ADA, adopting policies and practices consistent with its requirements, two legal concepts have been especially important. These concepts are essential functions and reasonable accommodations.

Essential functions are the fundamental duties that a qualified applicant must be able to perform on the job. Title I of the ADA holds that when an individual with a disability applies for a job, he or she must meet an essential-functions criterion to qualify for Title I protection. For example, if a job requires typing 75 words per minute, an applicant who can type only 65 words per minute would not meet the essential-functions requirement.

Essential functions are distinguished from marginal or incidental functions. If the essential functions requirement for a given job includes the ability to type 75 words a minute, and the job also requires that the employee make a weekly delivery to another office, the latter requirement might be deemed a marginal function—one that another employee could carry out. In such a case, the person able to type 75 words per minute might be deemed a qualified applicant for the job, even if he or she could not meet the marginal function of making the delivery.

While employers may insist that all employees be able to perform essential functions, employers also are required to make reasonable accommodations for workers with disabilities. The reasonable-accommodation concept may require a wide range of adjustments, depending on the job and the workplace environment. For example, a qualified worker who uses a wheelchair might not be able to enter a company lunchroom; in such a case, as a reasonable accommodation, the employer might be required to build a ramp or make other modifications to provide wheelchair access. Reasonable accommodation might also require modified work schedules and flexible leave practices, enabling workers with disabilities to take time during the week to visit the doctor. The employer might be required to purchase devices like special telephone equipment for use by hearing-impaired workers.

The Impact of the ADA

The ADA has been especially significant for small businesses. The employment provisions of the ADA apply to 87 percent of America's jobs in the private sector.

Accessibile Parking Spaces

Total Parking in Lot	Required Minimum Number of Accessible Handicap Spaces
1 to 25	1
26 to 50	2
51 to 75	3
76 to 100	4
101 to 150	5
151 to 200	6
201 to 300	7
301 to 400	8
401 to 500	9
501 to 1,000	2 percent of total
1,001 and over	20, plus 1 for each 100 over 1,000

Source: Department of Justice, *ADA Standards for Accessible Design*, Washington, D.C., Government Printing Office, 1994.

The ADA mandates how many parking spaces must be made available for people with disabilities.

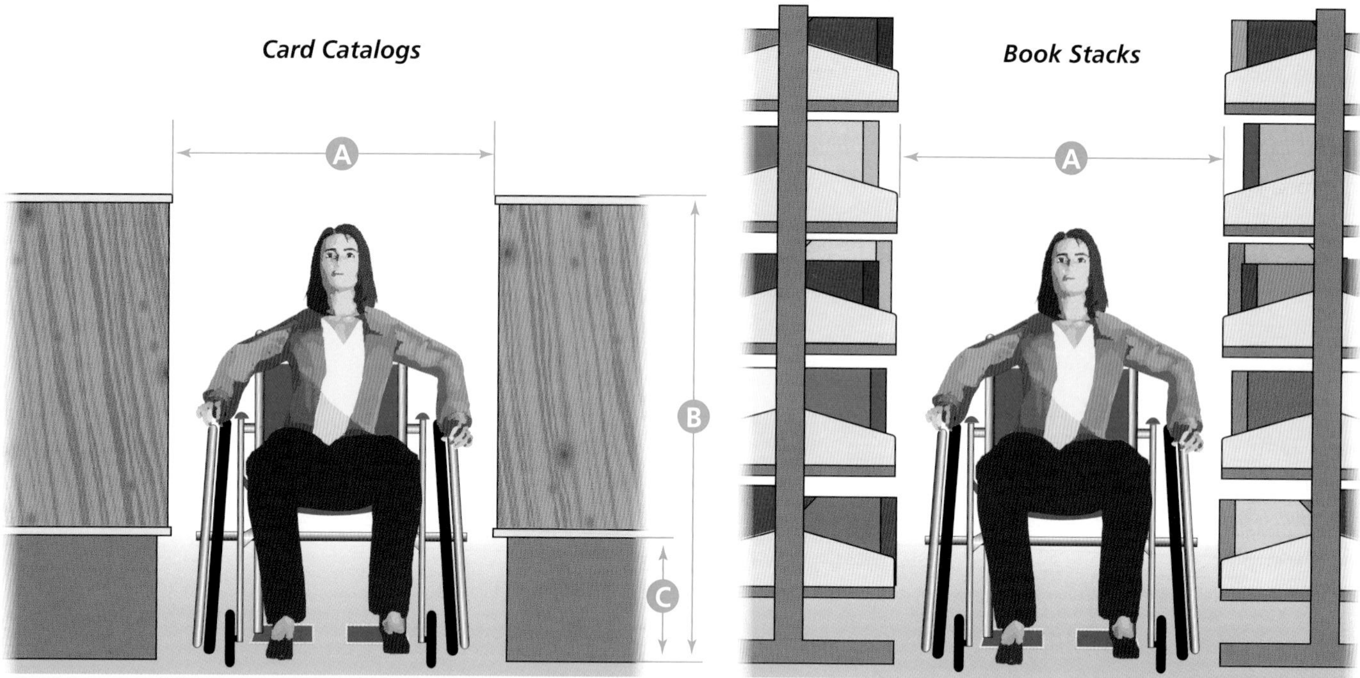

Among its many regulations, the ADA mandates that public facilities, including libraries, must be accessible to all. Libraries must observe particular standards as to the height of card catalogs and the width of aisles.

American small businesses account for 45 million of the more than 80 million jobs covered by the ADA, according to the Small Business Administration.

When enacting the ADA, Congress realized there would be new costs for business and industry in implementing the law. The costs in question are highly individual, thus generalizing about them is difficult. According to the Job Accommodation Network, 75 percent of employees hired under the ADA do not need a reasonable accommodation. The average cost of a reasonable accommodation, such as a device to assist a deaf worker, is about $300, according to the National Council on Disability. Some kinds of reasonable accommodation, like a modified or flexible work schedule, entail no new costs. A business that can demonstrate it has an "undue hardship" in financing the cost of a reasonable accommodation can be relieved of that obligation.

The ADA also holds out potential benefits for businesses; most significantly, the ADA has greatly enlarged the pool of potential workers. Flexible work schedules make employment at some firms more attractive to prospective employees. These potential benefits may help to explain why the ADA has the support of the Council of Better Business Bureaus, Inc., which has 270,000 members.

Further Reading

Bristo, Marco, ed. *Promises to Keep: A Decade of Federal Enforcement of the Americans with Disabilities Act.* Collingdale, Pa.: DIANE Publishing, 2001.

Fersh, Don. *Complying with the Americans with Disabilities Act.* Westport, Conn.: Quorum Books, 1993.

Gordon, Michael, ed. *Accommodations in Higher Education under the Americans with Disabilities Act.* New York: Guilford Publications, 1998.

West, Jane, ed. *Implementing the Americans with Disabilities Act.* Cambridge, Mass.: Blackwell Publishers, 1996.

—Don Fersh

Amortization and Depreciation

See also:
Accounting and Bookkeeping; Balance Sheet; Income Statement.

In accounting, amortization and depreciation are ways of recognizing the cost of an asset as an expense in each period of the asset's life. The difference between amortization and depreciation is that amortization is used with intangible assets (assets that have legal rather than physical substance, such as patents, trademarks, and copyrights), and depreciation is used with tangible assets (physical assets other than land). Depletion, a type of depreciation, is used to recognize the cost of a natural resource (such as a coal mine, oil pool, or mineral deposit) over the life of the asset.

The process of amortization and depreciation takes into account that most assets decrease in value over time. The decrease in value is caused by the consumption of an asset's services and can involve wear and tear or simply the passage of time. In accounting, land is the only physical asset that is excluded from being depreciated because land is not perceived to lose value as it is used; in fact, the value of the land tends to increase.

The methods for calculating depreciation and amortization are similar. After they are calculated, amortization and depreciation are both reported on the income statement in the period they are expensed. The amortization and depreciation expense is theoretically supposed to match the period that the asset contributes to the revenue of the firm. (A basic premise in accounting is that expenses should appear on the income statement to match the revenues that appear on the same income statement.) However, monitoring each asset to make sure it is expensed in the correct period is very difficult and not cost efficient for a company. Therefore, the company is permitted to choose one of several methods to approximate the matching of the expense of the asset with its revenue in each period of its useful life. These methods will be discussed in the next section.

Accumulated amortization and depreciation are also reported on the balance sheet. Accumulated amortization and depreciation are simply the cumulative expenses from the beginning of an asset's life until the end of the current accounting period. On the balance sheet, accumulated amortization and depreciation are subtracted from the original cost of an asset. The resulting number on the balance sheet is called the book value or carrying amount of the asset.

Depreciation Methods

Several methods are used to calculate depreciation. Each requires at least the following three pieces of information: acquisition cost, expected life, and an estimate of the residual value (or salvage value) at the end of the expected life. The acquisition cost is the actual price paid for the asset. If the asset was built instead of purchased, the acquisition cost is the cost of all the raw materials purchased plus the labor costs to build the asset. The expected life is the period an individual or business will benefit from the asset. Expected life can be either the estimation of the asset's physical life (until the asset can no longer perform) or an estimation of when the asset is planned to be sold. The residual value is also an estimate. It is the amount of cash or trade-in value the owner expects to receive for the asset at the end of its expected life. Typically this estimate is very low in relation to the purchase price of the asset.

Each asset declines in value differently. Some assets decline evenly each year while others vary year-to-year. Accordingly, the federal government permits businesses and individuals to use several depreciation methods that most accurately match the depreciation expense with the revenues generated from the asset. The four most common methods are the straight-line method, sum-of-the-years'-digits method, declining balance method, and the usage method.

Straight-Line Depreciation

The straight-line depreciation method spreads equal amounts of the asset's cost across each year of the asset's expected life. This method is the most common because it

Book Value of an Asset

On-Time Trucking Corp.
Balance Sheet
As of March 31, 2002

	Mar. 31, 2002
ASSETS	
Current Assets	
Checking/Saving	
Checking	20,627.20
Money Market	13,259.36
Vista	12,824.65
Total Checking/Savings	46,711.21
Accounts Receivable	
Accounts Receivable	136,444.09
Total Accounts Receivable	136,444.09
Other Current Assets	
Loan to Officers	-0.50
Tax Refund Receivable	-1.04
Salary Advance	560.00
Security Deposits	13,920.79
Total Other Current Assets	14,479.25
Total Current Assets	197,634.55
Fixed Assets	
Equipment	
Original Cost	30,595.00
Accumulated Depreciation	-20,303.00
Book Value	10,292.00
TOTAL ASSETS	207,926.55

Assets are depreciated as part of drawing up a balance sheet; the highlighted section here shows such a calculation for trucking equipment.

is the most typical way an asset (such as a factory or a machine) decreases in value. In addition, because this method requires only a simple calculation, it is the easiest to apply to a large number of assets.

The calculation of straight-line depreciation is based on an asset's depreciable cost. The depreciable cost is the asset's acquisition cost minus its residual value. In this and all other depreciation methods, the depreciable cost is also the total amount of depreciation that will be charged over the asset's estimated life. The only difference between the methods is how the total depreciation is spread over the estimated life. In the straight-line method depreciation is calculated in all periods as follows: acquisition cost less residual value divided by expected life of the asset.

For example, assume that a company buys a machine for $50,000. The company expects that it will use the machine for 10 years and at the end of the 10 years sell the machine for $5,000. The depreciation for each of the 10 years is ($50,000 – $5,000) / 10, or $4,500.

Sum-of-the-Years'-Digits

The sum-of-the-years'-digits is an accelerated depreciation method that multiplies the depreciable cost by a declining ratio each passing year. The method is accelerated because most of the depreciation occurs in the first few years. An example of an asset that depreciates more in its first few years is an automobile. The ratio is easy to calculate, but because a different ratio is used each year, this method is slightly more difficult to implement than the straight-line method.

To calculate the ratio for each year, the denominator is the sum of all the years of the asset's life (therefore, the denominator stays the same each year) and the numerator is the inverse of the year of depreciation. For example, assume the same $50,000 machine as above. The denominator of the ratio is always 55 for an asset with a 10-year life span (10 + 9 + 8 + 7 + 6 + 5 + 4 + 3 + 2 + 1 = 55). The numerator starts at 10, then 9, and so on from the first to the tenth year. The following is the calculation of the depreciation expense in the first two years and the final year:

Year 1: (10/55) × ($50,000 – $5,000) = $8,181.82
Year 2: (9/55) × ($50,000 – $5,000) = $7,363.64
Year 10: (1/55) × ($50,000 – $5,000) = $818.18

Declining Balance Method

Declining balance is another accelerated method of depreciation. However, it differs from sum-of-the-years'-digits in that it uses book value as a base rather than depreciable cost. This method is more difficult to implement than the previous two because the calculation requires the company to determine the book value before applying the depreciation rate. The calculation is as follows:

Straight-line rate × Accelerator × (Acquisition cost – Accumulated Depreciation)

The straight-line rate reflects the rate of depreciation as though the asset were being depreciated using the straight-line method. As in the above example, this would be 1/10, or one year divided by the total years of the asset's expected life. The accelerator is a number chosen by the company and its accountants after an analysis of the asset's wear and tear; many choose to use the number 2. Using the above examples, below is the calculation of the depreciation for the first three years:

Year 1: (1/10) × 2 × ($50,000 – $0) = $10,000
Year 2: (1/10) × 2 × ($50,000 – $10,000) = $8,000
Year 3: (1/10) × 2 × ($50,000 – $18,000) = $6,400
Year 10: The remaining book value is depreciated in the final year.

Usage Method

The usage method is the most difficult to implement because it is not based on a general percentage but on the actual usage of the asset. The calculation is similar to the sum-of-the-years'-digits:

Usage ratio × (Acquisition cost – Residual value)

The usage value is based on a specific base used to measure the entire life of the asset. For example, a trucking company may estimate that each truck will last 300,000 miles. Each year, the usage ratio is the actual miles driven that year divided by 300,000. Assume the truck drives 50,000 miles in year one and 45,000 miles in year two and has the same cost and salvage value as in the previous example. The depreciation is as follows:

Year 1: (50,000/300,000) × ($50,000 – $5,000) = $7,500
Year 2: (45,000/300,000) × ($50,000 – $5,000) = $6,750

Amortization

Amortization is the depreciation of intangible assets. The most common intangible assets are patents, copyrights, trademarks, leaseholds, organization costs, and franchises. The amortization of intangible assets can be calculated with methods similar to those used to calculate depreciation. However, estimating the useful lives of intangible assets is more difficult than estimating the useful lives of physical assets. Some intangible assets like patents and copyrights have legal lives dictated by the courts, but many of these assets do not have value for that length of time. Therefore, the useful life is typically shorter than the legal life. In addition, the salvage value is usually zero, or close to zero, and therefore does not affect the calculation of depreciation expense as much as the calculation physical assets.

Because physical and intangible assets are such a big part of a company's actual value, amortization and depreciation profoundly affect financial statements. Therefore, the most appropriate method must be chosen to accurately reflect the use of assets. Guidelines are available for determining the choice of the method to be used; however, some methods create more favorable financial pictures of a company's performance and value than others. Therefore, an incentive does exist to apply improperly a method that will craft a certain view of the company's assets and, far worse, misrepresent the value of the company as a whole.

Further Reading

Anthony, Robert, and Leslie Pearlman. *Essentials of Accounting*. New York: Prentice Hall, 1999.
Tracy, John A. *Accounting for Dummies*. New York: Hungry Minds, 2001.

—Andréa Korb and David Korb

See also:
Arts and Entertainment Industry; Brand Names; Information Technology; Internet; Publishing Industry.

AOL Time Warner

AOL Time Warner is a media colossus. Despite staggering losses in shareholder value, the company generates billions in annual revenues from movies, broadcast and cable television, music, book and magazine publishing, and the Internet.

AOL Time Warner controls an enormous range of familiar media brands including America Online Internet service, with more than 30 million subscribers, and the Internet software manufacturer Netscape. The company's Warner Bros. division produces and distributes popular movies and television shows. AOL Time Warner owns the Time Warner cable television network and the HBO premium cable channel. Turner Broadcasting System is a subsidiary of AOL Time Warner; it, in turn, owns the cable-television networks CNN, Turner Classic Movies, and the Cartoon Network, among others, as well as professional sports teams including baseball's Atlanta Braves. In addition, the company owns a majority stake in the WB broadcast television network.

The AOL Time Warner magazine publishing division produces such titles as *Time*, *People*, *Entertainment Weekly*, and *Sports Illustrated*. Book publishing includes Warner Books and Little, Brown. Record labels owned by the music division include Atlantic, Elektra, London-Sire, Reprise, and Warner Brothers; the company has ownership stakes in several other labels as well.

AOL Time Warner was formed in January 2001 through the $103 billion acquisition by Internet service provider America Online (AOL) of Time Warner. At that point, Time Warner was already a media giant, the product of the 1989 acquisition of entertainment conglomerate Warner Communications by magazine publisher and cable television company Time Inc.

The creation of AOL Time Warner reflects trends evident since the 1990s in the media industry. Internet operations are

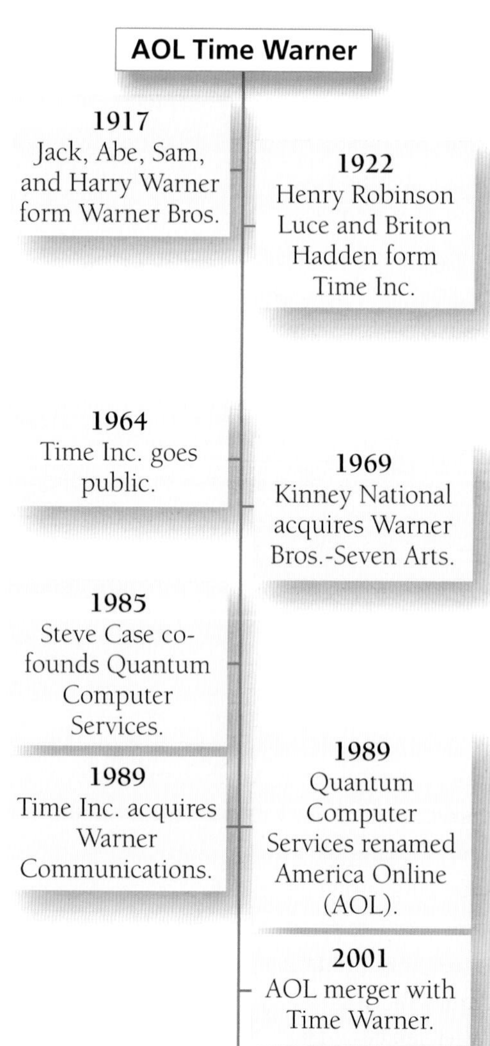

America Online

America Online (AOL) was founded in 1985 as Quantum Computer Services. This predates the general popularity of the Internet by several years, making AOL one of the oldest online services still operating.

Founder Steve Case claims he was born with entrepreneurial blood. His childhood venture, a lemonade stand, was profitable, as were four companies he founded while in college. In 1982 Case bought a personal computer, hoping to participate in the world of online bulletin-board systems (BBS). He had a tough time getting the equipment to work, but he was thrilled to be able to reach out via computer. His frustration with the difficulty of setting up his connection and his excitement communicating with others outside his community were experiences that likely influenced his focus on ease-of-use when he founded Quantum a few years later.

In 1989 Case gave Quantum a face-lift, renamed it America Online, and began recruiting members by appealing to a mainstream, technically illiterate audience. AOL expanded its services to offer general Internet access in the early 1990s and grew quickly, gathering 4 million members by 1994. Through some troubling times in 1995 and 1996—service bottlenecks and crashes, dissatisfied customers, and lawsuits—AOL emerged scathed but still strong.

In 2001 AOL surpassed more than 32 million subscribers, establishing itself as the world's largest Internet service provider. AOL continues to expand its global audience, building customized versions of its service for each country.

Announcing the merger of America Online and Time Warner in 2001 are (left to right) AOL Chairman Steve Case, Time Warner Chairman Gerald Levin, and Time Warner Vice Chairman Ted Turner. By early 2003 all three had given up their leading roles in the venture.

viewed as increasingly crucial to media companies because broadband Internet, which could be used to deliver video and audio entertainment, is expected to eventually have the great majority of market share. AOL Time Warner also embodies a long-standing historical trend toward ever-greater media conglomeration.

In the 1960s hooking together seemingly unrelated businesses was very popular, largely because accounting practices of the time made conglomerates seem more profitable. In 1969, a company called Kinney National acquired Warner Bros.-Seven Arts, a movie and music company. Kinney National, under the leadership of Steve Ross, was a typical conglomerate of the day—its diverse businesses included funeral homes, parking lots, home construction, and a talent agency.

After the acquisition, most of the businesses unrelated to entertainment were spun off. Ross greatly expanded the resulting company, Warner Communications, by moving it into cable television early in that industry's development and adding publishing operations as well. He also made forays into considerably less successful businesses, including ones into seemingly unrelated fields such as cosmetics. The company's most damaging move was the acquisition of the Atari video game company, which went through a spectacular boom-and-bust in the early 1980s that carried its parent company's earnings and stock price down along with it.

In the late 1980s Warner Communications became interested in merging with Time Inc. While Time Inc. was well known as a magazine publisher and a journalistic enterprise, by the 1980s close to half its revenues came from its entertainment-oriented cable television

Warner Bros.

Four Warner brothers founded Warner Bros. in 1917. The brothers—Jack, Abe, Sam, and Harry—had become fascinated after 1910 by a great novelty of the time, the motion picture. They experimented first with running a movie theater, then decided to make movies themselves, despite their lack of experience, connections, and capital. Their company, Warner Bros., started small, making short films, but soon became a full-fledged movie studio, expanding into music production in the 1920s.

In 1927 Warner Bros. released *The Jazz Singer*, starring Al Jolson. It was the first motion picture with sound. The great popularity of the talkies helped to establish Warner Bros. as a major studio. The studio developed motion picture stars, including Bette Davis and Humphrey Bogart, who worked under strict, exclusive contracts—a hallmark of the studio system. In the mid-1940s, however, an actress named Olivia de Havilland successfully sued Warner Bros. for release from her contract. Her suit marked the beginning of the end of the studio system. In 1952, the federal government barred studios from owning their own theaters, further weakening the system.

In 1956 Jack Warner engineered a secret buyout of his two surviving brothers, Abe and Harry, to obtain exclusive control of Warner Bros. A decade later, he sold his shares to Seven Arts Productions, Ltd., a music and movie production company that three years later was taken over by Kinney National, which changed its name to Warner Communications. Warner Bros. continues to produce films, but it is now a movie and television division of the massive media conglomerate AOL Time Warner.

Time Inc.

Time Inc. was founded in 1922 by Henry Robinson Luce and Briton Hadden, two journalists eager to launch a weekly magazine that would present world news in a concise fashion for people who did not have the time to read a newspaper. The magazine they founded is *Time*; its first issue appeared in March 1923. *Time* has become one of the most widely read newsweeklies in the United States.

Hadden died in 1929, and Luce took charge of Time Inc. The enterprise quickly expanded. In 1936 the company launched *Life*, a picture magazine so popular when it first appeared that the cost of printing enough copies to meet demand threw its parent company into financial difficulty. Later Time Inc. introduced *Fortune* and *Sports Illustrated* magazines, and it ventured into book publication and newsreel production.

Time Inc. became a public company (it offered ownership shares for sale to the public) in 1964; Luce died three years later. Following Luce's death Time Inc. expanded further, amassing a cable television network, developing the premium cable channel HBO, and, in 1989, acquiring Warner Communications.

division, which included HBO. The deal, closed in 1989, was technically an acquisition of Warner Communications by Time, but the resulting company looked much more like the product of a merger, with executives from both companies in top spots at the new company.

The merger created an enormous company that appeared to have holdings across all kinds of media. The 1990s would reveal a sizable gap—the Internet. Enter America Online, a provider of both Internet and proprietary services that enjoyed rapid growth but inflated value in the 1990s. The company's simple interface and personal touch created such brand loyalty among users that serious service problems created largely by the influx of new customers could not drive them away. In 2001 America Online acquired Time Warner, but Time Warner's chief executive, Gerald Levin, kept his position. America Online's chief executive, Steven Case, became chairman of the combined company.

Debating the Merger

The expansion of Time Warner into AOL Time Warner intensified controversies over the value of Internet-based media and the seemingly unstoppable growth of media companies. In investing circles, the controversy continues to focus on the benefits of merging, especially the much-touted notion of synergy, the idea that a success in one of a media conglomerate's businesses can be spread across others. For example, the reality show *Pop Stars*, which aired on the WB network in 2000 and tracked the development of the pop group Eden's Crush, resulted in strong sales for the group's album, which was released on Time Warner's London-Sire label.

Owning several different kinds of media businesses may prove important as a defensive strategy. Despite federal regulations designed to prevent companies that own cable systems and cable television networks from blocking programs produced by rivals, media companies like AOL Time Warner that own distribution networks are in a better position to ensure that their products actually get seen by the public than are media companies that do not. The power of owning a distribution network was demonstrated in 2000, when Time Warner pulled the ABC Network (owned by rival Walt Disney Company) off its cable systems because of a payment dispute with Disney—a move that resulted in intense negative publicity and regulatory disapproval.

Consumer advocates worry that large players like AOL Time Warner will eventually squeeze out all smaller media companies, using their control over distribution networks to make inaccessible competitors' television programs, movies, records, and books. These fears become especially pronounced where news is concerned. Respected news outlets like *Time* magazine and CNN are now only small subdivisions of enormous corporations; some journalists worry that media conglomerates will pressure their news outlets to be uncritical of them and their products, while at the same time shutting off access to news outlets that they do not control.

Further Reading

Bruck, Connie. *Master of the Game: Steve Ross and the Creation of Time Warner.* New York: Simon & Schuster, 1994.

Byron, Christopher. *The Fanciest Dive: What Happened When the Media Empire of Time/Life Leaped without Looking into the Age of High-Tech.* New York: W. W. Norton, 1986.

Swisher, Kara. *aol.com: How Steve Case Beat Bill Gates, Nailed the Netheads, and Made Millions in the War for the Web.* Rev. ed. New York: Times Books, 1999.

—*Mary Sisson*

Arbitration

Arbitration is a method by which two parties involved in a dispute agree to have a neutral third party, the arbitrator, hear both sides of the argument, consider the facts, reach a decision and, when appropriate, make a monetary award. As part of the arbitration process, both parties customarily agree to abide by the decision of the arbitrator. While arbitration carries the weight of a legal proceeding, arbitrators are not necessarily lawyers or judges. Arbitrators may be persons with specialized knowledge in a field pertinent to the particular arbitration hearing.

Arbitration is often used as a way to avoid a long, costly court battle. Rather than have their case heard in a public court of law, the parties agree to have their differences privately arbitrated. Arbitration is usually quicker and less expensive than the trial process.

Sometimes arbitration may be the only available course. For example, credit card companies may ask their customers to sign an agreement that requires the customer to submit disputes to arbitration when differences are not routinely resolved. In some cases, employers ask prospective employees to sign arbitration agreements as a condition of their employment. Arbitration clauses may be included in any contract between two parties; the parties involved can be two individuals, an individual and a company, two companies, a labor union and management, or even two nations.

Although decisions reached through arbitration proceedings are usually binding on both parties, nonbinding arbitration does exist. In nonbinding arbitration, each party retains individual rights to have the case heard in a court of law.

History of Arbitration

Resolving international differences through arbitration dates to the first Hague Conference in 1899. The 26 nations participating agreed to consider questions of disarmament, methods of warfare, and the establishment of a permanent vehicle for the resolution of international disputes. Along with the other participating nations, the United States agreed to the creation of a Permanent Court of International Arbitration. However, arbitration was not made mandatory. In 1907, at the urging of President Theodore Roosevelt, a second Hague Conference was called. The apparatus for voluntary arbitration was enlarged at that time.

In 1925 the United States Congress passed the Federal Arbitration Act. As

See also:
Collective Bargaining; Labor Union; Regulation of Business and Industry; Screen Actors Guild.

In an 1886 cartoon by Joseph Keppler, two men set the hands (labor) of the clock (business). Arbitration, as the pendulum, swings in between them.

Individuals can use an arbitrator to mediate disputes.

originally envisioned, the act addressed arbitration of commercial contract disputes. Over time, however, federal arbitration procedures have been used to resolve civil rights violations, securities fraud, antitrust claims, and employment disputes. The commercial aspect of the act remains important, however, and enforcement of arbitration agreements and awards, both in interstate commerce and in international contracts, is addressed in the federal act.

The Arbitration Society of America, the Arbitration Foundation, and the Arbitration Conference joined forces in 1926 to form the American Arbitration Association (AAA). That year, the Actors' Equity Association was one of the first organizations to include an arbitration clause in its contracts between actors and managers. Today, the AAA offers a wide range of services for alternative dispute resolution (ADR). A nonprofit organization, the AAA annually provides assistance to more than 100,000 persons seeking remedies outside the courtroom. AAA handles disputes in business, labor relations, employment, automobile accidents, and in other areas.

Mediation is another approach to conflict resolution. In mediation, a neutral third party hears both sides of the argument and may offer suggestions on better ways to communicate about the conflict, or ways to see the other's point of view, but does not offer a specific, binding resolution. Thus, a mediator helps the parties arrive at their own solution while an arbitrator provides the solution.

Why Arbitrate?

Arbitration or mediation offers many advantages in dispute resolution. For many people, avoiding the cost and complexity of a lawsuit is advantage enough; but there are others. In addition to the cost of a lawsuit, cases brought before the judicial system can take months or even years to be heard. Once a decision is reached, if a party to the lawsuit chooses to appeal the ruling, still more time may be added to the process.

Unlike a trial by jury, where the parties involved do not choose the members of the jury charged with weighing the evidence, arbitration allows the parties to choose their arbitrators from a pool of neutral individuals who have expertise in the field. Because courts must abide by complex rules of evidence and procedure, an arbitration hearing can seem quite informal. During arbitration, the parties involved in the dispute have the opportunity to present their story in a relaxed and private setting.

Because the hearings and awards in arbitration are kept private, less opportunity arises for the acrimony that sometimes accompanies the publicity surrounding a high-profile court case. This is especially important if the parties involved must continue to work together after the dispute is settled.

Both arbitration and mediation as methods of dispute resolution are gaining more adherents. Arbitration clauses are increasingly being written into contracts of every kind across virtually all industries. The methods of ADR have even made it to the classroom; the value of constructive conflict resolution is being recognized by a growing number of educators in both elementary and high schools. Workshops are being offered, journal articles written, and teachers are using ADR techniques to address conflicts among students.

In some schools, students are being trained in ADR methods to enable them to act as mediators when a conflict erupts among their peers. Before a dispute reaches that step, the students involved in the conflict are encouraged to negotiate their differences in an attempt to reach an understanding. If negotiation fails to produce results, student mediators become involved. Finally, if the situation cannot be resolved through mediation, a teacher is brought in to arbitrate the dispute.

Further Reading

Abersold, John R., and Wayne E. Howard. *Cases in Labor Relations: An Arbitration Experience.* Englewood Cliffs, N.J.: Prentice-Hall, 1967.

Böckstiegel, Karl-Heinz, ed. *Acts of State and Arbitration.* Köln: C. Heymanns, 1997.

Bognanno, Mario, and Charles J. Coleman, eds. *Labor Arbitration in America: The Profession and Practice.* New York: Praeger, 1992.

Friedman, Clara H. *Between Management and Labor: Oral Histories of Arbitration.* New York: Twayne Publishers; London: Prentice Hall International, 1995.

Kellor, Frances. *American Arbitration: Its History, Functions and Achievements.* Washington, D.C.: Beard Books, 1999.

—*Connie Tuttle*

A demonstration by United Farm Workers (UFW) in support of 2002 legislation that would give the union greater control during arbitration of contract negotiatons. UFW President Arturo Rodriguez, left, is pictured with union co-founder Dolores Huerta. A poster depicting Cesar Chavez is in the background.

See also:
Agriculture Industry;
Business Ethics;
Commodities; Price Fixing;
Subsidy.

Archer Daniels Midland Company

The self-styled "Supermarket to the World," Archer Daniels Midland Company (ADM) is a global leader in the processing and sale of agricultural commodities. Roughly two-thirds of the company's sales come from oilseeds like peanuts and soybeans; the company also processes corn, wheat, cocoa, and other commodities. ADM, headquartered in Decatur, Illinois, was once considered to be a wonder, racking up ever-increasing profits in the ordinarily low-margin, fiercely competitive business of agricultural commodities. However, a string of controversies, culminating in a massive price-fixing scandal in the mid-1990s, has cast a shadow over the company from which it has yet to emerge.

Until the 1960s, ADM was a relatively obscure midwestern operation. Formed in 1923 by the merger of Archer Daniels Linseed Company and Midland Linseed Products Company, for much of its history the firm focused on plant oils like linseed and castor oils that had a variety of industrial uses.

By the mid-1960s, sinking earnings led the Archer and Daniels families to turn control of ADM over to Dwayne O. Andreas and his family. Andreas, who officially became ADM's chief executive in 1971, had had a remarkably successful career at his family's company and at the commodities giant Cargill Co. Dwayne Andreas and the various members of his family, who quickly took leadership positions in the company and were awarded seats on its board, soon divested ADM of its more industrial businesses to focus on agricultural products. Unlike other commodity companies, which were satisfied to sell raw product, ADM also handled processed commodities, including high-fructose corn syrup or ethanol from corn, that command better profit margins.

Helping the bottom line was Dwayne Andreas's focus on efficient management. Under his leadership, ADM became famous in management circles for being a "nimble giant," a large corporation that was nonetheless almost devoid of bureaucracy. At ADM, executives were given complete authority to make decisions, and those decisions were executed with remarkable speed.

Critics charged, however, that Dwayne Andreas's real genius was for cultivating political friendships. Agriculture is an industry where subsidies and import controls are still more the norm than the exception, and political lobbying is common. ADM often benefited from government policies. For example, ADM's high-fructose corn syrup business came into existence in the late 1970s largely because federal policies propped up the price of sugar through price supports and import quotas. The company's ethanol business also owes its existence largely to federal policies promoting ethanol-and-gasoline mixes as automotive fuel.

Dwayne Andreas routinely denied demanding favorable treatment in exchange for political donations. Nonetheless, he has

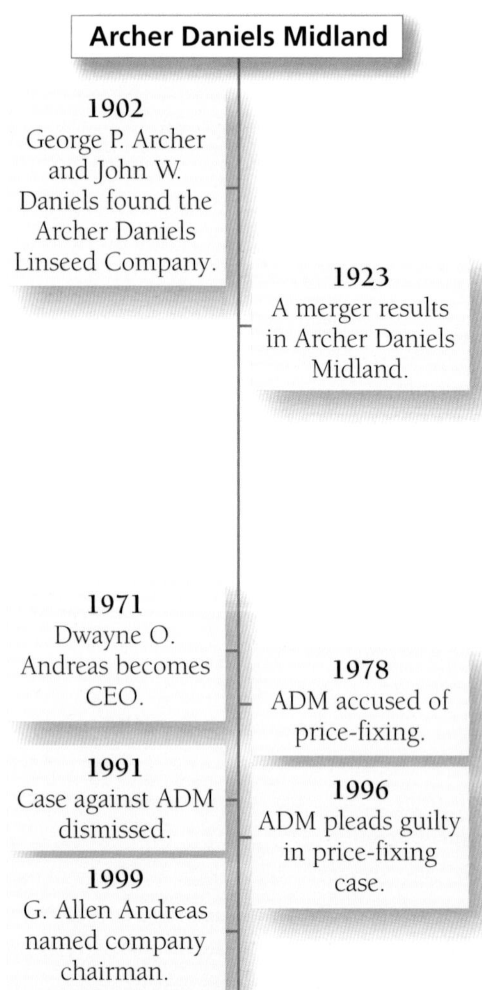

donated lavishly to both political parties since the 1940s, and he never denied the impact government policy could have on ADM. Dwayne Andreas is quoted in a 1991 biography as likening the government to a sow and agricultural companies to piglets. "When she rolls over, either you get a teat in your mouth or you get squashed," he said.

During the 1970s, when the United States focused on campaign finance following the Watergate affair, many of Dwayne Andreas's large donations to politicians became fodder for scandal, although none led to any criminal convictions. In 1978, however, ADM faced the first of what would be a more damaging series of price-fixing scandals when the company pleaded no contest to charges that it had conspired with two other businesses to fix prices on federal Food for Peace contracts. Four years later, federal prosecutors filed an antitrust action charging that ADM had fixed the price of fructose, but the case was dismissed in 1991 for lack of evidence. In 1992 and 1994, ADM paid a total of $1.5 million to settle two civil suits alleging that it had conspired to fix the price of carbon dioxide.

Late in 1992 Mark Whitacre, president of ADM's bioproducts division, confessed to an agent of the Federal Bureau of Investigation that ADM was involved in international conspiracies to fix the prices of commodities like the feed additive lysine. With the cooperation of Whitacre, the FBI spent more than two years recording conversations and meetings about the price-fixing schemes. In 1995, the FBI raided the corporate headquarters of ADM and the houses of many of its high-ranking executives. On October 15, 1996, ADM pleaded guilty in federal court to fixing the prices of lysine and citric acid and paid a fine of $100 million—the largest fine by far ever paid in a criminal price-fixing case.

In September 1998 three high-ranking ADM executives were convicted of fixing the prices of lysine. Among them were Michael D. Andreas, Dwayne Andreas's only son and the heir apparent to ADM's chief executive position; Terrance Wilson, head of the company's corn-processing division; and Whitacre himself, who had lost his immunity from prosecution when it was discovered that he had been embezzling money from ADM while an informant. The three were sentenced to prison terms ranging from two to two-and-a-half years for price-fixing; Whitacre had earlier received another nine years on fraud charges stemming from his embezzlement.

The price-fixing affair put ADM's family-dominated corporate governance under close and continuing scrutiny. The company has promised reform, adding nonfamily members to the board, but critics charge that these so-called outsiders have close personal and business ties to the family. Dwayne Andreas stepped down as chief executive in April 1997 and as chairman in January 1999, naming as his replacement in both positions his nephew, G. Allen Andreas. In August 2001, ADM announced that Dwayne Andreas was retiring from the board; the nomination for his replacement was his daughter, Sandra Andreas McMurtie. While Dwayne Andreas has given up much formal responsibility at ADM, he is believed to retain considerable influence behind the scenes.

In 2001 a freighter sails into the port of Havana, Cuba, carrying more than 26,000 tons of corn from ADM—the first direct commercial export of goods from the United States to Cuba since 1963.

Further Reading

Eichenwald, Kurt. *The Informant: A True Story.* New York: Broadway Books, 2000.

Kahn, E. J., Jr., *Supermarketer to the World: The Story of Dwayne Andreas, CEO of Archer Daniels Midland.* New York: Warner Books, 1991.

Lieber, James B. *Rats in the Grain: The Dirty Tricks and Trials of Archer Daniels Midland.* New York: Four Walls Eight Windows, 2000.

—*Mary Sisson*

See also:
Henson, Jim; Internet; Miramax Films; Recreation Industry; Walt Disney Company; Winfrey, Oprah.

Arts and Entertainment Industry

The arts and entertainment industry encompasses many different art forms, including fine arts, music, dance, theater, film, and television. It involves using skills, knowledge, and creative imagination to produce an artistic work that strives to capture an audience's attention, inspire the imagination, and enable members of the audience to explore new ideas by viewing life from another perspective. As the amount of time and money Americans devote to leisure activities has increased throughout the twentieth century, the arts and entertainment industry has played an ever-expanding role in U.S. society.

The arts and entertainment industry has had a major impact on the development and sharing of cultures. Ancient Egyptian priests used hieroglyphic picture-scripts to record historical events. Greek poets recited their epic poems aloud, while actors presented plays to delight their audiences. Throughout Europe, musicians, singers, and dancers were sought to perform in the courts of kings and queens. Minstrels would take their talents on the road to share a story in song.

Millions of people across the United States attend events in one or more of the four art disciplines—visual arts, music, dance, and drama. They buy tickets to art museums, festivals, professional theater, community theater, symphony orchestras, dance companies, and many other outlets of the arts. Yet a large percentage of the population opts for other leisure activities, sports or gambling among them. Therefore, the industry must continually find ways to

A dancer awaits her entrance in a community theater production of The Nutcracker.

Performing Arts: Selected Data 1985 to 1999

	1985	1990	1995	1999
Broadway theater [1]				
Broadway shows:				
New productions	33	40	33	39
Playing weeks [2,3]	1,078	1,070	1,120	1,441
Attendance (in millions)	7.3	8.0	9.0	11.7
Gross ticket sales (in millions)	$209	$282	$406	$588
Broadway road tours:				
Playing weeks	993	944	1,242	1,082
Attendance (in millions)	8.2	11.1	15.6	14.6
Gross ticket sales (in millions)	$226	$367	$701	$707
Nonprofit professional theaters [4]				
Companies reporting	217	185	215	313
Productions	2,710	2,265	2,646	3,921
Performances	52,341	46,131	56,608	64,556
Total attendance (in millions)	14.2	15.2	18.6	18.0
Gross income (in millions)	$234.7	$307.6	$444.4	$740.0
OPERA America professional member companies [4]				
Number of companies reporting [5]	97	98	88	95
Performances [6]	1,909	2,336	2,251	2,200
Total attendance (in millions)	6.7	7.5	6.5	6.7
Symphony orchestras [7]				
Concerts	19,573	18,931	29,328	31,549
Attendance (in millions)	24.0	24.7	30.9	30.8
Gross revenue (in millions)	$252.4	$377.5	$536.2	$671.8

[1] For season ending in year shown. [2] All shows (new productions and holdovers from previous seasons). [3] Eight performances constitute one playing week. [4] For years ending on or prior to Aug. 31. [5] United States companies. [6] Prior to 1993 and for 1999, United States and Canadian companies; 1993 to 1998, U.S. companies only. [7] For years ending Aug. 31. Prior to 1995 represents 254 U.S. orchestras; beginning 1995, represents all U.S. orchestras, excluding college/university and youth orchestras. Also, beginning 1995, data based on 1,200 orchestras.
Sources: The League of American Theaters and Producers, Inc., New York; Theatre Communications Group, New York; OPERA America, Washington, D.C.; American Symphony Orchestra League, Inc., Washington D.C.

attract new audiences while seeking to keep its loyal subscribers.

Impact on the Community

The arts and entertainment industry is much larger than Hollywood-created films and New York–based television shows. It enhances the quality of life in, and has a powerful economic impact on, every community. The industry fosters community involvement, increases cultural awareness, promotes the sharing of ideas, provides leisure activities, and creates jobs. The industry's multiple effects add up to an economic return on investment that is then channeled back to the community.

Many state agencies as well as business organizations recognize the great importance of arts and entertainment programs. Public and private sectors work hand in hand to invest millions of dollars to promote the industry, which in turn has provided jobs and money. A state's arts and entertainment resources provide a valuable means of recruiting new, highly skilled employees.

Research on human development has also made government and business increasingly aware that the arts strengthen higher-order thinking skills. The business community has identified these skills as essential for the workforce of the future. Businesses want to hire people who can be creative as they work; thus they donate millions of dollars to nonprofit organizations that support art education programs.

Incorporating arts into education programs for children helps them to connect more positively with society and with the community in which they live. Because dance, music, photography, and other visual arts go beyond spoken language, they can build a bridge across cultural and racial divides and among ethnic groups. The arts can promote an understanding of similarities and differences among religions, races, and cultural traditions. The arts help children develop originality and imagination by encouraging discovery and innovation.

Current Trends

The arts and entertainment industry has always been faced with a steady stream of new media forms. Each new media form is expeced to hurt the industry: Films were expected to be the death of radio, television to be the death of films, and so on. While there is no doubt that new media have negative effects on old ones in the short term, the arts and entertainment industry as a whole has proven to be extremely flexible. In the long term, new media trends have had positive effects, expanding the reach of the industry and creating more job opportunities.

The digital revolution of the late twentieth century increased convenience for consumers and offered lower prices. For example, downloading music from the Internet is fast and easy. Big record companies, fearing for their lives in the face of free music-swapping, are introducing services that will enable users to rent or buy songs without ever purchasing the compact disk. Movie studios know that they are next—the increasing accessibility of high-speed Internet connections will, in the not-too-distant future, make downloading and sharing films easy.

Although the motion picture industry is still predominantly using film, digital technology and computer-generated imaging are rapidly evolving; film pioneer George Lucas made history by shooting his high-tech extravaganza *Star Wars II: Attack of the Clones* (2002) entirely with digital cameras. Once again convenience and reduced costs are good selling points, as editing a picture is much faster and easier using digital techniques. Backgrounds can be inserted after actors perform and the location can be digitally modified to reflect the script. Characters can also be digitally created. The character of Yoda in the *Star Wars* films has traditionally been a puppet, manipulated by Frank Oz of Muppets fame; in *Attack of the Clones*, Yoda was a purely digital creation.

Digital technology will affect not only big budget filmmaking, but also smaller productions. By using digital technology, independent filmmakers can lower production costs and thus increase the chance that they will succeed in getting their films released nationally. The use of satellites or fiber-optic cable to distribute movies to theaters is also possible with digital technology.

With the global availability of cable television, digital videodisks (DVDs), video

Arts and Entertainment Careers

Each year thousands of new hopefuls are attracted to the arts and entertainment industry, lured by the prospect of bright lights, glamour, and superstardom. Most of these individuals are performing artists who plan to sing, dance, or act their way into the spotlight. Career opportunities for artists, musicians, singers, dancers, and actors are quite limited however. Competition in these fields is great, and success depends on talent, confidence, determination, and no small amount of luck. Very few people are able to attain the celebrity status of Maya Angelou, Madonna, or Tom Hanks.

Fortunately, the arts and entertainment industry offers many non-performing careers that can satisfy creative instincts. Many careers are by nature both entertainment and art forms. For example, costume designers, fashion designers, hair stylists, and makeup artists each use their skills to create art for entertainment. Behind-the-scenes careers are more various and plentiful than those in front of the camera.

For the individual who seeks a career in the field of arts and entertainment, research is crucial when choosing an arts program, a school, or a workshop. Ask for background information about instructors, get referrals from former students, and observe a class before signing up. Another good idea is to study two or three different disciplines, as this will provide added job opportunities.

The entertainment industry employs thousands of professionals and the prospect of finding employment—as something other than a performer—is excellent. Many jobs require the appropriate educational background, but entry-level jobs typically go to those with some experience. The best way to acquire experience is by working as a volunteer or an intern. This allows for the opportunity to sample a career and get to know those who have knowledge about job openings.

A scene from Monsters, Inc., *a film made with the sophisticated digital technology that is changing the face of the arts and entertainment industry.*

recorders, and the Internet, the demand for feature films has increased. Many new independent filmmaking companies have been formed in response to this demand. The great amount of programming needed to fill cable and satellite television channels and the demand for in-home videos, DVDs, and films over the Internet make the employment outlook for the motion picture production and distribution industry very good. According to the Bureau of Labor Statistics, career opportunities in the motion picture industry alone will increase by an additional 80,000 jobs by the year 2006.

One expected development will be interactive television, which will merge television and the Internet. A television show could be stopped midway through; the viewer can walk away and then come back later to resume watching. Viewers could respond to a commercial by placing an order at that very moment. Interactive television will also make possible checking for e-mail messages while watching television, viewing a buddy list to see if friends are watching the same show, and the sending of short messages.

Whatever the medium—a big-budget film, a regional theater production, or a tiny art gallery in a small town—the arts and entertainment industry has the power to influence, educate, motivate, and inspire. In addition to being one of the fastest growing industries for employment in the twenty-first century, this multifaceted industry reaches into every aspect of daily life. Cutting-edge technology and a global arena will certainly keep the arts and entertainment industry moving forward.

Further Reading

Eberts, Marjorie, and Margaret Gisler. *Careers for Culture Lovers and Other Artsy Types.* New York: McGraw-Hill, 1999.

Field, Shelly. *Career Opportunities in Theater and the Performing Arts.* New York: Facts On File, 1992.

Mauro, Lucia. *Careers for the Stagestruck and Other Dramatic Types.* Chicago: NTC Publishing Group, 1997.

—Scarlet Bolden

See also:
Brand Names; Entrepreneurship; Women in the Workforce.

Ash, Mary Kay

1918–2001
Cosmetics entrepreneur

Few corporate leaders are more closely identified with their companies than Mary Kay Ash, the founder and former chairwoman of Mary Kay Inc. She put a strong personal stamp on the second-largest direct seller of cosmetics in the United States—known for its pink packaging and for awarding lavish prizes, like pink Cadillacs, to top sellers.

Ash was born Mary Kay Wagner in Hot Wells, Texas, and grew up in the Houston area. The exact date of her birth is a bit of a mystery. After refusing for years to give her age, Ash began saying in the 1990s that she was born on May 12, 1918. Other evidence suggests she was born some years earlier. Whatever the year, Ash was born into hardship. Her father, Edward Wagner, contracted tuberculosis and became an invalid when his daughter was seven years old. Her mother, Lula Wagner, worked full time, while Mary Kay cared for her father and the house. At age 17, she married a musician who was a local radio star; her family eventually included three children.

Mary Kay Ash in an undated portrait.

At that time the United States was in the midst of the Great Depression of the 1930s, and Ash's husband's income was not sufficient to support the family. To earn money, Ash went into direct sales, joining Stanley Home Products in Houston, which sold cleaners and brushes. By 1939 she had become a manager at Stanley Home. Her experience there led to an insight that would influence her later: She realized she would work harder for a prize than she would for a monetary bonus—especially if the prize were some outlandish luxury that she would never buy for herself.

By 1942 Ash had made enough money to attend college. She intended to become a doctor, but after a year she decided to drop out and focus on her career in sales. Her husband enlisted in the military during World War II, and the family moved to Dallas. After the war, he asked for a divorce, leaving Ash to support the family.

In 1952 Ash left Stanley Home and became a sales training director for World Gift Co. There, her gender was a serious impediment to her career. She trained male employees, only to see them promoted over her head. She was routinely

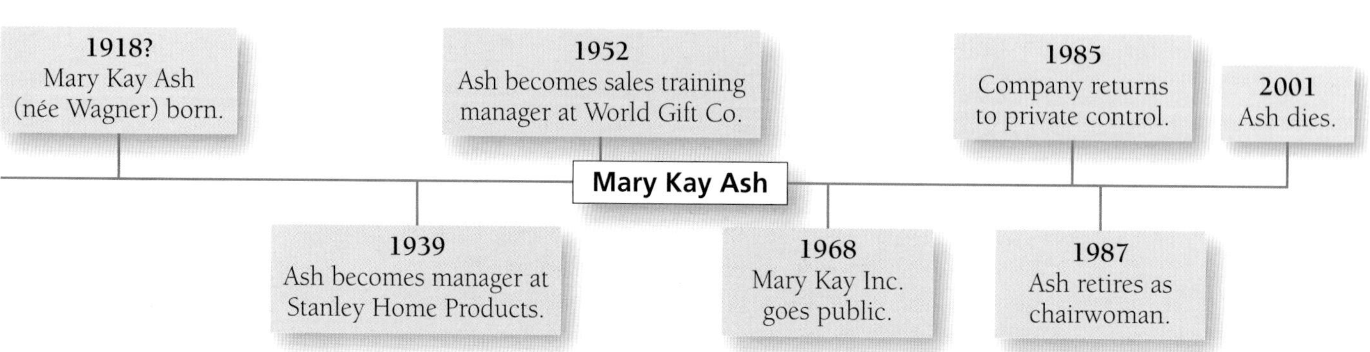

told her ideas were no good because she "thought like a woman."

By 1963 Mary Kay had remarried and her children were grown, easing her financial situation. She retired and began working on a book about her "dream company," one where women were treated with respect and where their salaries would not be limited. After a few weeks, she decided to start the dream company herself—she would handle marketing while her husband would manage the finances.

She bought the rights to a cosmetic formula with a cult following in Dallas. The family put its savings—about $5,000—into a storefront. A month before the store was to open, Ash's husband died unexpectedly. The money had been invested, however, and it was too late to turn back. Ash tapped her younger son, the 20-year-old Richard Rogers, to manage the business, and the store opened in September 1963. By the end of 1964, the company had sales of almost a million dollars.

The 1960s and 1970s were good times for Ash and for Mary Kay Inc. In 1966, Ash married Melville Ash, a businessman. The marriage was happy, ending only with Melville's death in 1980. Mary Kay Inc. went public in 1968 and soon became famous—and mocked—as an extension of its founder's personality. The company reflected many of its founder's predilections, including an emphasis on spirituality (Ash was a devout Baptist) and a skirts-only dress code.

Sales slumped in the early 1980s, and the company's stock price tumbled, leaving the company vulnerable for takeover. In 1985 Mary Kay and her family conducted a $450 million leveraged buyout to take the company private and gain more control over it. The move risked the family's fortune but appears to have paid off—the company had sales of $1.2 billion in 2000. Mary Kay retired as chairwoman in 1987, handing the reins to Richard Rogers. Despite repeated illnesses, Ash continued to embody her company's philosophy until her death on November 22, 2001.

Our company was founded with one purpose in mind and that was to give women an opportunity to climb the corporate ladder, because for those of you who still remember what was happening in the early '60s, there were no opportunities for women. I wondered time and again after training one person after another and coming back to Dallas to find one of those people was my superior . . . if I could teach them how to do it, why I couldn't be the superior. But the real reason was, you are in the wrong body, honey!

And so I decided that women were not getting a fair break and I was going to do something about it. Women responded to what I wanted to do! They wanted the same things that I did. . . . Today the question was asked, "How did you do this? How did you get so far so fast?" Well I was middle-aged, had varicose veins, and I didn't have time to fool around!

And so we started with that measly $5,000. Had I tried to go to the bank to borrow money they would have laughed me right out of the bank. . . . so we started out in a meager way. We started with one of those little Sears Roebuck shelves, one tier of it filled with cosmetics. Today our newest consultant has more inventory than that, but we began with great hopes and great dreams.

—Mary Kay Ash

Speech to Northwood University, 1990

Further Reading

Ash, Mary Kay. *Mary Kay.* Rev. ed. New York: Harper & Row, 1986.

———. *Mary Kay on People Management.* New York: Warner Books, 1984.

Hollandsworth, Skip. "Hostile Makeover." *Texas Monthly,* November 1995, 128–133.

—Mary Sisson

A training session for Mary Kay, Inc., sales associates.

See also: Environmentalism; Globalization; Sustainable Development; World Bank.

Asian Development Bank

Asian Development Bank (ADB) is a non-profit financial institution devoted to poverty reduction in Asia and the Pacific. Often acting in association with other development banks like the World Bank, it carries out activities that aim to promote economic growth, develop human resources, improve the status of women, and protect the environment. Other objectives, including private-sector development, law and policy reform, social development, and regional cooperation, contribute to its primary mission of reducing poverty.

Since its establishment in 1966, membership in the ADB has grown from 31 nations to 59 by the end of 2001. Members are both Asian and other countries; the United States and Japan are the largest shareholders, each accounting for nearly 16 percent of the ADB. With headquarters in Manila and 21 other offices around the world employing about 2,000 workers, ADB is the leading organization of its kind in Asia.

An employment-creation program for rural women in Bangladesh, 1993.

Asian Development Bank

1966 Asian Development Bank (ADB) established.

1992 Earth Summit in Rio de Janeiro establishes environmental priorities.

1999 ADB adopts poverty reduction strategy.

2001 Member nations of ADB number 59.

In 1999 ADB adopted a poverty reduction strategy, shifting its central focus from the promotion of economic growth to the eradication of poverty in Asia. This new strategy rests on three pillars: pro-poor, sustainable economic growth; social development; and good governance. The overarching objective is to improve the welfare of the 900 million Asians living on less than one dollar a day.

ADB's projects focus on energy, transport and communications, industry, finance, and agriculture. Many of these programs involve nongovernment organizations (NGOs) and community-based organizations (CBOs). ADB's principal tools in development are the granting of loans and technical support to specific high-priority development projects and programs. Funding is given to a nation's government and then distributed for use. The amount of assistance a project is granted is based upon placement on its county's priority list. In 2000 ADB granted a total of U.S.$5.8 billion, with the average loan being U.S.$65 million. Of its members, Indonesia, China, India, and Pakistan have been the largest recipients of funds.

Development Initiatives

ADB's human development initiatives seek to reduce poverty by improving the health, living standards, and livelihood of people living in Asia. The bank's priorities include policy reform initiatives and aid programs in the areas of education, health and nutrition, water supply and sanitation, and urban development.

Education is a primary focus of ADB's human development program. ADB believes that education can provide people with the ability to improve their earning potential, therefore enabling them to break the poverty cycle and better the lives of current and future generations. ADB invests in programs that seek to ensure equal access to primary education and provide opportunities for transition to higher education and training for children of its member nations.

Because the majority of the poor population in Asia is female, one of ADB's new focuses is improving the status of women. ADB's Gender and Development (GAD) policies work to provide women with greater access to education, employment opportunities, and primary health services such as programs that address maternity care and the prevention of sexually transmitted diseases. GAD also promotes gender equality through equal opportunity employment in all ADB operations. Gender specialists hired by ADB help supervise GAD projects and provide training programs for women.

ADB also aids in the environmental management efforts of its member nations. ADB assists member nations in improving their capabilities in environmental planning and management through loans and technical assistance. It seeks to address

During a 2001 protest in Honolulu, the president of ADB, Tadao Chino, center, speaks with Darwan Chantarahesee of Thailand about the effects of a bank-supported water project in her country.

An agrarian reform project in the Philippines, 2001.

regional and subregional environmental problems as well as transborder environmental issues, including climate change, acid rain in northeast Asia, and the impact of atmospheric haze brought about by forest fires in southeast Asia. Over the years, the environmental protection policies of the ADB have helped achieve significant progress but are short of the goals set at the Earth Summit in Rio de Janeiro in 1992.

Climate change is a primary focus of the Environmental Protection Program. ADB, in collaboration with the Hans Seidel Foundation, International Union for the Conservation of Nature, and United Nations Environment Programme, provides technical assistance and funds for member nations to develop inexpensive greenhouse gas reduction strategies. This program also promotes environmental awareness through workshops, seminars, conferences, and forums.

Controversies Confront the Bank

ADB's development work does not come without controversy. Its most scrutinized investment has been its many dam projects in the Mekong River basin, located in Southeast Asia. These projects, which have been labeled "destructive development" by critics, will profoundly affect a river that provides food, water, transportation, and economic sustenance to more than 50 million people. Many critics have accused ADB of putting the interests of private corporations and investors before the welfare of the people of the region. Environmentalists have pleaded with the bank to reconsider its investment. So far their pleas have not succeeded, and numerous environmental concerns remain unaddressed.

Even amid this cloud of controversy, ADB is still welcomed by many in the region. As a leading force for economic and social development in Asia and the Pacific, Asia Development Bank continues to aid struggling nations in the fight against poverty. Its programs supply monetary and technical assistance for the citizens of member nations, aiding them on a path toward modernization and prosperity.

Further Reading

Asian Development Bank. "Asian Development Outlook 2001." http://adb.org/Documents/Books/ADO/2001/ (December 5, 2002).

———. "Policies and Strategies." http://adb.org/Development/policies.asp (December 5, 2002).

Wihtol, Robert. *The Asian Development Bank and Rural Development: Policy and Practice.* Basingstoke, England: Macmillan, 1988.

—Bill Z. Tan

Assembly Line

An assembly line is an arrangement of machines and workers designed to manufacture products with the greatest efficiency. Although assembly lines are used in a variety of industries, they were pioneered by the Ford Motor Company in the early twentieth century and remain strongly associated with auto manufacturing.

Making a bacon-lettuce-and-tomato (BLT) sandwich illustrates the challenge of assembly line production. What is the best sequence of assembly: lettuce first or mayonnaise? Should the bacon be microwaved or fried? If the task is to make one sandwich, there is probably no best way; if it is necessary to make 10,000 BLTs, day after day, then organizing an efficient production method becomes crucially important.

Problems of scale and complexity create the need to think about optimal arrangements for mass production. For a BLT with its five ingredients—bread, lettuce, bacon, tomato, and mayonnaise—there are only 32 (2^5) different ways to assemble the product. For a more complex product like a car, with more than 5,000 parts, making optimal production decisions becomes far more complex, because the production possibilities are nearly infinite in number.

Assembly line manufacturing provides a means for addressing such problems, making mass production possible on a scale unimaginable in earlier days of handcraft industry. Development of the assembly line in the twentieth century was influenced by earlier innovations. An assembly line requires standardized parts, uniform in size and shape. Eli Whitney, known to most people for his invention of the cotton gin, pioneered the use of standardization in arms manufacture early in the nineteenth century. The agricultural products industry had switched from hand labor to belts and moving hoppers for processing grain as early as 1791. The Swift Company developed an early version of mechanical movement in the Chicago meatpacking industry (for the *dis*assembly of pigs) in the 1870s.

Ultimately, however, the most important element in assembly line manufacture was systemization and standardization of

See also:
Division of Labor; Ford, Henry; Industrial Revolution; Manufacturing Industry.

In 1917 completed Model T's roll off the assembly line.

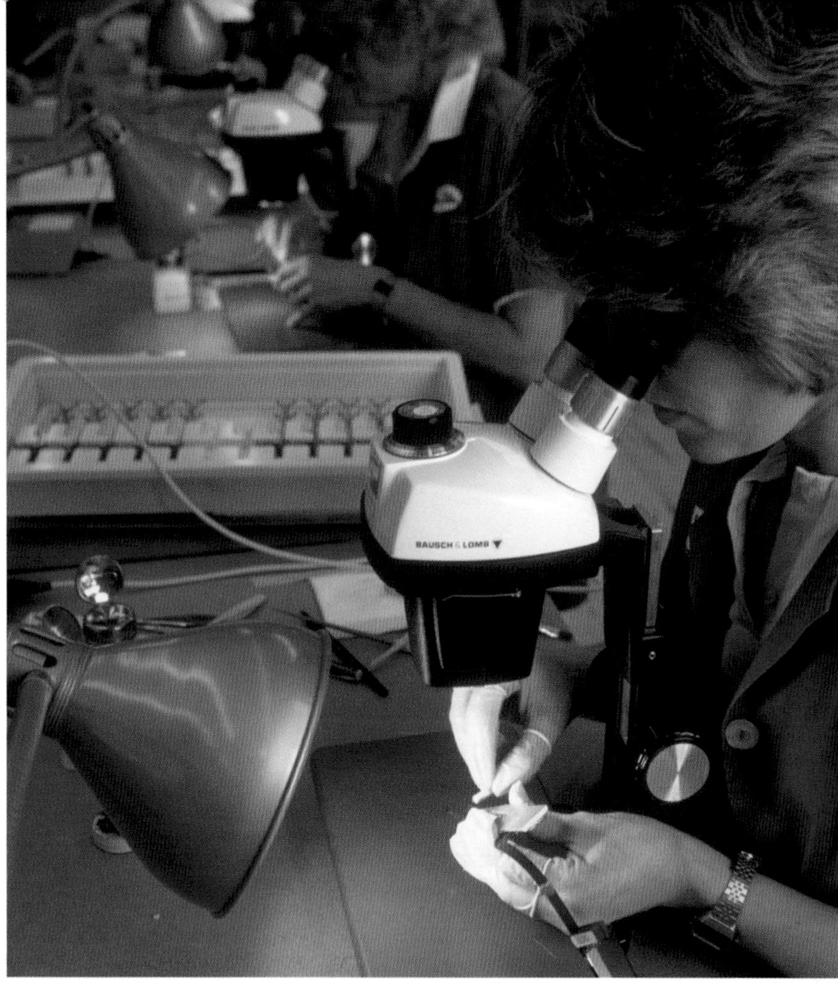

Assembly lines are used to create many products; the women pictured here are making computer hardware in Minneapolis.

the feeder lines. These subsystems kept assembly operations supplied with materials and parts. For this element, Henry Ford's contribution was crucial. The Ford plant in Dearborn, Michigan, brought in raw materials on one end and put out finished automobiles at the other. Dozens of subassembly systems made component parts that eventually became complete automobiles, assembled on the line.

Dispute exists about who invented the moving assembly method of automobile manufacture. A key player at Ford was Charles Sorenson. Sorenson claims to have built the first car ever assembled on a moving line. The Model N car had been manufactured at static workstations at Ford's Piquette factory in 1906. In 1908 Sorenson noticed that assembly would be easier if the chassis moved and had parts added to it rather than bringing the parts to the chassis. Sorenson began at one end of the plant with a frame, added axles, wheels, and other parts, and, in his own words, moved the whole thing past the stockroom instead of moving the stockroom to the chassis. In another account, Ford employee Clarence Willard Avery claims to have developed the first assembly line at Ford's Model T factory in Highland Park, Michigan, in 1913.

Henry Ford provided the managerial impetus for assembly line methods. He once wrote that true leadership means planning and that management's goal should be to arrange material and machinery in such a way as to make operations so simple that practically no orders need be given. Each person and machine on the line should do only one thing. Pushing the limits of this view, Ford sought exact divisions of labor on the assembly line to secure a competitive advantage in automobile manufacturing.

Once early innovations had established a new direction for manufacturing methods at Ford, Avery led a subsequent effort to improve the assembly line method. Successive waves of engineers at Ford designed systems—for auto body stamping and automated welding, for example—that cut auto production time from about eight hours in the 1950s to less than 20 minutes today.

Assembly line manufacturing now produces goods in several continuous-process industries including oil refining, chemicals, telecommunications equipment, and computers. Some modern assembly lines are governed by computers and self-regulating equipment. Although many products today are still assembled by hand, the mass production techniques made possible by assembly lines developed in the automobile industry bring reliable and affordable products to millions of consumers.

Further Reading

Batchelor, Ray. *Henry Ford, Mass Production, Modernism and Design.* Manchester, England: Manchester University Press, 1994.

Ford, Henry. *Today and Tomorrow.* 1926. Reprint. Cambridge, Mass.: Productivity Press, 1988.

Ford Motor Company. *Ford at Fifty, 1903–1953.* New York: Simon & Schuster, 1953.

Sorenson, Charles. *My Forty Years with Ford.* New York: W. W. Norton, 1956.

—Stephen Haessler

Assets and Liabilities

See also:
Accounting and Bookkeeping; Balance Sheet.

Assets are items of value owned by a business or an individual; examples include cash, machinery, and real estate. Liabilities are debts of a business or an individual; examples include payments due on loans or lease agreements. Businesses need to keep track of assets and liabilities to stay solvent, profitable, and operating. Assets and liabilities are therefore important for reasons that go beyond technicalities of accounting.

To keep track of important financial information, businesses prepare financial statements. A financial statement is a list that presents financial information in an organized way so that the owners of a business can understand how the business is performing. Information about assets and liabilities is presented in one type of financial statement—a company's balance sheet. What assets and liabilities might be listed on a balance sheet? The following discussion of the Acme Baseball Bat Company illustrates the possibilities.

Assets

Assets constitute the resources of a business. They have value to a firm because the firm can use them directly, or because it can exchange them for goods or services it wishes to obtain. For example, finished baseball bats are an asset for Acme because the bats can be sold during the next year.

On balance sheets, assets are presented in decreasing order of liquidity (the ease with which the assets can be converted into cash without a large decline in value). Highly liquid assets, known as current

Workers taking inventory in a warehouse, 2000.

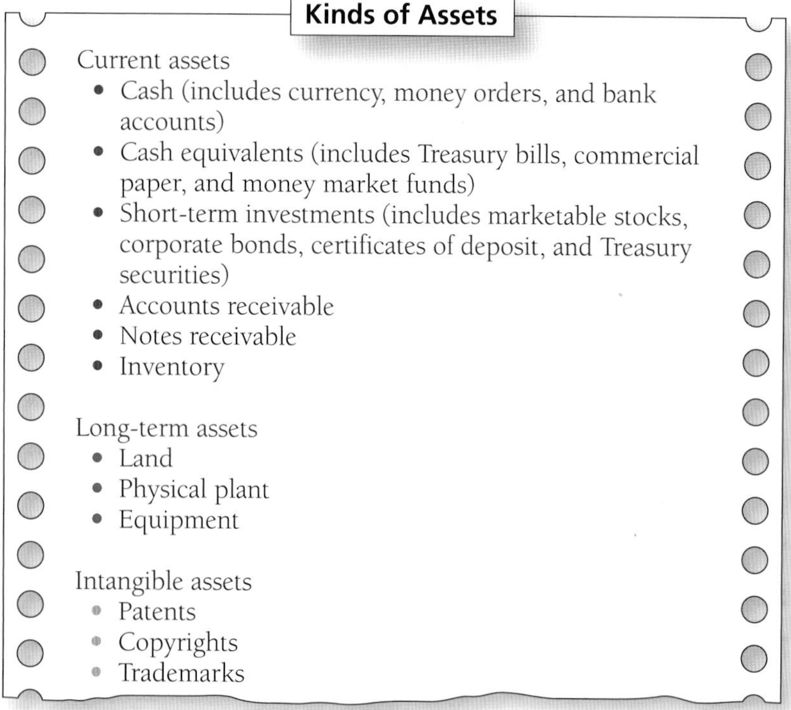
Kinds of Assets

Current assets
- Cash (includes currency, money orders, and bank accounts)
- Cash equivalents (includes Treasury bills, commercial paper, and money market funds)
- Short-term investments (includes marketable stocks, corporate bonds, certificates of deposit, and Treasury securities)
- Accounts receivable
- Notes receivable
- Inventory

Long-term assets
- Land
- Physical plant
- Equipment

Intangible assets
- Patents
- Copyrights
- Trademarks

assets, are listed first. Assets with the least liquidity are listed last; they are known as long-term or intangible assets.

For the Acme Baseball Bat Co., current assets include cash and other assets that Acme expects to convert into cash, or to sell or use up, within the next year. Examples of Acme's current assets include cash, cash equivalents, short-term investments, accounts and notes receivable, and inventories. Cash includes coins and currency, of course, but it may also include money orders, travelers' checks, and checking and savings accounts, including the company checking account Acme uses to pay its employees. Cash equivalents may include Treasury bills (IOUs issued by the U.S. government), commercial paper (IOUs issued by major corporations), and money market funds (funds in a special kind of checking account that pays interest). An item must have a maturity (or come due) within 90 days to be a cash equivalent.

Acme's short-term investments include highly marketable stocks, such as shares in Microsoft and IBM, corporate bonds (representing a special type of long-term loan), certificates of deposit (for money deposited in an interest-bearing bank or savings and loan account), and Treasury securities due in more than 90 days.

Certain Acme customers, such as sporting goods stores and large retailers (Wal-Mart, perhaps), are allowed to buy baseball bats on credit. These customers do not have to pay for the baseball bats right away; they may pay later, when a certain period (often, 30 days) has elapsed after delivery of the bats. A sale of baseball bats on credit creates a current asset for Acme known as an account receivable. An account receivable is typically supported by a sales invoice rather than a formal written promise to pay.

Another type of current asset on Acme's books is a note receivable. If a customer (to whom baseball bats have been sold and delivered) cannot pay after 30 days, that customer must sign a promissory note. A promissory note is an unconditional written promise to pay by a certain date, signed by a borrower or debtor. Most promissory notes stipulate an explicit charge or rate for interest to be paid by the borrower.

Inventory typically represents the largest category of current assets for manufacturing and retail firms. For Acme, inventory includes finished baseball bats awaiting sale as well as partly completed baseball bats. Depending upon the nature of a company's business, inventory may include almost any tangible good or material, including component pieces of equipment, bulk commodities (such as wheat or milling flour), fuel oil awaiting sale during winter, or even unused storage space.

Noncurrent or long-term assets are assets that a company will not convert to cash during the next year. Instead of selling these assets, the company will use them in the production or sale of goods. Acme's noncurrent assets include the buildings in which the company will, for 20 years or longer, make its baseball bats, store its supplies and inventory, and house its business offices (along with the necessary office furniture, computers, and supplies). Other noncurrent assets include Acme's milling machines and lathes, used in the production of baseball bats, and the small fleet of trucks Acme uses for delivering bats to customers and for transporting raw materials used in the manufacture of bats.

Acme owns several acres of land not currently in use. This land is a long-term asset. Acme acquired it several years ago in anticipation of future growth. The owners of Acme bought the property before they intended to begin using it to avoid paying a much higher price for the property later, when the company would be ready to expand.

Acme also owns some intangible long-term assets. Intangible assets are assets that have no physical substance and are expected to provide economic benefits beyond the next year. Examples include patents, copyrights, and trademarks. A patent is a federal government grant that gives an inventor the exclusive right to make, use, or sell an invention for a limited time period (anywhere from 14 to 20 years). Acme has several patents on various steps it has invented for use in manufacturing baseball bats. A copyright is an exclusive right to publish, print, or sell certain products for a given period. Copyrights apply exclusively to works of art, literature, and other authored works, including software. Acme has a copyright on some software it has designed for the automated lathes it uses in tapering baseball bats. A trademark is a distinctive mark, motto, device, or emblem that a manufacturer stamps, prints, or otherwise affixes to the goods it produces so that they may be identified on the market and their origins made known. Acme has a distinctive emblem that is emblazoned on each bat manufactured in its facilities.

Liabilities

Liabilities are the debts owed by a firm. Typically, the debts must be paid by a definite date. A liability is classified as current if it must be paid off within the next year; it is a long-term liability if payment is not due for more than a year.

For example, a current liability arises when Acme purchases wood for baseball

A computer manufacturing plant in 1998. The knowledge these workers have represents an asset for the firm; the workers' salaries, however, represent a liability.

Types of Liabilities

Current liabilities	Long-term liabilities
• Short-term debt	• Mortgage and rent
• Notes payable	• Loans
• Salaries and wages	
• Unearned revenues	
• Taxes	

bats from forest products firms. Typically, Acme must pay the forest products company within 30 days after delivery of the wood to Acme's factory. Until Acme actually pays for the wood, a debt or financial obligation equal to the cost of the wood remains on Acme's books. Another kind of current liability, known as a note payable, arises if Acme fails to pay on time for purchases it has made (say, for varnish used on baseball bats). A note payable is created when Acme signs a promissory note, promising to pay its balance due.

Current liability also includes salaries or wages payable. Acme's employees work in exchange for payment of wages or salaries. For every day of work completed, Acme owes money to its employees. Acme pays its employees every two weeks; a liability for salaries and wages is created on the company's books until it is discharged on the next pay day.

Another kind of current liability is unearned revenues. These occur when one of Acme's customers pays in advance for baseball bats. A liability arises from the payment because Acme is obligated to manufacture and deliver baseball bats to the customer who has already paid.

Taxes that must be paid by Acme to the local, state, or federal government within the next year are also a current liability. One example is the real estate taxes that Acme must pay on the buildings and land it owns. Many communities use revenue from real estate taxes to pay for the public services they provide—police and fire protection, schools, and so on. Another liability is the taxes Acme must pay the federal government on the profits it makes from the sale of baseball bats.

Any debt or obligation that does not have to be paid within the next year is a long-term liability. Acme's long-term liabilities include mortgage payments it must make, long-term notes it must pay off, and rent and pension payments it must make according to its lease and pension obligations.

When Acme built its factory and offices, it had to borrow several hundred thousand dollars from a local bank to pay for construction. The bank allows Acme to make monthly payments over a 20-year period to repay the loan. The payments that are not due within the next year are a long-term liability. Another long-term liability on Acme's books is a five-year loan that Acme obtained from the local bank to purchase a new delivery truck. Acme makes a monthly payment to the bank until the loan is paid off.

The long-term survival of a business requires that its assets must, on average, exceed its liabilities. When liabilities exceed assets over a long term, the business will not generate enough earnings and cash flow to pay its debts as they come due. If employees and suppliers are not paid in a timely fashion for goods and services provided, the business will not be able to continue its operations. Then employees may lose jobs and shareholders may lose money on their investments. Careful attention to assets and liabilities helps companies to avoid such unwelcome outcomes.

Further Reading

Kremer, C. *Managing By the Numbers: A Commonsense Guide to Understanding and Using Your Company's Financials.* Cambridge, Mass.: Perseus Publishing, 2000.

Peterson, Raymond H. *Accounting for Fixed Assets.* 2nd ed. New York: J. Wiley, 2002.

Sveiby, K. E. *The New Organizational Wealth: Managing & Measuring Knowledge-Based Assets.* San Francisco: Berrett-Koehler Publishers, 1997.

Westhem, A. D. *Protecting Your Assets: How to Safeguard and Maintain Your Personal Wealth.* New York: Carol Publishing Group, 1996.

—*Carl Pacini*

AT&T

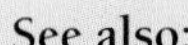

See also: Merger and Acquisition; Monopoly; Patent; Regulation of Business and Industry; Sherman Antitrust Act; Telecommunications Industry.

AT&T, nicknamed Ma Bell, is the largest telecommunications company in the United States. Originally the initials stood for American Telephone and Telegraph Company, but since 1994 the name has been shortened to just the initials. AT&T held a monopoly on long-distance telephone services that was broken up by a U.S. government antitrust suit in 1984. The transition to a new arena of competitive markets has been difficult for AT&T. Stiff competition has reduced overall profit margins as well as the company's market share in long-distance services, and the company has been wrenched by structural changes.

AT&T came into existence at the same time the telephone did. The Bell Telephone Company was founded in 1877 and initially was owned in part by the inventor of the telephone, Alexander Graham Bell. The company was a monopoly from the beginning. For roughly the first 15 years of its existence, Bell's patents assured that his company was the nation's sole provider of telephone equipment and service. Bell Telephone charged what it liked, forced users to lease its telephones, and offered service only in profitable markets.

In the 1880s Bell acquired Western Electric, a manufacturer of telephone

Alexander Graham Bell at the 1892 opening of the long distance line from New York to Chicago.

A telephone repairman in Atlanta, Georgia, in 1950.

equipment, and embarked on a strategy of expansion. Bell would supply small providers of local telephone service with equipment and access to its network in exchange for a major ownership stake; companies that did not cooperate were denied access to Bell local or long distance networks. An 1899 corporate reorganization resulted in a name change and American Telephone and Telegraph was born.

By the turn of the nineteenth century Bell's patents had expired, more Americans were subscribing to cheaper competing services, and regulators were agitating for AT&T to open its networks to competitors. In response, AT&T, with the backing of financier J. P. Morgan, began secretly buying up competitors; in 1910 it acquired the telegram company Western Union. The acquisitions triggered an investigation by the U.S. attorney general into whether AT&T was violating the Sherman Antitrust Act, the first antimonopoly law in the United States. In 1913, AT&T agreed to shed Western Union, to seek approval from the Interstate Commerce Commission before acquiring competitors, and to open its networks. The company also began to change its focus, treating telephone service increasingly as a public utility in exchange for favorable treatment from regulators. That strategy did not prevent the 1918 nationalization of AT&T, which placed it under the control of the U.S. Post Office. Nationalization lasted only a year, however, because the Post Office promptly hiked telephone rates.

In 1921 the federal government declared AT&T to be a natural monopoly and exempted it from some provisions of the Sherman Act (see box). In that year, AT&T initiated its famed $9-a-share dividend for shareholders. The dividend, which the company paid regardless of its financial performance, made AT&T shares famous as a "widows and orphans" stock—an unexciting but safe investment with guaranteed returns. It was an attractive prospect for many buyers; by the 1970s, AT&T shares were the most widely held stock in the United States.

Nonetheless, AT&T continued to experience an uneasy relationship with regulators. In 1934 the federal government replaced the Interstate Commerce Commission with the Federal Communications Commission (FCC) as the agency overseeing telecommunications. AT&T's Western Electric unit was placed under scrutiny, and in 1949 the U.S. Justice Department filed a lawsuit under the

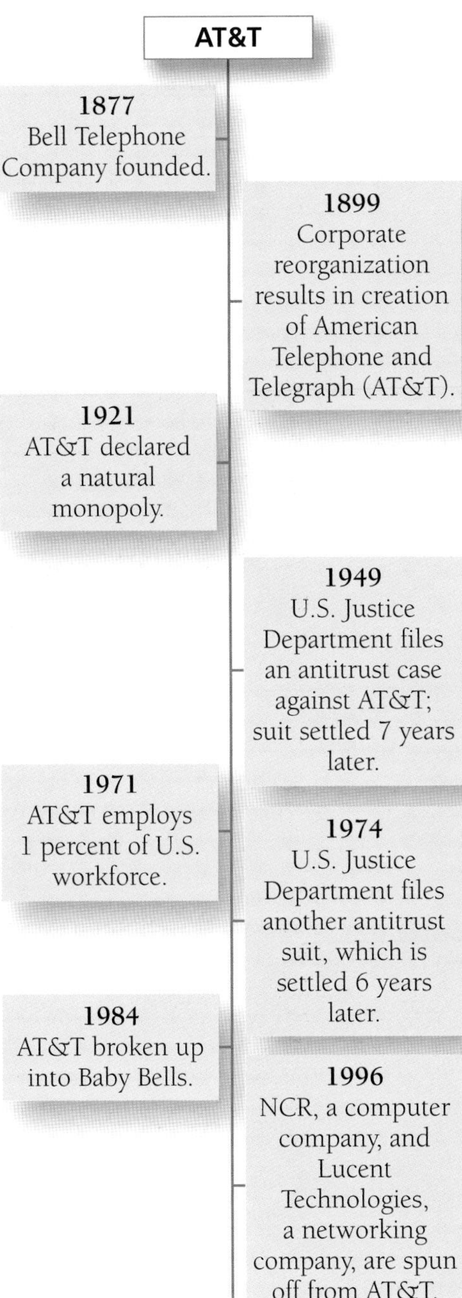

Sherman Antitrust Act demanding that AT&T shed its equipment division. The lawsuit was settled after seven years by a consent decree in which AT&T agreed to restrict its business to telephones and to weapons development for the U.S. government—a settlement blasted by critics as a sweetheart deal arranged by government officials who had gotten too cozy with a powerful monopoly.

Difficulties for AT&T continued in the late 1960s and '70s. The FCC ruled that people could purchase their own telephone equipment rather than having to lease equipment manufactured by Western Electric. The FCC also ruled that other telecommunication companies could offer private lines to businesses, using networks that largely bypassed those of AT&T. AT&T's public image suffered in 1969 and 1970 when service failures, some lasting weeks, hit a number of urban areas. The company was still a giant, however; by 1974 AT&T employed one million people, or more than 1 percent of the U.S. workforce.

In 1974 the Justice Department again filed suit against AT&T, this time seeking to break up the company. The case went to trial in 1981; a year later, AT&T settled with the Justice Department, signing a consent decree calling for the dismemberment of the company.

In 1984 AT&T's operating companies, which handled local service, were spun off into seven separate companies that were promptly

The Rise and Fall of a Natural Monopoly

For decades the telecommunications industry in the United States was seen as a natural monopoly, an industry in which a single firm can provide cheaper services for consumers than could several competing firms. Because of its early monopoly on telephone service, AT&T got a jump on its competitors and built an extensive and expensive network of copper telephone lines. While other companies had entered the local-service market by 1910, it seemed unlikely that they could raise the capital necessary to replicate AT&T's network. The concept of a natural monopoly was attractive to some regulators, because AT&T's top executives had agreed to make telephone service universally available, even in unprofitable rural markets.

However, AT&T seemed willing to use its natural monopoly on long distance telephone service to establish "unnatural" monopolies in other areas, such as telephone equipment, and that prospect was bothersome to regulators. In 1913, therefore, AT&T was essentially granted a monopoly on long-distance telephone service provided it agreed to stay out of unrelated businesses. Throughout most of the twentieth century, antitrust investigations into AT&T tended to focus on business activity unrelated to telephone service, such as AT&T's ownership of telephone equipment manufacturer Western Electric.

In the mid-1970s Microwave Communications, Inc.—later known as MCI and now part of WorldCom—a company that provided private telephone lines to businesses, began using its microwave-relay network to offer long-distance service. The ability of Microwave Communications to provide long-distance service suggested that the only thing keeping competitors out of telephone service was regulation.

The idea that AT&T held a natural monopoly on supplying telephone services had been so weakened by the early 1980s that the company was broken up in a way that would have been inconceivable a generation earlier. Instead of leading to unreliable service, competition in the long-distance market has spurred technical innovations and lowered prices for consumers.

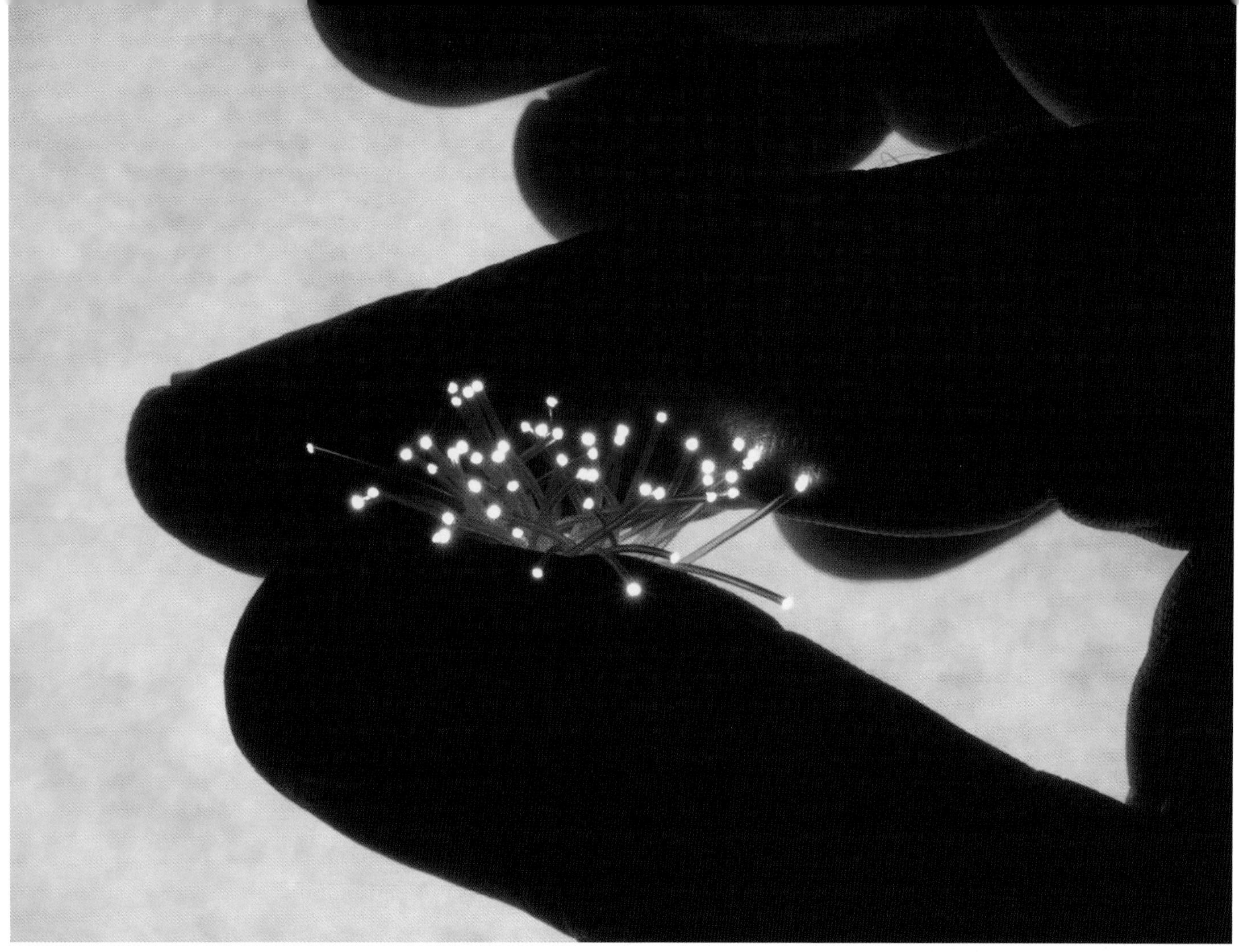

Fiberoptic cable.

dubbed the Baby Bells. (Almost 20 years later, four remain: Verizon Communications, SBC Communications, BellSouth Corp., and Qwest Communications International.) The breakup divested AT&T of roughly 75 percent of its assets, 65 percent of its employees, and 50 percent of its revenues. AT&T kept its long-distance service, Western Electric, and its Bell Labs research division, but all of its businesses were thrown open to competition.

AT&T was able to hold on to its share of the long distance market throughout the 1980s; by the 1990s, however, competition for its core business became more intense, and AT&T has struggled to remain viable. The company attempted to enter the computer market by purchasing NCR Corp., only to spin that business off in 1996, along with Lucent Technologies, created out of the former Western Electric and Bell Labs.

In the late 1990s, the company aggressively purchased cable-television operations in an effort to become a one-stop telecommunications and broadband provider, only to reverse itself in October 2000, when then chief executive, C. Michael Armstrong, announced that he would split the company into four separately traded businesses: consumer telecommunications, business services, wireless telephones, and cable television. In 2001 AT&T was still the largest provider of long-distance telephone service in the United States, but stiff competition had reduced overall profit margins as well as the company's market share in long distance services.

Further Reading

Brooks, John. *Telephone: The First Hundred Years.* New York: Harper & Row, 1976.

Coll, Steve. *The Deal of the Century: The Break-up of AT&T.* New York: Atheneum, 1986.

Evans, David S., ed. *Breaking Up Bell: Essays on Industrial Organization and Regulation.* New York: North-Holland, 1983.

—*Mary Sisson*

Balance of Payments

Individuals produce, trade, and borrow to satisfy their economic needs. These exchanges can become complicated; therefore, many people keep careful records of their transactions. These records tell them how much they have earned, the amount of their debts, what they own, and so on. Reviewing these documents will reveal their financial strengths and will show potential problems. National economies can be understood and evaluated in the same way, in a process economists call the balance of payments. This is the record of all transactions that take place between the residents of one nation (including individuals, businesses, and governmental units) and the residents of all other nations. (A related concept, the balance of trade, focuses more narrowly on goods exchanged between nations.)

The balance of payments has three components: goods, services, and money. All are exchanged with other countries in equal trades. Therefore, if all of one nation's exchanges are totaled, the inflows and outflows must be equal. If one nation buys more goods and services from another nation than it sells to that country, the difference is made up by the second nation gaining assets from the first. For example, if Americans buy computers from Taiwan and make no other exchanges with Taiwan, the Taiwanese retain the dollars that they realized from the sale. They may keep this money in a bank or buy something with it. The result: The United States gains computers and Taiwan gains dollars or property in the United States.

The table shows the different parts of the United States' balance of payments in 2000. The top half of the table is called the Current Account; it records trades in goods and services. It shows that the United States sold $772 billion worth of merchandise and $293 billion of services to people in other countries. However, after totaling U.S. imports and other transactions, the table reveals that the United States has a $382 billion trade deficit; the United States buys far more from other countries than it sells to them.

The bottom half of the table records the Capital Account. It shows the flow of money for the purchase or sale of financial and real assets that occurred in 2000; financial assets include stocks and bonds, while real assets include factories, office buildings, and so on. Many foreigners invest in the United States, buying financial and real assets, and Americans also frequently invest abroad. The Capital Account shows how the United States paid for its trade deficit. Capital inflows—foreign borrowing and purchases—exceeded

See also:
Balance of Trade;
Mercantilism; Smith, Adam;
Trade Policy.

The 2000 balance of payments for the United States. Foreign investment makes up for the deficit in U.S. exports.

U.S. Balance of Payments
2000
(in billions of dollars)

THE UNITED STATES OF AMERICA

Current Account	
U.S. merchandise exports	772
U.S. merchandise imports	–1,224
Balance of trade	–452
U.S. exports of services	293
U.S. imports of services	–217
Balance of services	76
Balance of goods and services	–376
Net investment income	–16
Net transfers	–54
Balance of current account	–382
Capital Account	
Capital inflows into the United States	1,024
Capital outflows from the United States	–581
Balance of capital account	443
Current and capital account balance	67
Official reserves	–67
Total balance	0

Note: Numbers are rounded to the nearest billion. *Source: Survey of Current Business*, June 2002.

capital outflows by $443 billion, more than making up for the Current Account deficit.

This demonstrates one reason why the balance of payments calculations can result in controversy: Overspending on imports by a country results in foreigners owning assets in that country. This became a great concern in the United States in the late 1980s when other countries' nationals bought such properties as Rockefeller Center in New York City and Pebble Beach golf course in California. Many people were also concerned that jobs were leaving the United States as fewer people bought goods produced in the United States.

Another reason why balance of payments calculations can be controversial is related to the concept of national wealth. Eighteenth-century economists, called mercantilists, argued that a nation's wealth should be measured by how much gold and silver it had. Having more specie made a nation more powerful, they reasoned, therefore governments should actively interfere with trade and the economy to create a trade surplus. The result was that European kings frequently attempted to manage their economies by granting monopolies, imposing heavy taxes on trade, and other policies.

Adam Smith was the most famous opponent of this view. He convincingly argued that the mercantilists were wrong because increasing the supply of specie resulted in inflation, or an increase in prices. Instead, Smith asserted that a nation's wealth was best measured by what it could produce and proposed a policy called laissez-faire, or hands off. Smith's policy called for minimizing government involvement in the economy and allowing individuals the right to trade freely.

Economists generally agree that a nation's balance of payments is a matter of perspective. A trade deficit suggests that a nation's industries are not competitive and may suffer job losses as a result. On the other hand, consumers gain because they are able to buy foreign goods that are more appealing because of price or quality. Whether deficits are helpful or harmful depends on how long they last and the events causing them.

Further Reading

Mansfield, Edwin, and Nariman Behravesh. *Economics U$A*. 6th ed. New York: Norton, 2001.

McConnell, Campbell, and Stanley Brue. *Macroeconomics*. 15th ed. New York: McGraw-Hill, 2002.

—*David Long*

The famed Pebble Beach golf course in California was bought by Minoru Isutani in 1990; two years later he sold it to a Japanese golf resort company, the Lone Cypress Co., for approximately $500 million. A consortium of U.S. investors, including Arnold Palmer and Clint Eastwood, bought the course in 1999.

Balance of Trade

The balance of trade is the difference between the amount of goods that a country sells to other countries and the amount it imports from other countries. If a country sells more than it buys, it has a trade surplus. If it buys more goods from abroad than it sells, it has a trade deficit. A nation's balance of trade depends on several factors, including the spending habits of its citizens and how competitive its leading industries are.

The consequences of a persistent trade deficit can be serious. One concern is that such a deficit indicates an economy that is not very competitive. If a country cannot produce appealing goods at reasonable prices or fails to produce new and innovative goods, it will tend to export less and import more. The result: Employment will fall as domestic industries fail, thereby reducing incomes. Another concern is that nations seem to lose wealth when they run consistent trade deficits. Trade deficits result in foreigners gaining assets—money or property—in the deficit nation. This sale of a nation's assets can cause discontent and resentment among voters, because foreigners seem to be buying the country.

See also:
Balance of Payments; North American Free Trade Agreement; Protectionism; Tariff; World Trade Organization.

U.S. Balance of Trade 1947 to 2000
(in million dollars)

	Exports	*Imports*	*Balance on goods*		*Exports*	*Imports*	*Balance on goods*
1947	16,097	-5,973	10,124	1974	98,306	-103,811	-5,505
1948	13,265	-7,557	5,708	1975	107,088	-98,185	8,903
1949	12,213	-6,874	5,339	1976	114,745	-124,228	-9,483
1950	10,203	-9,081	1,122	1977	120,816	-151,907	-31,091
1951	14,243	-11,176	3,067	1978	142,075	-176,002	-33,927
1952	13,449	-10,838	2,611	1979	184,439	-212,007	-27,568
1953	12,412	-10,975	1,437	1980	224,250	-249,750	-25,500
1954	12,929	-10,353	2,576	1981	237,044	-265,067	-28,023
1955	14,424	-11,527	2,897	1982	211,157	-247,642	-36,485
1956	17,556	-12,803	4,753	1983	201,799	-268,901	-67,102
1957	19,562	-13,291	6,271	1984	219,926	-332,418	-112,492
1958	16,414	-12,952	3,462	1985	215,915	-338,088	-122,173
1959	16,458	-15,310	1,148	1986	223,344	-368,425	-145,081
1960	19,650	-14,758	4,892	1987	250,208	-409,765	-159,557
1961	20,108	-14,537	5,571	1988	320,230	-447,189	-126,959
1962	20,781	-16,260	4,521	1989	359,916	-477,665	-117,749
1963	22,272	-17,048	5,224	1990	387,401	-498,435	-111,034
1964	25,501	-18,700	6,801	1991	414,083	-491,020	-76,937
1965	26,461	-21,510	4,951	1992	439,631	-536,528	-96,897
1966	29,310	-25,493	3,817	1993	456,943	-589,394	-132,451
1967	30,666	-26,866	3,800	1994	502,859	-668,690	-165,831
1968	33,626	-32,991	635	1995	575,204	-749,374	-174,170
1969	36,414	-35,807	607	1996	612,113	-803,113	-191,000
1970	42,469	-39,866	2,603	1997	678,366	-876,485	-198,119
1971	43,319	-45,579	-2,260	1998	670,416	-917,112	-246,696
1972	49,381	-55,797	-6,416	1999	684,553	-1,029,987	-345,434
1973	71,410	-70,499	911	2000	772,210	-1,224,417	-452,207

Source: Economic Report of the President, 2002.

Economists and politicians therefore try to create trade surpluses to increase the wealth and power of their nation. In the second half of the twentieth century, the world steadily moved toward more open trade. Treaties like the North American Free Trade Agreement (NAFTA) and organizations like the European Union are predicated on the gains expected from free trade. These include access to goods and services that otherwise would not be available, lower prices for consumers, and the chance to create jobs by exporting goods and services to other countries.

However, free trade is not universally recognized as a positive force because capitalism is based on competition. Businesses that can satisfy consumers on price, quality, and innovation will profit and prosper. Those that cannot will be forced into bankruptcy and their workers into unemployment. Foreign trade increases the amount of competition and therefore presents a threat to both business profits and workers' jobs. Accordingly, both workers and employers have an incentive to appeal for government action against foreign trade. Consumers, a far larger but less united group, have less incentive to act and are thus less involved.

Almost all nations have trade barriers in place to protect domestic industries against foreign competitors, frequently citing a balance of trade deficit as the reason for government action. Common strategies include tariffs (taxes on imported goods that raise their prices) and quotas (set limits on the amount of goods foreign competitors may import).

These strategies benefit domestic employers and, to a lesser extent, their workers. Their costs can be quite large, however. In various studies of different industries, economists have found that protecting jobs through tariffs costs more than retraining the workers in other fields. This gap between intentions and results leads many economists to conclude that

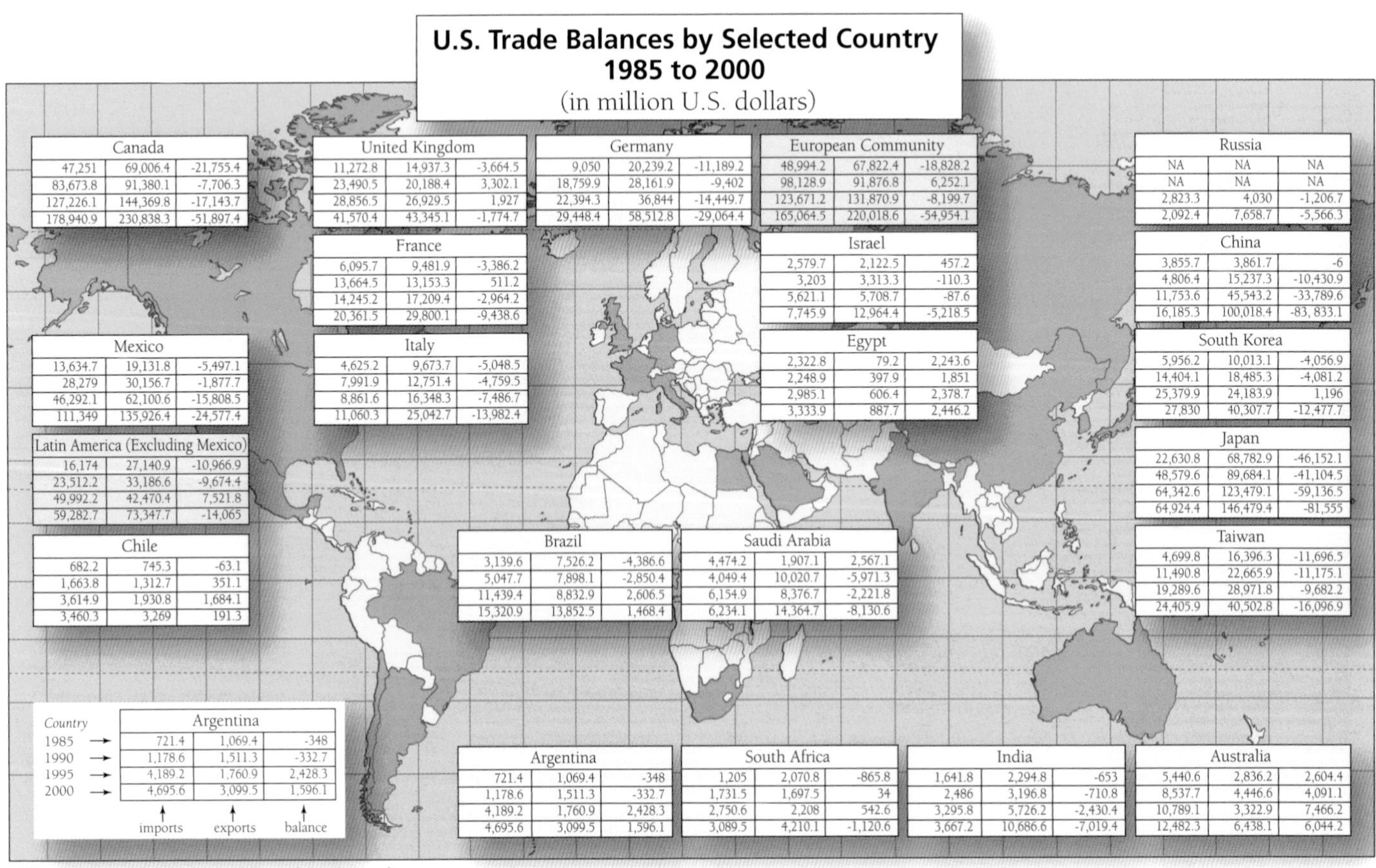

U.S. Trade Balances by Selected Country
1985 to 2000
(in million U.S. dollars)

Country	Argentina		
1985 →	721.4	1,069.4	-348
1990 →	1,178.6	1,511.3	-332.7
1995 →	4,189.2	1,760.9	2,428.3
2000 →	4,695.6	3,099.5	1,596.1
	↑ imports	↑ exports	↑ balance

Canada		
47,251	69,006.4	-21,755.4
83,673.8	91,380.1	-7,706.3
127,226.1	144,369.8	-17,143.7
178,940.9	230,838.3	-51,897.4

United Kingdom		
11,272.8	14,937.3	-3,664.5
23,490.5	20,188.4	3,302.1
28,856.5	26,929.5	1,927
41,570.4	43,345.1	-1,774.7

Germany		
9,050	20,239.2	-11,189.2
18,759.9	28,161.9	-9,402
22,394.3	36,844	-14,449.7
29,448.4	58,512.8	-29,064.4

European Community		
48,994.2	67,822.4	-18,828.2
98,128.9	91,876.8	6,252.1
123,671.2	131,870.9	-8,199.7
165,064.5	220,018.6	-54,954.1

Russia		
NA	NA	NA
NA	NA	NA
2,823.3	4,030	-1,206.7
2,092.4	7,658.7	-5,566.3

France		
6,095.7	9,481.9	-3,386.2
13,664.5	13,153.3	511.2
14,245.2	17,209.4	-2,964.2
20,361.5	29,800.1	-9,438.6

Israel		
2,579.7	2,122.5	457.2
3,203	3,313.3	-110.3
5,621.1	5,708.7	-87.6
7,745.9	12,964.4	-5,218.5

China		
3,855.7	3,861.7	-6
4,806.4	15,237.3	-10,430.9
11,753.6	45,543.2	-33,789.6
16,185.3	100,018.4	-83, 833.1

Mexico		
13,634.7	19,131.8	-5,497.1
28,279	30,156.7	-1,877.7
46,292.1	62,100.6	-15,808.5
111,349	135,926.4	-24,577.4

Italy		
4,625.2	9,673.7	-5,048.5
7,991.9	12,751.4	-4,759.5
8,861.6	16,348.3	-7,486.7
11,060.3	25,042.7	-13,982.4

Egypt		
2,322.8	79.2	2,243.6
2,248.9	397.9	1,851
2,985.1	606.4	2,378.7
3,333.9	887.7	2,446.2

South Korea		
5,956.2	10,013.1	-4,056.9
14,404.1	18,485.3	-4,081.2
25,379.9	24,183.9	1,196
27,830	40,307.7	-12,477.7

Latin America (Excluding Mexico)		
16,174	27,140.9	-10,966.9
23,512.2	33,186.6	-9,674.4
49,992.2	42,470.4	7,521.8
59,282.7	73,347.7	-14,065

Japan		
22,630.8	68,782.9	-46,152.1
48,579.6	89,684.1	-41,104.5
64,342.6	123,479.1	-59,136.5
64,924.4	146,479.4	-81,555

Chile		
682.2	745.3	-63.1
1,663.8	1,312.7	351.1
3,614.9	1,930.8	1,684.1
3,460.3	3,269	191.3

Brazil		
3,139.6	7,526.2	-4,386.6
5,047.7	7,898.1	-2,850.4
11,439.4	8,832.9	2,606.5
15,320.9	13,852.5	1,468.4

Saudi Arabia		
4,474.2	1,907.1	2,567.1
4,049.4	10,020.7	-5,971.3
6,154.9	8,376.7	-2,221.8
6,234.1	14,364.7	-8,130.6

Taiwan		
4,699.8	16,396.3	-11,696.5
11,490.8	22,665.9	-11,175.1
19,289.6	28,971.8	-9,682.2
24,405.9	40,502.8	-16,096.9

Argentina		
721.4	1,069.4	-348
1,178.6	1,511.3	-332.7
4,189.2	1,760.9	2,428.3
4,695.6	3,099.5	1,596.1

South Africa		
1,205	2,070.8	-865.8
1,731.5	1,697.5	34
2,750.6	2,208	542.6
3,089.5	4,210.1	-1,120.6

India		
1,641.8	2,294.8	-653
2,486	3,196.8	-710.8
3,295.8	5,726.2	-2,430.4
3,667.2	10,686.6	-7,019.4

Australia		
5,440.6	2,836.2	2,604.4
8,537.7	4,446.6	4,091.1
10,789.1	3,322.9	7,466.2
12,482.3	6,438.1	6,044.2

Note: Some totals may not add up, due to rounding.
Source: U.S. Census Bureau, Foreign Trade Division, Data Dissemination Branch, Washington, D.C.

the costs of protectionism far outweigh the benefits.

A second drawback of trade barriers is that they often result in international friction. Nations commonly accuse each other, often with reason, of cheating and threaten retaliation. Nations commonly subsidize, or give loans or other funds, to producers of certain goods. This allows those companies to offer cheaper prices and reap greater profits, often driving their foreign competition into bankruptcy. Cheating makes sense to politicians because they have more incentive to please their potential campaign donors and voters than the citizens of other countries.

A series of international trade agreements called the General Agreement on Tariffs and Trade (GATT) strives to address these issues. The 1994 GATT agreement called for international reductions in tariffs, quotas, and other trade barriers between 1995 and 2005. The World Trade Organization (WTO) was created in 1995 to quickly and fairly resolve trade disputes. Formerly, nations had very little recourse to solve trade issues and often resorted to retaliating against tariffs or quotas with similar measures, leading to trade wars and economic losses. Ideally, the WTO acts as a neutral third party to mediate disputes.

In 2002 steelworkers in Chile protest U.S. tariffs on steel imports, which were imposed to protect the U.S. steel industry from foreign competition.

Further Reading

Heilbroner, Robert, and Lester Thurow. *Economics Explained: Everything You Need to Know about How the Economy Works and Where It Is Going*. New York: Simon & Schuster, 1998.

McConnell, Campbell, and Stanley Brue. *Macroeconomics*. 15th ed. New York: McGraw-Hill, 2002.

U.S. Trade Deficit Review Commission. "The U.S. Trade Deficit: Causes, Consequences and Recommendations for Action." 2000. http://www.ustdrc.gov/reports/reports.html (November 15, 2002).

—David Long

See also:
Accounting and Bookkeeping; Amortization and Depreciation; Assets and Liabilities; Capital; Income Statement.

Balance Sheet

A balance sheet is one of the many statements used by a business to report and assess its financial position. These statements are also known as position statements, statements of financial condition, or statements of financial position. While the workings of a business are ongoing, a balance sheet is like a snapshot of the worth of the business, measuring its value on a specific date. Typically a balance sheet is prepared at the end of a month or business cycle to list and compare a business entity's assets, liabilities, and owner's equity.

A balance sheet may be presented in two ways. The first is to list the assets on the left and the liabilities and owner's equity on the right. The second is to list these three components one beneath the other. Either way, the statement is based on what is commonly known as the basic accounting equation or balance sheet equation: Assets = Liabilities + Owner's Equity.

Assets are anything of monetary value that is currently owned or scheduled to be received in the future. Assets are typically divided into current and long-term assets. Cash, stocks and bonds, land, buildings, and machinery and equipment are assets, as well as any money owed by customers (called accounts receivable). The balance sheet gives a description of each asset and its accounting value, which in most cases is its cost, or amount paid, rather than its current value. For example, a building purchased 10 years ago for $45,000 may be worth more or less than that today; however, it is still listed at $45,000.

Liabilities, which may also be current or long-term, are amounts owed. They are listed on a balance sheet as items payable

The Sweet Tooth Candy Shoppe
Balance Sheet
As of December 31, 2002

Current Assets		Current Liabilities	
Cash	$7,000	Notes Payable	$10,000
Inventory	8,000	Accounts Payable	3,000
Accounts Receivable	16,000	Salaries Payable	3,000
		Taxes Payable	5,000
Long-Term Assets		Long-Term Liabilities	
Land	13,000	Notes Payable	10,000
Building	45,000	Total Liabilities	$31,000
Equipment	8,000		
		Owner's Equity	
		Capital	$50,000
		Retained Earnings	16,000
		Total Equity	66,000
Total Assets	$97,000	Total Liabilities and Equity	$97,000

One way to structure a balance sheet is to put all assets on the left side and liabilities on the right.

The Sweet Tooth Candy Shoppe
Balance Sheet
As of December 31, 2002

Current Assets			
Cash			$7,000
Inventory			8,000
Accounts Receivable			16,000
Long-Term Assets			
Land			13,000
Building			45,000
Equipment			8,000
	Total Assets		$97,000
Current Liabilities			
Notes Payable			$10,000
Accounts Payable			3,000
Salaries Payable			3,000
Taxes Payable			5,000
Long-Term Liabilities			
Notes Payable			10,000
	Total Liabilities		$31,000
Owner's Equity			
Capital		$50,000	
Retained Earnings		16,000	
	Total Equity		66,000
	Total Liabilities and Equity		$97,000

An alternative structure for balance sheets is to put assets on the top and liabilities on the bottom.

and indicate a business's debts or responsibilities for future payments. Examples include loans (or notes), any money owed to other businesses for goods or services already provided, salaries to be paid, and taxes that are due.

Owner's equity is the amount invested in a business by the owners, as well as cumulative profits or losses from business operations. Often owners contribute cash or other assets to their businesses, both initially and later on. These contributions are called capital. When a business makes a profit, the owners may choose to leave a portion of the earnings in the business as a reinvestment rather than take the earnings out of the business as income. Profit is known as retained earnings. Collectively, capital and retained earnings make up the owner's equity.

The balance sheet of a particular business reveals the ability of the business to run its daily operations. A business cannot place orders with suppliers or pay its employees without a clear picture of funds available.

To help ensure accurate bookkeeping, the balance sheet has a built-in check system: The numbers must always come out equal, or balance. If they do not, an error has been made. Although the balance sheet reports a business's position on a single day, it is affected by every transaction of that business; indeed, transactions affect the balance sheet not once but twice. Each transaction must be recorded

Transactions

Every transaction affects the balance sheet not once but twice, as illustrated below:

Example 1

$1,000 worth of inventory is bought for cash.

- Cash is decreased by $1,000, while inventory is increased by $1,000.
- Both cash and inventory are assets, thus the asset total is not affected.

Assets = Liabilities + Owner's Equity
Assets + $1,000 – $1,000 = Liabilities + Owner's Equity
$97,000 + $1,000 – $1,000 = $31,000 + $66,000
$97,000 = $97,000

Example 2

A debt of $500 is paid in cash.

- Cash (an asset) is decreased by $500, while Accounts Payable (a liability) is decreased by $500. (Total debt owed is $500 less.)
- Each side of the equation is decreased by $500, leaving it equal.

Assets = Liabilities + Owner's Equity
Assets – $500 = (Liabilities – $500) + Owner's Equity
$97,000 – $500 = ($31,000 – $500) + $66,000
$96,500 = $96,500

Example 3

A business receives a delivery from a supplier with an invoice for $3,500.

- Inventory (an asset) is increased by $3,500, while Accounts Payable (a liability) increases by the same. (The debt is being increased.)
- Each side of the equation is increased by $3,500, leaving it equal.

Assets = Liabilities + Owner's Equity
Assets + $3,500 = (Liabilities + $3,500) + Owner's Equity
$97,000 + $3,500 = ($31,000 + $3,500) + $66,000
$100,500 = $100,500

Example 4

An owner takes $2,000 in cash out of the business for personal use.

- Cash (an asset) decreases by $2,000, while Owner's Equity decreases as well.
- Each side of the equation is decreased by $2,000, leaving it equal.

Assets = Liabilities + Owner's Equity
Assets – $2,000 = Liabilities + (Owner's Equity – $2,000)
$97,000 – $2,000 = $31,000 + ($66,000 – $2,000)
$95,000 = $95,000

to assess the financial position of a business accurately. Watching the balance sheet allows business owners to make informed decisions regarding future activity. Inaccurate financial statements can be detrimental to the success, or even survival, of a business.

Further Reading

Costales, S. B., and Geza Szurovy. *The Guide to Understanding Financial Statements.* 2nd ed. New York: McGraw-Hill, 1994.

Tracy, John A. *How to Read A Financial Report.* 5th ed. New York: John Wiley & Sons, 1999.

— *Andréa Korb*

Bankruptcy

When individuals and businesses get into financial difficulty, they sometimes file for bankruptcy. In the United States, bankruptcy proceedings are governed primarily by federal law and, to a lesser extent, by state law. The law allows debtors—both individuals and businesses—to seek relief from existing debts; the purpose of relief, when it is granted, is to enable debtors to get a fresh start. The law also provides for the quick, equitable distribution of debtors' assets among creditors when claims against debtors are sustained.

One of America's founding fathers, Benjamin Franklin, once remarked that creditors observe "set days and times" and expect to be paid at agreed-upon times. Traditionally, debtors were subjected to punishment, including debtors' prison and involuntary servitude, for not paying debts. Today's legal system does not follow a punitive philosophy in its approach to bankruptcy.

Bankruptcy Law in the United States

Federal bankruptcy law is contained in Title 11 of the U.S. Code. Chapter 7 provides for liquidation proceedings (the selling of various assets and the distribution of proceeds to creditors). Chapter 11 governs reorganizations. In reorganization cases, creditors usually look to the debtor's future earnings as a source for repayment, whereas in liquidation cases creditors look to the debtor's property. Chapter 12 (applying to family farms) and Chapter 13 (applying to individuals) provide for the adjustment of debts of parties with income; that is, these chapters provide for repayment plans.

Chapter 7 governs what is called straight (or ordinary) bankruptcy. In straight bankruptcy proceedings, debts are liquidated; the debtor's assets are sold and proceeds are distributed to creditors. The debtor may be an individual, a partnership, or a corporation. (Railroads, insurance firms, banks, savings and loans, and credit unions cannot be debtors under Chapter 7.)

See also:
Contracts and Contract Law; Debt; Enron; Finance, Personal; Rule of Law.

An illustration of a debtors' prison in England; the origins of U.S. bankruptcy law were partly inspired by the harsh treatment of debtors in Europe.

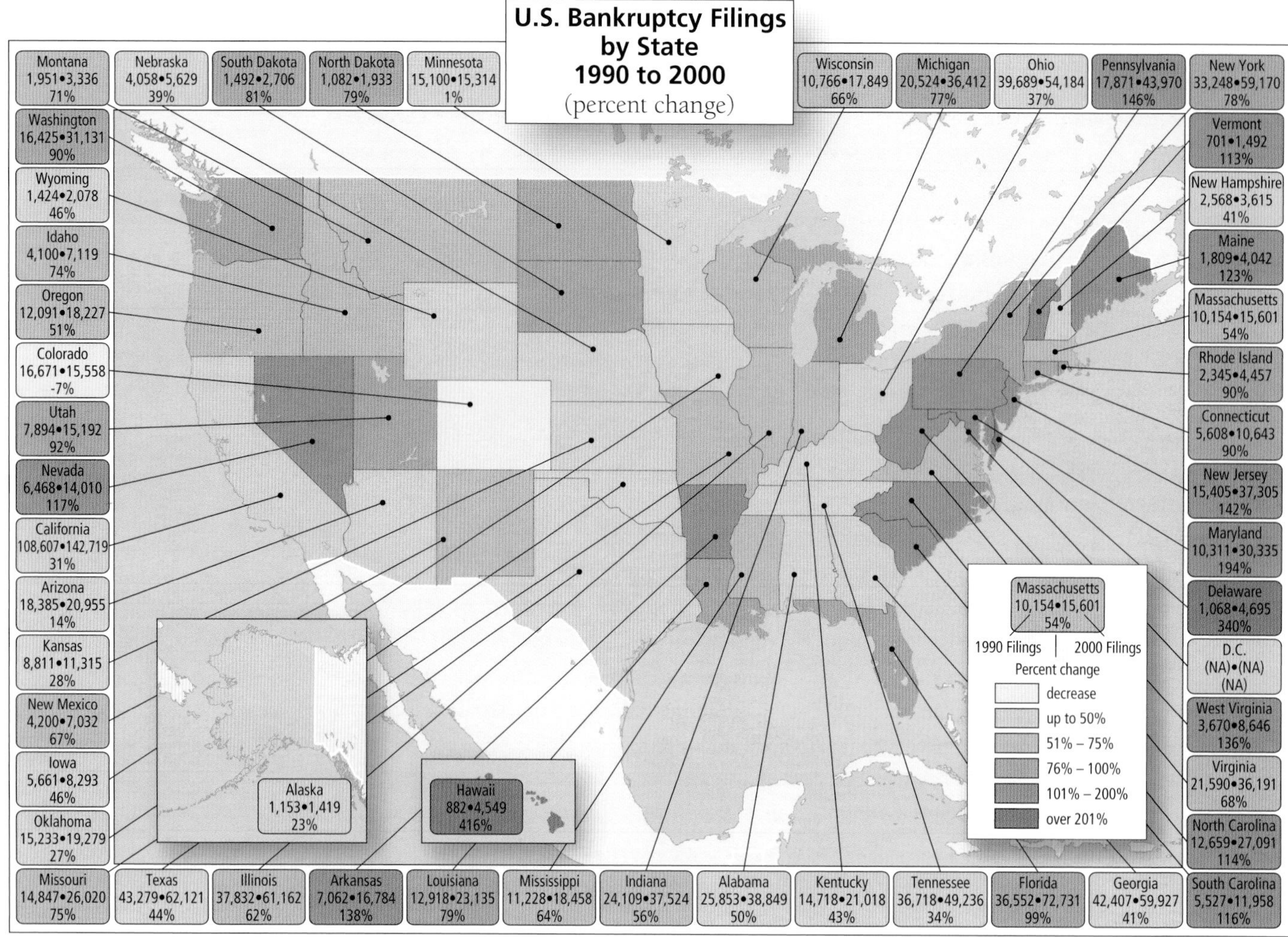

Source: American Bankruptcy Institute.

Certain debts, however, are not dischargeable under Chapter 7; the debtor cannot be released from them even if he or she has filed for bankruptcy. These include debts arising from customs duties and taxes, alimony, maintenance, or child support awards, fraud, embezzlement, larceny, or violation of a fiduciary duty (for example, the duty a lawyer owes to a client). Certain consumer debts and cash advances are also nondischargeable.

An ordinary bankruptcy proceeding is initiated by the filing of a voluntary or an involuntary petition. More than 99 percent of all bankruptcy petitions are filed voluntarily. Any person who is a debtor may file a voluntary petition and need not be insolvent to do so. (Insolvency is a financial condition in which an individual is unable to pay his or her debts as they come due or a condition in which liabilities exceed assets.) A voluntary petition results in an automatic stay (a court order that suspends creditors' claims until the issues have been resolved). The petition must include a list of all creditors, a list of all property owned by the debtor, a list of property claimed by the debtor to be exempt, and a statement of those assets considered necessary for a fresh start. Precisely what is exempt from claims of creditors depends on state law. To be official, a bankruptcy petition must be given under oath and signed by the debtor. Concealing assets or knowingly supplying false information in a bankruptcy petition is a crime.

An involuntary petition under Chapter 7 occurs when creditors force a person (or a business) into bankruptcy. An involuntary petition cannot be filed against a farmer, bank, insurance company, nonprofit corporation, railroad, or a person who owes less than $10,775. If a debtor opposes an involuntary petition, the court must hold a hearing. If the court finds that legal grounds for involuntary bankruptcy exist, the court will order relief on behalf of creditors.

Chapter 13 of the bankruptcy law provides for adjustment of debts (repayment plans) of an individual with regular income, under specified conditions. After a debtor completes all or nearly all payments under a Chapter 13 plan, the court will grant a discharge of all debts (except alimony and child support, student loans, criminal restitution and fines, and debts requiring payment over a period longer than that of the plan). Even if the debtor does not complete the plan, a hardship discharge may be granted under certain conditions—for example, if failure to complete the plan was caused by circumstances beyond the debtor's control.

Chapter 11 Bankruptcy

When corporations fall into deep debt, they often use a Chapter 11 reorganization proceeding. Late in 2001, America's seventh-largest corporation, Enron, filed for Chapter 11 reorganization. Other well-known companies that filed for Chapter 11 reorganization proceedings in 2001 include the Internet service provider Excite@Home and the airline TWA.

Chapter 11 reorganization allows debtors to restructure finances, the business to continue, and creditors to be paid. A bankruptcy case under Chapter 11 is started by the filing of a petition requesting an order for relief. Petitions may be voluntary or involuntary. A petition will result in a stay or suspension of creditors' actions against the debtor.

An individual or company filing for bankruptcy under Chapter 11 is usually allowed to operate as a debtor-in-possession (the debtor may continue to operate the business) unless a creditor or a party-in-interest (another party with a claim against the debtor) requests appointment of a trustee. A debtor-in-possession has 120 days after the order for relief to file a plan and 180 days to obtain acceptance before others can file a plan. After creditors have approved the plan, the court holds a hearing to confirm the approval, and the debts not provided for in the plan are discharged.

For many years, banks and other creditors have complained to Congress that current bankruptcy law permits debtors to avoid their debts too easily. Some of the more common creditor objections are that debtors' homes receive too much protection, that businesses can stay too long in Chapter 11 reorganization, and that credit card debts are too easily discharged. By summer 2001, such complaints had generated strong support in Congress, and bills had been drafted to tighten bankruptcy procedures under Chapters 7 and 13. According to some proposed reforms, consumers also would have found discharging credit card debt more difficult. By the fall of 2001, however, legislators were confronted with a steep downturn in the U.S. economy, aggravated by the September 11

Largest U.S. Bankruptcies 1983 to 2001

	Company	Bankruptcy Date	Total Assets Pre-Bankruptcy
1.	Enron Corp.[1]	12/2/2001	$63,392,000,000
2.	Texaco, Inc.	4/12/1987	$35,892,000,000
3.	Financial Corp. of America	9/9/1988	$33,864,000,000
4.	Global Crossing Ltd.	1/28/2002	$25,511,000,000
5.	Pacific Gas and Electric Co.	4/6/2001	$21,470,000,000
6.	MCorp	3/31/1989	$20,228,000,000
7.	Kmart Corp.	1/22/2002	$17,007,000,000
8.	First Executive Corp.	5/13/1991	$15,193,000,000
9.	Gibraltar Financial Corp.	2/8/1990	$15,011,000,000
10.	FINOVA Group, Inc., (The)	3/7/2001	$14,050,000,000
11.	HomeFed Corp.	10/22/1992	$13,885,000,000
12.	Southeast Banking Corporation	9/20/1991	$13,390,000,000
13.	Reliance Group Holdings, Inc.	6/12/2001	$12,598,000,000
14.	Imperial Corp. of America	2/28/1990	$12,263,000,000
15.	Federal-Mogul Corp.	10/1/2001	$10,150,000,000
16.	First City Bancorp.of Texas	10/31/1992	$9,943,000,000
17.	First Capital Holdings	5/30/1991	$9,675,000,000
18.	Baldwin-United	9/26/1983	$9,383,000,000

[1] Enron's financials were under review at the time of filing.
Source: BankruptcyData.com, New Generation Research, Inc., Boston, http://www.BankruptcyData.com (December 2, 2002).

An employee of the bankrupt Pan Am Airlines passes baggage loaders and machines headed for the auction block in 1992.

terrorist attacks on New York City and Washington, D.C. As unemployment rates rose and business failures increased early in 2002, the movement for bankruptcy reform was eclipsed by congressional attention to issues of national security and proposals for stimulating economic recovery. Bankruptcy reform issues are likely to resurface, however, as circumstances change and legislators reexamine how best to reconcile the legitimate interests of creditors with the public's interest in fostering resilience on the part of debtors.

Web Resources on Bankruptcy

www.BankruptcyData.com is the premier business bankruptcy resource Web site. It provides access to updated information on business bankruptcy filings.

www.abiworld.org, the Web site of the American Bankruptcy Institute, is a great resource for information on bankruptcy.

www.swiggartagin.com/lawfind provides information on all legal aspects of bankruptcy; it is maintained by the Boston law firm Swiggart and Agin, LLC.

www.nacba.com is the home page of the National Association of Consumer Bankruptcy Attorneys, serving the needs of consumer bankruptcy attorneys and consumer debtors in bankruptcy.

www.bankruptcy-expert.com, a service of the Moran Law Group in California, provides information on personal and business bankruptcies.

www.hg.org/bankrpt.html is a useful research guide to every aspect of bankruptcy law.

Further Reading

Bhandari, J. S., and L. Weiss, eds. *Corporate Bankruptcy: Economic and Legal Perspectives*. London: Cambridge University Press, 1996.

Kilpi, Jukka. *The Ethics of Bankruptcy*. New York: Routledge, 1998.

Levy, Nathan. *Bankruptcy Handbook*. Boston: Little, Brown, 1993.

Sitarz, D. *Debt Free: The National Bankruptcy Kit*. Carbondale, Ill.: Nova Publications, 1999.

—*Carl Pacini*

Bar Code

See also:
IBM; Inventory;
Retail and Wholesale.

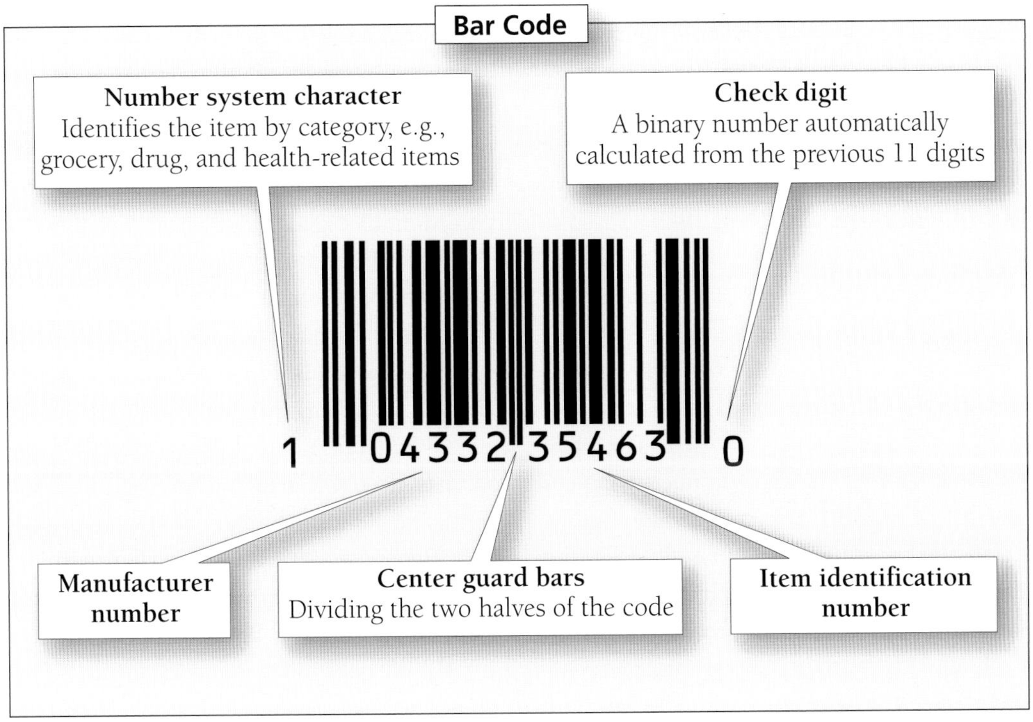

A bar code is a series of vertical, parallel lines, or bars, that symbolize a number assigned to a given product. The U.S. grocery industry introduced the bar code in its basic form in the 1970s as a way to speed the costly, labor-intensive checkout process; bar codes were simple to print on packages and labels and were easily read by a scanning device.

As computer-processing power and scanning devices have improved, bar codes have been put to a variety of uses around the globe. They enabled retailers to tighten control over their stock, helping to make possible the development of superstores with enormous inventories and the maintenance of huge databases of information about sales and customers' purchasing preferences. The scannable bar code, in conjunction with a computer database of product information, also made providing customers with detailed receipts possible. Bar codes improved efficiency and reduced errors in manufacturing, package delivery, health care, and other industries. Bar codes printed on ID cards facilitate quick identification of people. They have even been employed to keep track of animals. Esoteric versions of bar codes have been used by researchers to label genes and other molecules.

A key objective in efforts to develop a machine-readable pattern symbolizing a product number was that the pattern be scannable from both left to right and right to left, in order to minimize the time and labor required for scanning. A rectangular array of bars was not the only kind of pattern that could meet this criterion. Indeed, in 1972 a Cincinnati supermarket started a trial run of a code using a bull's-eye pattern created by RCA; at the time, RCA was the leading producer of cash registers, so the bar code was a natural expansion of its product line. The following year, however, a grocery industry committee endorsed an IBM proposal for a rectangular bar pattern, which was less vulnerable to printing problems than the bull's eye. The IBM proposal, slightly modified, is the basis of the standard now known as the Universal Product Code (UPC). At 8:01 A.M. on June 26, 1974, the first purchase of a product bearing a UPC code was made at a Marsh's supermarket in Troy, Ohio; the item bought was a pack of Wrigley's gum.

In the basic version of the UPC, a pair of thin vertical lines mark the left and right

The parts of a bar code.

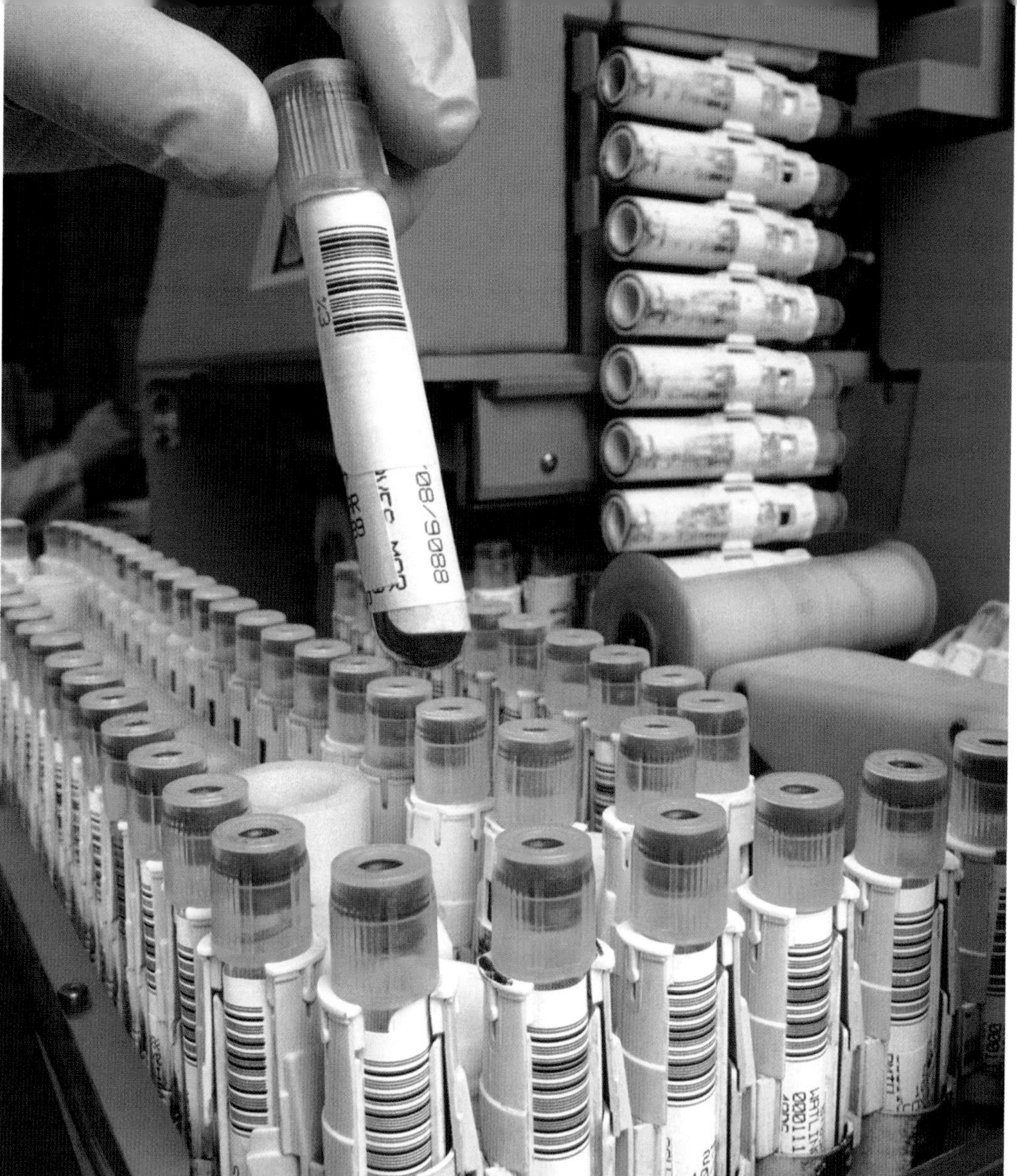

Bar codes may have been created for groceries, but they can now be found everywhere, from express packages to ID cards and even, as in this 1998 photo, on blood samples.

boundaries of a series of dark and light bars of varying widths. The bars encode an ID number keyed to specific information in a computer database. When a product's UPC is scanned, the number can be used to look up price or other data in the database and also to record in the database information about, for example, the quantity sold. The basic UPC is constructed in two halves, separated by a pair of thin vertical lines. Either half may be read first. Indeed a half may read in either direction, left to right, or right to left. The basic UPC represents a 12-digit number, which is usually printed in human-readable figures below the bar pattern. The first digit signifies the general category of the product. The five following digits, assigned by the Uniform Code Council, indicate the manufacturer or other company associated with the product. Next comes a five-digit code, assigned by the company; it commonly is the same or similar to the product's stock-keeping unit (SKU) number. The twelfth digit is a check digit, helping to detect errors in the scanning of the preceding 11 digits.

The UPC was the first of what are now hundreds of machine-readable bar code formats. These formats, or "languages," are called symbologies. Outside the United States and Canada, the symbologies most commonly used with retail products are two fixed-length formats closely related to the UPC: the EAN (European Article Numbering) system and the JAN (Japanese Article Numbering) system. Among the better-known examples of other symbologies are the Bookland code, which is used on books and is based on the ISBN, or International Standard Book Number;

Codabar, used on FedEx airbills; and Code 128, a quite dense variable-length format sometimes used in the shipping industry. Another important format is Postnet, used by the U.S. Postal Service to encode ZIP codes; the bars in Postnet codes, however, differ in height, not in width.

While the original UPC and similar formats can convey only a reference number, so-called two-dimensional, or 2D, bar codes, developed later, have a far greater capacity, enough to hold a digitized picture or fingerprint or the text of U.S. president Abraham Lincoln's Gettysburg Address. Some 2D formats are essentially stacks of one-dimensional bar codes, making them look to the eye like a minute checkerboard. Other 2D formats do not use checkerboard-like bars. United Parcel Service's MaxiCode, for example, is based on hexagons.

In principle, bar codes make possible the full automation of the customer checkout process, dispensing with the need for a cashier. Some companies, among them the Winn-Dixie supermarket chain, have experimented with self-checkout lanes. Whatever advances the future holds for code systems in commerce and manufacturing, they may well not involve the bar code, which is expected to be supplanted by "smarter," more interactive technologies, such as wireless radio-frequency identification (RFID) tags.

RFID microchip tags can automatically both send and receive data when they detect the presence of a radio-frequency reader. In contrast to bar code scanners, which use laser light, an RFID reader does not require that the product be in its line of sight. RFID tags have a larger data capacity than bar codes; thus every individual product item in the world (not just every product type, as with bar codes) could be assigned its own unique ID number. Such identification would allow information about an item's status within the distribution chain to be made available to manufacturers, retailers, and others linked in networks of readers, perhaps connected via the Internet.

Given an appropriate network infrastructure, RFID tags could permit complete automation of the mechanics of shopping, dispensing with the need for a checkout procedure. Sensors on shopping carts could automatically detect items selected by the customer, and the appropriate deduction could be automatically made from the customer's bank account. Radio-frequency chips have been used for years to keep track of livestock and railroad cars and to facilitate toll collection on highways. At the beginning of the twenty-first century, the chief obstacle blocking RFID tags from becoming as ubiquitous as bar codes is the cost of the RFID system, but researchers hope that costs will eventually decline to a competitive level.

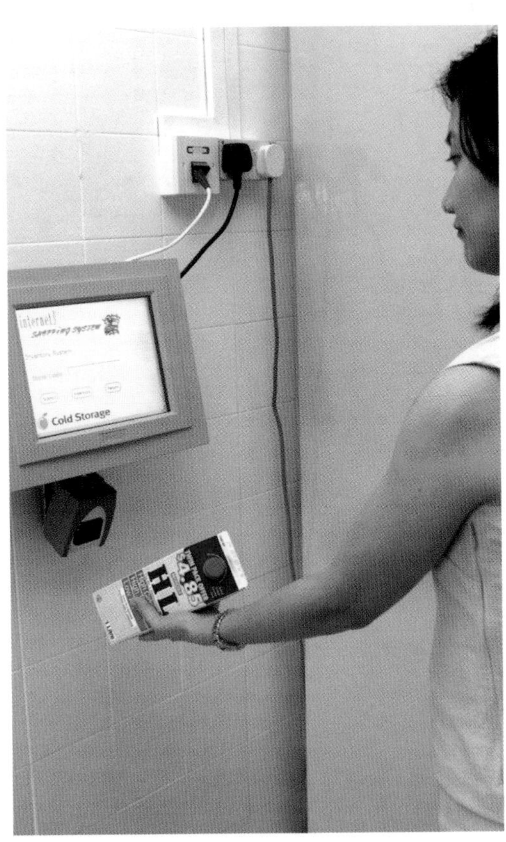

In 2000 a woman in Singapore swipes a carton of milk under a bar-code reader on her refrigerator; the order is relayed to a local grocery store via the Internet.

Further Reading

Brown, Stephen A. *Revolution at the Checkout Counter: The Explosion of the Bar Code.* Cambridge, Mass.: Harvard University Press, 1997.

Leibowitz, Ed. "Bar Codes: Reading between the Lines." *Smithsonian*, February 1999, 130 ff.

Nelson, Benjamin. *Punched Cards to Bar Codes: A 200 Year Journey.* Peterborough, N.H.: Helmers Publishing, 1997.

Schmidt, Charlie. "Beyond the Bar Code." *Technology Review*, March 2001, 80–85.

—Richard Hantula

See also:
Corporate Social Responsibility; Entrepreneurship.

Ben & Jerry's Homemade

Business success was sweet for Ben Cohen and Jerry Greenfield, two longtime friends who joined their talents to build a unique multimillion-dollar corporation based on ice cream and principles of social responsibility.

The boys' association began early. Born just four days apart in 1951 in Brooklyn, New York, the two first met in eighth grade. The heavy-set boys struggled together when running the track in gym class. By high school they had become good friends, sometimes double-dating in Cohen's Camaro, listening to tapes on the eight-track cassette player. After graduating from Calhoun High School in Merrick, New York, each attended a different college.

Greenfield, a National Merit Scholar, enrolled at Oberlin College in Ohio. He hoped to become a medical doctor, but he was not accepted into medical school after graduation, so he took his skills to New York and began working as a lab technician. He remembers, not fondly, that the job involved stuffing pieces of cow hearts into test tubes. He subsequently reapplied to medical school and was once again rejected. During these otherwise unpromising years, he reunited with Cohen. They were roommates in New York City and, later, in Saratoga Springs, New York.

Cohen took a different path after high school. Completing just a year and a half at Colgate, he left to pursue other interests. Working at minor jobs, he attended college part-time, taking courses like pottery and sound recording. Eventually he moved to Paradox, New York, where he took a job teaching crafts at Highland Community School.

In various ways ice cream was a point of interest for both boys throughout their early lives. Greenfield remembers dishing up ice cream in the college cafeteria where he worked. Cohen recalls his own experiments in dessert making, mixing ice cream and mashed cookies; later, as a high school senior, he worked as an ice-cream seller, peddling treats to neighborhood children. When he dropped out of Colgate, Cohen returned to selling ice cream.

While the two were roommates in Saratoga Springs, they decided to pool their skills and pursue their longtime dream of starting a food business together. Cohen says they might have set out to make bagels had the necessary equipment not been so expensive; instead, after researching the industry, they launched their ice-cream business. According to their biographies, their research included taking a five-dollar Penn State correspondence course on ice-cream-making, for which they received perfect scores.

Because Saratoga Springs already had an ice-cream store, they located their shop in the thriving college town of Burlington, Vermont. There, in May 1978, Ben & Jerry's Homemade Ice Cream Parlor opened in a converted gas station on a busy street corner. The rich and flavorful ice cream quickly became a hit in town, and the young men and their organization

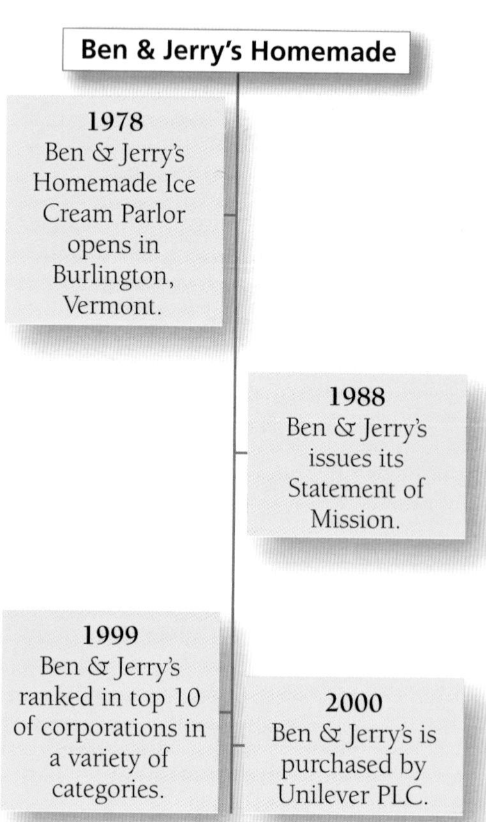

Ben Cohen (standing) and Jerry Greenfield (seated) in 1992.

became well known. From the beginning, Ben & Jerry's was committed to making high-quality ice cream from all-natural Vermont dairy products; for example, the company rejected milk and cream from cows treated with rBGH, an artificial growth hormone. In addition, Cohen and Greenfield committed themselves to being good citizens of their community. They actively participated in local celebrations and festivals, and in 1985 they established a foundation to serve the community. All the while, they were equally committed to running a profitable business.

What began as a small shop blossomed into a large, lucrative organization. Throughout the growth, Ben & Jerry's was loyal to the concept of linked prosperity—selling a high-quality and interesting product through a profitable enterprise that is also socially responsible. The men offered a wide variety of products with off-the-wall names like Chunky Monkey, Chubby Hubby, and Cherry Garcia. They worked diligently to maintain a lively workplace—instituting Ben & Jerry's Joy Gang, a group aimed at making the organization a happy place to work. The Joy Gang plans events (such as Elvis Day) for the staff and periodically surprises employees with snacks, neck massages, and the occasional clown or juggler. Together, Cohen and Greenfield became spokesmen for Business for Social Responsibility, an organization that promotes socially responsible business models. As a part of its commitment, Ben & Jerry's has always given 7.5 percent of its pretax profits to charity and operated according to policies that favor family farms and sustainable agriculture.

What we feel Ben & Jerry's represents is that including a concern for the community adds value to the company. It doesn't take it away despite what the skeptics might say. Our products are competitively priced, we are consistently profitable, and we have not forgotten the community. The question is, as one business leader is known to have phrased it in looking at our success, "If those idiots at Ben & Jerry's can do it, why can't we?"

Could others do the same sort of thing we are doing? Yes, and a growing number are. But the numbers of companies are too few, and their size is too small. We need more companies engaging in pioneering work, so that the frontier of social responsibility gets pushed out ever further. And we need bigger companies to get in on the act; it's not enough to have Benetton, Body Shop, or Patagonia working on social or environmental innovation, we need the Exxons, Toyotas, and Westinghouses.

What exactly would the world look like if the Fortune 500 suddenly got religion and joined Business for Social Responsibility? Imagine what we could do together to address our environmental and social problems. We have to find ways to unleash our corporate imagination, creativity and, indeed, our spirituality, and construct a vision of doing things better. And we simultaneously need to cajole, plead with, threaten, boycott, beg, persuade and argue with the megacorporations in an effort to turn them around, to expand their conception of the bottom line to include two parts. We must find the way to make business want to make itself part of the solution to our problems.

—Ben Cohen, from "What Does Business Do?" *MBA Perspectives,* January 1996

The concept of linked prosperity brought nationwide, and eventually worldwide, respect to the company. In September 1999 the *Wall Street Journal* rated corporations according to a Harris public opinion poll about corporate image: Ben & Jerry's ranked sixth in the nation. Ben & Jerry's high overall standing was attributed to its ranking among the top five corporations in four categories: Emotional Appeal, Social Responsibility, Products and Service, and Workplace Environment.

On April 12, 2000, Ben & Jerry's Homemade, Inc., was purchased by Unilever PLC for $326 million. The buyout agreement provided for the ice-cream maker to remain in Vermont, operating with its own board of directors, independent of Unilever. Announcing the purchase, Unilever's president told the Associated Press, "Much of the success of the Ben & Jerry's brand is based on its connections to basic human values, and it is our hope and expectation that Ben & Jerry's continues to engage in these critical, global economic and social missions."

Ben & Jerry's remains a maker of premier ice cream as well as a contributor to society through the philanthropic foundation it established more than two decades ago. The company also seeks to inspire community participation through the sponsorship of charity events and activist projects.

Further Reading

Cohen, Ben, and Jerry Greenfield. *Ben & Jerry's Double Dip: Lead with Your Values and Make Money, Too.* New York: Simon & Schuster, 1997.

Gumpert, David E. Inc. *Magazine Presents How to Really Create a Successful Business Plan: Featuring the Business Plans of Pizza Hut, Software Publishing Corp., Celestial Seasonings, People Express, Ben & Jerry's.* 3rd ed. Boston: Inc., 1996.

Lager, Fred. *Ben & Jerry's, The Inside Scoop: How Two Real Guys Built a Business with Social Conscience and a Sense of Humor.* New York: Crown Publishers, 1994.

—*Karen Ehrle*

Benchmarking

See also:
Comparative Advantage; ISO 9000; Management; Manufacturing Industry.

Benchmarking is best defined as the process of comparing a current state against a desired state. Companies in almost every industry use benchmarking to create a baseline for constant improvement. Benchmarking is also used by individuals in their quest for higher savings, to find a quicker way to get from point A to point B, and so forth. Benchmarking is certainly not a new concept, but only in the 1990s did a demand arise for a standardized benchmarking process. Previously, every company used benchmarking differently. While this is still the case in many situations, standards have been developed for use in various industries.

Benchmarking Process and Results

The result of any benchmarking study is a deficiency listing, or gap analysis. To arrive at this result, one must identify the process to be analyzed or improved. Next, one must study the process step-by-step to understand how it works, how much time it takes, how much it costs, and so forth. Understanding the process can be achieved in a number of ways, including asking questions of the people in charge of the process, and taking a tour of the operations and simply watching for a while. For example, in an automobile factory, one may be analyzing the painting process. A tour of the conveyer belt and surrounding areas would come first. Then, workers would be interviewed to find out where the paint comes from, how many cars can they paint in an hour, how many hours they work, and how much downtime they have during the day. Finally, one would view the process for a while to find out how fast cars are painted, how many defects occur, how many times the paint runs out, and how much inventory is waiting.

Once the process is fully understood, something with which to compare it must be found. For a company identifying a process within a plant, the best comparison would be to another company with a similar plant that may be more efficient. Thus, a new automobile manufacturer might want to compare its painting process to the painting process in Toyota's plants. A comparison is preferably made to what is called best-practice processes—companies or individuals who operate the most efficiently, or most profitably for that particular process. Most companies or individuals do not have the best practice for all processes; therefore each process must be compared separately. If Toyota has the best paint process but Ford has the best brake installation process, then the new automobile company would use Toyota to benchmark the painting process and Ford to benchmark the brake installation.

Finally, results must be studied. If the new automobile company produces two defects each hour and Toyota produces only one each hour, this is a gap. The reasons for the gap must be understood and a plan to improve the process based on this knowledge must be devised and implemented. Perhaps the reason is the kind of paint used or the skill of the workers. Either way, to become a best-practice company, the problems must be resolved.

Benchmarking results can range from extremely simple to correct to extremely complex. For example, an individual commutes to work every day by bus. This person needs 45 minutes to get to work. This person later finds out that a neighbor commutes to the same location by train and needs only 30 minutes. This is a very simple benchmarking situation and result. The

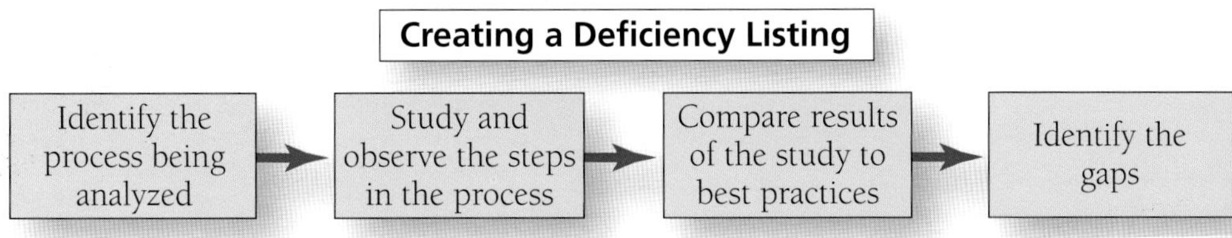

commuter would simply take the train like her neighbor to be more efficient. However, what if the train costs twice as much as the bus or the commuter must drive to the train but does not have a car? This makes the resolution of the gap more complex. Nonetheless, the commuter has the information needed to decide whether becoming more efficient is cost beneficial.

The same kinds of decisions are made every day in large corporations. For example, the new car company may have to buy higher quality and more costly paint, or spend time and resources to train its workers better. It may cost more to do so than to lower defects to one per hour. Either way, this would not be known without going through a benchmarking study.

Benchmarking Standards

As noted, benchmarking standards have been developed for many industries. These standards call for a minimum level of care for each process. If these levels are met, a company receives a certification proving that it is a company of sufficient operations.

One such standard is called ISO 9000. ISO 9000 is a standard for quality-management systems. ISO 9000 is unique because it is a generic standard that does not apply

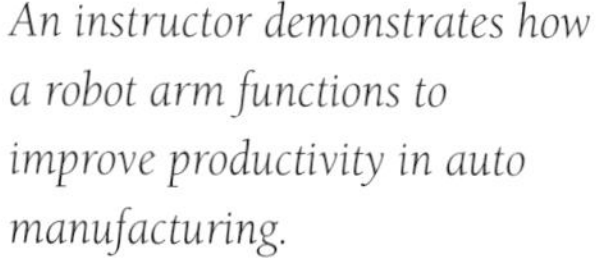

An instructor demonstrates how a robot arm functions to improve productivity in auto manufacturing.

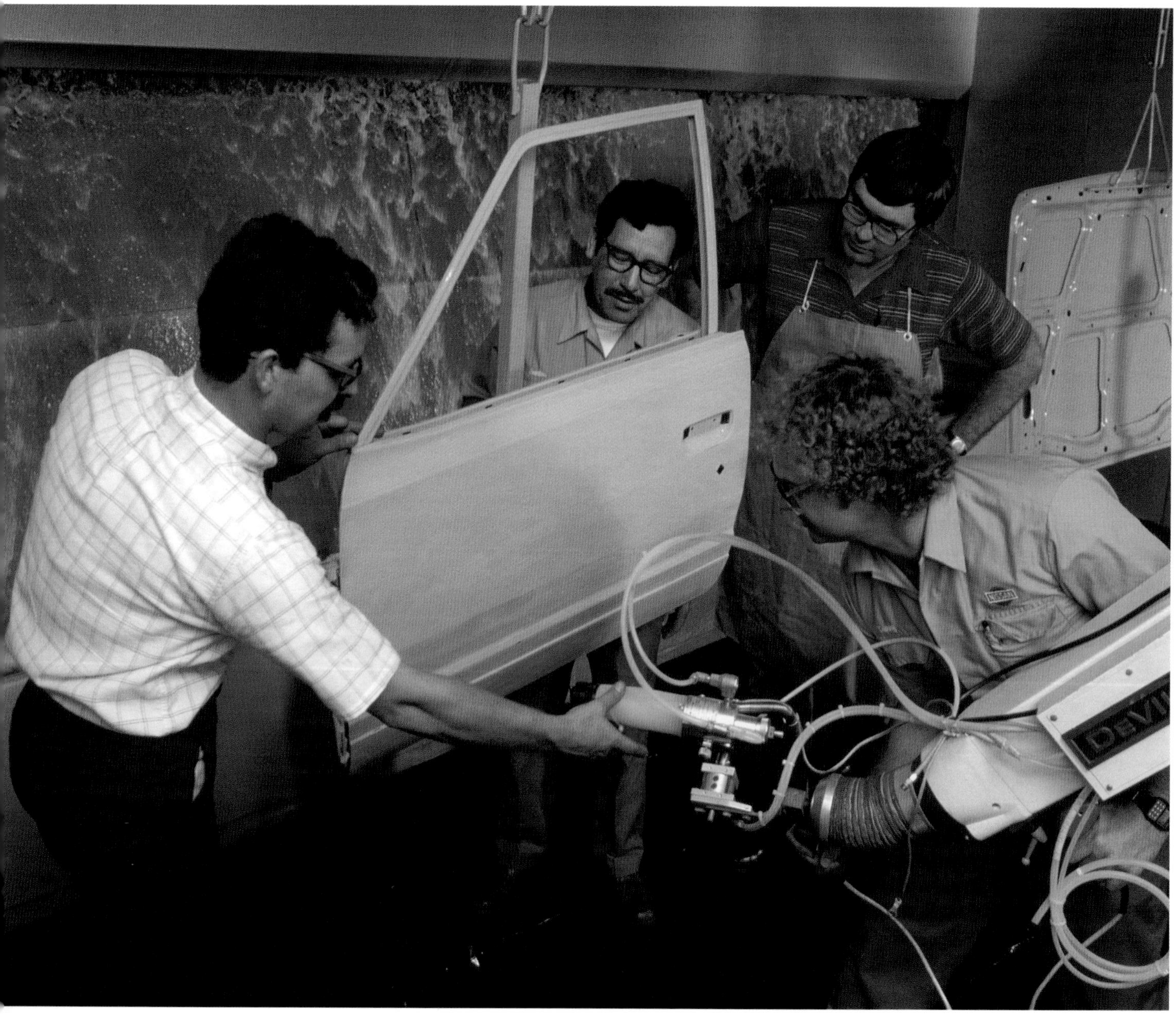

Benchmarking in Daily Life

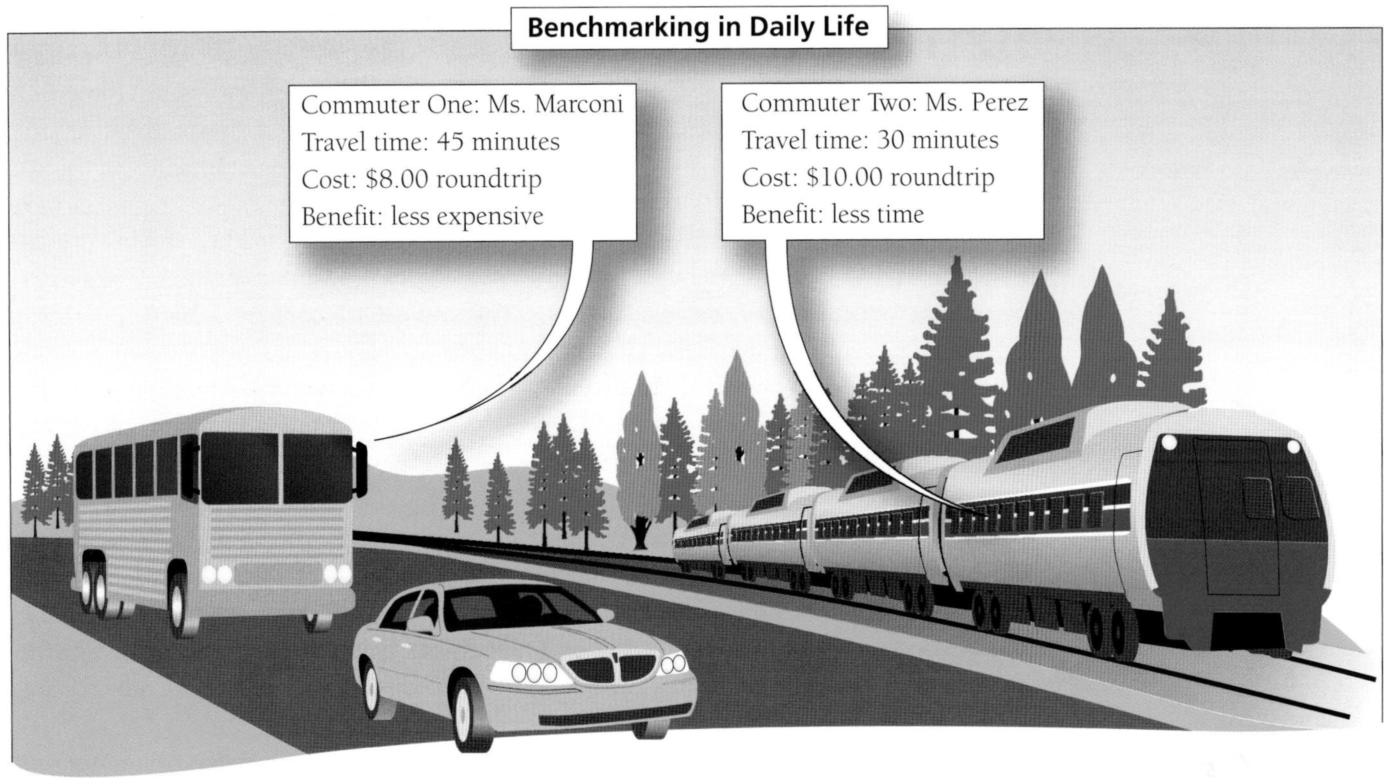

to a specific industry. It applies in general to the management operations of all companies because it analyzes levels of customer satisfaction and product defects. These issues arise in all companies.

Many companies and individuals require suppliers to obtain ISO certification to keep their business. To become ISO-certified, a company must engage a certified auditor to review the company's operations and identify gaps. Unlike gaps to best practices discussed above, these are gaps to the minimum level of acceptance. Once these gaps are filled, the company can obtain its certification.

ISO 9000 is only one example of a standard benchmark. Others are QS 9000 for the automotive industry, AS 9100 for the aerospace industry, and ISO 13485 for the medical device industry. Many more exist and more are being developed.

Although many standard certifications are available, many companies still do not fit into any standard. These companies typically use external consultants to perform gap analyses based on their experiences with other clients. While the result of this kind of gap analysis is not a certification, the consulting firm will typically produce a report that lists the gaps and resolutions. Such a report will usually suffice for outside parties that require efficient customers or suppliers.

For individuals, benchmarking is solely a personal process as it mostly benefits the individual and a few others. For companies within the services or product-producing industries, standards for benchmarking are becoming increasingly important, as some customers will not buy from uncertified suppliers. Benchmarking has been around unofficially for a long time and has finally become a widely accepted, transparent method for understanding the operations of a company.

Further Reading

Bogan, Christopher E., and Michael J. English. *Benchmarking for Best Practices: Winning through Innovative Adaptation.* New York: McGraw-Hill, 2001.

Harrington, H. James, and James S. Harrington. *High Performance Benchmarking: 20 Steps to Success.* New York: McGraw-Hill, 1995.

—Andréa Korb and David Korb

See also:
Advertising, Business Practice; Advertising Industry; Business Ethics; Professional Associations; Regulation of Business and Industry.

Better Business Bureau

The Better Business Bureau (BBB) was created by businesspeople to police business practices. Its 145 local offices in the United States and Canada, usually incorporated as independent nonprofit businesses, gather information on local businesses, handle millions of consumer complaints and inquiries each year, and monitor local advertising. These efforts provide consumers with information; indirectly, BBBs regulate advertising and sales practices—a feat all the more impressive because the BBB operates as a voluntary association with little means to punish those who violate its guidelines.

Local BBB offices in the United States are affiliated with the National Council of Better Business Bureaus. The council's National Advertising Division (NAD) monitors the accuracy of national advertisements. The council is a supporting member of the independent National Advertising Review Board (NARB), which examines advertiser appeals of NAD rulings.

Both locally and nationally, the BBB is supported by membership fees. Member businesses agree to follow BBB guidelines. Such participation is strictly voluntary; attempts to force businesses to follow BBB guidelines have been struck down in U.S. courts as violations of antitrust law.

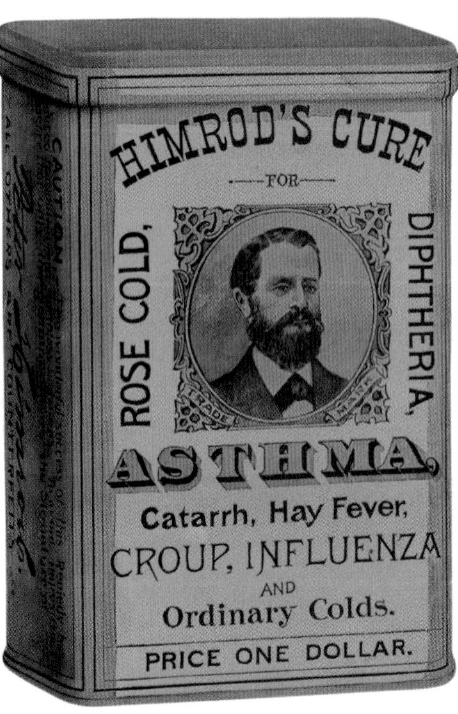

The BBB was created to protect consumers from fraudulent advertising like this nineteenth-century ad for Himrod's Cure, which promises to cure everything from hay fever to diphtheria.

The BBB arose from the "truth in advertising" movement of the early twentieth century in the United States. At the turn of the nineteenth century, advertising claims made for some products were so outrageous that several magazines refused to carry any medical advertising. Advertising professionals, fearing that the entire industry's reputation would be sullied beyond repair, began to push for reform. In 1912, a New York City association of advertising professionals formed a vigilance committee. The 33-member committee began investigating complaints about misleading advertising, turning fraudulent ads over to law enforcement officials. Although the committee was established only to investigate advertising, the members quickly found themselves handling complaints by consumers about the sales practices of retailers. This experience prompted the Associated Advertising Clubs of America to establish a National Vigilance Committee later that year. In 1921 the National Better Business Bureau of the Associated Advertising Clubs of the World was incorporated, becoming an independent entity in 1926. In that year, the BBB had 45 local offices; by 1962 the number had increased to 122.

Although the BBB provides consumer information, it differs from consumer organizations in important ways. It focuses narrowly on good business practices rather than consumer protection (although the two goals sometimes overlap). Thus, the NAD and NARB focus on the accuracy of claims made in national advertising, but whether an advertisement aimed at adults is in good taste is outside the purview of either organization. In addition, while the BBB sometimes makes recommendations regarding consumer-protection legislation, it is not a lobbying organization and generally avoids drafting laws and trying to influence policy.

In 1996 James Bast, president of the BBB, introduced the new BBBOnline service, which helps customers evaluate businesses that advertise on the Internet.

The BBB also has no legal authority to regulate companies. It establishes guidelines for business practices but, unlike government agencies that issue regulations, has no way to enforce its guidelines. Occasionally a local BBB office will sue a business in court, but the main weapon in the BBB's arsenal is publicity. For example, if an advertisement is found by the NAD to be deceptive, the punishment imposed on the advertiser is simply that the division publishes a report of its findings. A local BBB office can also suspend the membership of a business that does not follow its guidelines; in such a case the office will usually issue a press release explaining its action to the local media, which tend to cover BBB suspensions and admonitions closely. These tactics often prove to be effective. Indeed, consumer organizations that strongly criticized the creation of the NAD and NARB in the early 1970s as simply a ploy by the advertising industry to avoid government regulation have largely dropped their opposition and now work with BBB organizations.

To preserve its influence, the BBB cultivates a reputation as an honest broker between businesses and consumers. Local offices have full-time staff and seek a wide range of business support to prevent them from becoming beholden to a single company. Businesses and business associations sometimes charge the BBB with going overboard in its efforts to be impartial. The BBB has maintained its support within business circles, however, because it is seen as protective of legitimate businesses and as a workable alternative to government regulation.

Further Reading

Miracle, Gordon E., and Terence Nevett. *Voluntary Regulation of Advertising: A Comparative Analysis of the United Kingdom and the United States.* Lexington, Mass.: Lexington Books, 1987.

Smith, Ralph Lee. *Self-Regulation in Action: Story of the Better Business Bureaus 1912–1962.* New York: Association of Better Business Bureaus, 1961.

—*Mary Sisson*

Basic Principles of Truth in Advertising

1. The primary responsibility for truthful and non-deceptive advertising rests with the advertiser. Advertisers should be prepared to substantiate any claims or offers made before publication or broadcast and, upon request, present such substantiation promptly to the advertising medium or the Better Business Bureau.

2. Advertisements which are untrue, misleading, deceptive, fraudulent, falsely disparaging of competitors, or insincere offers to sell, shall not be used.

3. An advertisement as a whole may be misleading although every sentence separately considered is literally true. Misrepresentation may result not only from direct statements but by omitting or obscuring a material fact.

—Better Business Bureau Code of Advertising

See also:
Gordy, Berry, Jr.; Johnson, John H.; Publishing Industry; Winfrey, Oprah.

Black Enterprise

Black Enterprise is a leading financial journal and the only one to directly address the needs and concerns of black business owners and professionals. As the magazine's first editorial put it, "Lacking capital, managerial and technical knowledge, and crippled by prejudice, the minority businessman has been effectively kept out of the American marketplace. We want to help change this."

The founder and guiding spirit of *Black Enterprise* is Earl Graves. In the spring of 1969, Graves, a graduate of West Point and former administrative assistant to Senator Robert Kennedy, and his consulting firm were working with the Small Business Administration, studying ways to improve economic conditions for African Americans. Struck by the lack of concrete, practical

The November 2002 issue.

information available to help black people start, manage, and enlarge their businesses, Graves conceived the idea of a newsletter. He began by assembling a blue ribbon panel of black business and political leaders to advise on the proposed newsletter's content and direction. The panel included Senator Edward W. Brooks, Representative Shirley Chisholm, and Charles Evers, a well-known civil rights leader.

With the help of the panelists, Graves managed to attract $500,000 worth of advertising for the first issue, which was released in August 1970. Evers, then the mayor of Fayette, Mississippi, and a small-business owner himself, was the subject of *Black Enterprise*'s first cover article. The issue was distributed free to a select list of 100,000 black businesspeople, community leaders, and institutions. By its ninth issue in 1972 the magazine had attracted paying subscribers, had begun turning a profit, and was available on some newsstands.

In 1973, the magazine came up with an innovation that helped cement its reputation as a valuable source of information for black businesspeople: the BE index, a ranking of the top 100 black-owned businesses across the United States. Over the years, the BE index has become a reliable tool to assess economic development and opportunities in the black community. With the exception of Motown Records, which topped the inaugural list with $40 million in revenue, the vast majority of the 1970 BE index businesses were small mom-and-pop operations with less than $1 million in sales. The original BE index of the top 100 black-owned businesses has been supplemented with other lists, such as the top 100 black-owned insurance companies, investment banks, and the top 100 asset managers.

The core of *Black Enterprise* is profiles of successful black business leaders, but the magazine also features stories of failure and struggle, as well as articles intended to help young black professionals handle racism as they move up the corporate ladder. Profiles of famous black sports figures and entertainers, including Tiger Woods and Oprah Winfrey, have also become a common feature of the magazine; the articles often focus on how these celebrities have used their fame to gain entrance to successful sidelines like becoming commercial spokespersons, entrepreneurial ventures, and marketers of their own subsidiary products.

Black Enterprise has begun to focus on the young black market, publishing lists of the top 50 colleges for African Americans and launching two subsidiary publications, *Teenpreneurs* and *Kidpreneurs*, aimed at introducing young people to the basic concepts of finance and entrepreneurship. Thus, 30 years after the magazine began offering a hand up to struggling black businesspeople, *Black Enterprise* continues to expand its fundamental mission while covering the considerably wider horizons of black enterprise that it helped to create. Such dedication and focus contribute not only to the continued success of the magazine but also to the success of its readership.

In 1997 Earl Graves poses in New York's Times Square with a copy of his book, How to Succeed in Business without Being White.

Further Reading

Daniel, Walter C. *Black Journals of the United States.* Westport, Conn.: Greenwood Press, 1983.

Graves, Earl G. "Why Black Enterprise?" *Black Enterprise,* August 2000, 30.

—Colleen Sullivan

See also:
Advertising Industry;
Trademark.

Brand Names

Brand names provide a means of identification of products, differentiation from competition, and assurance of a consistent level of quality. Without brand names, buyers would have to choose from individual products each time they shopped, as when they choose fresh meats or fish from a butcher's counter. Buyers reduce their shopping time as they easily identify familiar brands. At the same time, brands create financial value for the seller. Every time shoppers buy Campbell's Tomato Soup, they expect to see the familiar lettering on the red and white can. They are assured that the soup will taste the same each time they buy it and will be at the level of quality they have learned to expect.

A brand name is that part of a brand that can be spoken aloud, as contrasted to a brand mark that is a design or symbol. The word *Nike* is a brand name, while the swoosh design is a brand mark. Along with product performance, packaging, and advertising, brands help to create an image for products. Buyers identify some brands so closely with a particular product category that the brands are referred to as master brands. The Kleenex brand, for example, means facial tissues. The phenomenon of brand loyalty occurs when a buyer purchases one brand fairly consistently and has a positive attitude toward that brand. In some instances, the loyalty is so strong that buyers display brands prominently, in effect associating their own images with those of the brands. Harley-Davidson Motorcycle buyers sometimes go so far as to tattoo the Harley brand name and the eagle brand mark on their bodies.

What Makes a Good Brand Name?

When companies create new products, they usually spend considerable time choosing brand names that will convey the image they want. Brand names fall into a number of categories. Some brand names are people's names, such as Ford or Dell. Other brand names are made-up words

Many companies depend on the concept of brand loyalty to influence customers to choose one product over another, virtually identical, product.

such as Exxon or Kodak. Clean Shower and Windex illustrate the third category of brand names, those that show product benefits or describe products in some way.

Good brands typically have several characteristics. They are easy to say, spell, and remember. A shorter name is preferable to a longer one. The brand should also be readily differentiated from the competition. Brand names showing product benefits and contributing to a desirable product image are usually good choices. Finally, a good brand name should be appropriate to international markets. Tide brand laundry detergent is an example of positive brand name characteristics. The word *Tide* is easy to say, spell, and remember. It is short. When Tide is printed on the side of a box of detergent, its letters can be large and commanding on the shelf, fairly shouting at the supermarket shopper. The word *Tide* means water and sea, conjuring the image of waves washing in and out; the name supports a positive, clean concept appropriate to a detergent. Intending to compete with the Tide brand, a newer laundry detergent made an obvious brand name choice with similar meaning when it chose the name *Surf*.

Brand names, whether they are for tangible or intangible products, may be legally registered. Once they have been registered, they are official trademarks, and the owners have the exclusive right to use of these brand names. The owner is responsible to police the trademark and to bring legal action against organizations that may be using the brand without permission.

Short History of Branding

The first kinds of companies to promote brand names heavily were those making consumer goods—products sold in supermarkets and discount stores. These consumable brands were followed by durable goods like appliances and automobiles.

Sports star Michael Jordan turned himself into a brand name, which enables him to have successful side businesses like his own cologne and this Chicago restaurant.

Some extremely successful brands are recognized the world over: Here, shoppers seek the Gap clothing brand at a store in Tokyo.

Next, companies aiming their products at businesses began to emphasize their brand names. Then services like financial institutions and not-for-profit organizations embarked on a process of creating images through emphasizing their brand names and marks. Educational institutions, government agencies, vacation locations, and even individuals have all realized the importance of creating brand identities. Michael Jordan, Madonna, and Martha Stewart are all people, but they are brand names as well.

The late twentieth century saw an increased emphasis on branding in the marketplace. Historically, with the occasional exception of long-established brands such as Dole or Chiquita, produce tended not to have brand names, but now many fruits and vegetables like mushrooms and tomatoes come packaged with pronounced brand names and marks. Formerly, the only meats branded tended to be luncheon or processed meats. Now the shopper sees branded fresh poultry products and sometimes beef.

Competition exists not only between individual brands but also between kinds of brands. The "battle of the brands" is sales competition between manufacturer's brands, also known as national brands, and private or store brands. Manufacturer's brands carry a name chosen by the producer. Examples would be Sony, Kellogg's, or Oxydol. Private or store brands carry names chosen by wholesalers or retailers such as Gap, Kroger, or Sam's American Choice. Although manufacturer's brands still outsell private labels, these private brands are gaining sales in discount stores and supermarkets because of their good value. In clothing stores, private label brands provide the seller the advantage of exclusivity and usually higher profits. The only place to buy Old Navy clothing is at an Old Navy store.

Brand names are a means of identifying and differentiating products, of creating images, and of assuring buyers of a consistent level of quality and reliability. The movement in the marketplace is definitely toward placing more emphasis on brand names. The use of brand names has expanded beyond consumer goods to business-to-business markets and to services, government agencies, and not-for-profit organizations.

Further Reading

Gobé, Marc. *Emotional Branding: The New Paradigm for Connecting Brands to People*. New York: Allworth Press, 2001.

Khermouch, Gerry, Stanley Holmes, and Moon Ihlwan. "The Best Global Brands." *Business Week*, August 6, 2001, 50–58.

—*Lois Smith*

Breakeven Point

In accounting and finance, the breakeven point is the point at which sales revenue equals the expenses of making and distributing a product. This can be measured in many ways through breakeven analysis. A breakeven analysis yields either the number of items that must be sold within a particular period or the amount of time needed to break even. Breakeven analysis is important to most businesses because it tells investors how long they will have to wait to begin earning back their principal investment—a major concern of any investor.

To calculate the breakeven point, the number of unit sales must be adjusted until the unit sales multiplied by the selling price minus all costs of doing business yields a result of zero: (unit sales × selling price) – all costs and expenses = 0. Unfortunately, this calculation can require a good deal of trial and error, as different types of business costs react differently when unit sales change. An easier way to calculate the breakeven point is available: One needs only to understand the difference between fixed costs and variable costs.

Fixed costs are charges to the business that are not directly affected by the number of units sold. Examples of these are rent, insurance, and fixed salaries (the salaries of the president and senior executives). Many fixed costs are fixed for a certain range of unit sales but increase when the capacity is reached. Thus, if too many products are produced, they have to be stored in a new warehouse. The company will have to find a new warehouse and pay new fixed rental charges. For this discussion, all analysis of fixed cost is assumed to be within current capacity; so, assume that fixed costs for a company that sells widgets are $1,000,000.

Variable costs are charges that are directly related to the number of units sold—for example, cost of materials used to produce the product, selling costs, transportation costs, and direct labor costs. Variable costs can be expressed in per unit costs, because they are directly related to each unit produced. Thus, to produce one widget, costs are $5 to buy the raw materials, $9 in direct labor to assemble the widget, $1 to sell it, and $2 to transport it to the customer. Therefore, the variable cost per unit is $17.

The sales price per unit (assume here it is $37) less the variable cost per unit ($17) is called the per-unit contribution margin. The contribution margin is an important concept because it represents the amount each unit is contributing to profits. In this case, the per unit contribution margin is $20 ($37 – $17). For each unit sold, the company is better off by $20.

To calculate the breakeven point, the company must divide total fixed costs by the unit contribution margin:

$$\frac{\$1{,}000{,}000}{\$20/\text{unit}} = 50{,}000 \text{ units}$$

See also:
Accounting and Bookkeeping; Income Statement; Interest; Overhead; Profit and Loss.

The salaries of these executives, the rent for the office they are in, and the price of the computer they are using are all costs that must be factored into the breakeven point.

The Breakeven Equation

(Unit Sales x Selling Price) – All Costs and Expenses = 0

The company must sell 50,000 widgets to recoup its investment in fixed costs. If the company knows it can sell only 20,000 units per year, it knows that 2½ (50,000 / 20,000) years will be needed to recoup its fixed costs.

Although this analysis is very useful, it does have flaws. Most important, the analysis does not take into consideration the time value of money. It assumes that a dollar earned or spent today has the same value as a dollar earned or spent in the future. This is not the case. The money invested in fixed costs today carries more value than the contribution margin earned in the future. In this respect, breakeven analysis is overstated. Additionally, for companies with several products, accurately allocating fixed costs to each product is difficult, thus the breakeven point for each product may inadvertently be calculated incorrectly.

However, even with its flaws, the breakeven point is used by most corporations to analyze new projects, by most banks to decide whether to lend to corporations, and by most investors to understand how soon they will earn a return on their investment. These parties are aware of the flaws involved in breakeven analysis but use it as a baseline result that should be adjusted appropriately based on each situation.

Further Reading

Anthony, Robert, and Leslie Pearlman. *Essentials of Accounting.* New York: Prentice Hall, 1999.

Higgins, Robert. *Analysis for Financial Management.* New York: McGraw-Hill Higher Education, 2000.

—Andréa Korb and David Korb

Kinds of Costs in the Breakeven Calculation

Concepts	Definition	Examples
Fixed Costs	Expenses not directly affected by the number of units sold	Rent
		Insurance
		Management salaries
Variable Costs	Expenses directly related to the number of units sold	Material
		Labor
		Selling costs (e.g., commissions)
		Transportation

Bristol-Myers Squibb

In 1989 pharmaceutical companies Bristol-Myers and Squibb merged in what was the largest such merger up to that time. The two companies had been ranked the number 12 and number 14 pharmaceutical companies in the world, but the merger created the second largest pharmaceutical company in the world (after Merck & Company).

Bristol-Myers Squibb

1856
E.R. Squibb founded in Brooklyn, N.Y.

1887
William McLaren Bristol and John Ripley Myers found Clinton Pharmaceutical Company (later Bristol, Myers).

1906
Pure Food and Drug Act passed by U.S. Congress.

1944
Squibb opens world's largest penicillin plant in New Jersey.

1959
Bristol-Myers acquires Clairol.

1975
Squibb researchers create Capoten, the first in a new class of antihypertensive agents.

1989
Bristol-Myers and Squibb merge.

2001
Bristol-Myers Squibb agrees to sell AIDS drugs in Africa at reduced prices.

Bristol-Myers Squibb has 14,000 employees worldwide and thousands of products marketed in more than 130 countries.

Although Bristol-Myers Squibb is a recent creation, the history and impact of each company reach back to the mid-nineteenth century. Bristol-Myers and Squibb were both founded in the mid-to-late 1800s as ethical pharmaceutical companies. At that time, ethical pharmaceuticals had a somewhat different meaning than it does today. In the 1800s, shelves were filled with various forms of snake oil, most of which were ineffective or downright dangerous. The designation *ethical pharmaceuticals* referred to medicines of proven scientific value, often medicines sold directly to doctors.

Bristol, Myers

In 1887 William McLaren Bristol and John Ripley Myers decided to sink $5,000 into a failing drug manufacturing firm, the Clinton Pharmaceutical Company, located in Clinton, New York; Bristol was president and Myers was vice president. Bristol and Myers had two business rules: Insist on high quality and maintain the firm's good financial credit standing at all costs. In May 1898 they renamed the company Bristol, Myers Company (a hyphen replaced the original comma after Myers died in 1899). The company operated for 13 years before breaking even, but it has turned a profit in every year since.

The company's first nationally recognized product, Sal Hepatica, was termed the poor man's spa by chief chemist J. Leroy Webber. It was a laxative mineral salt that, when dissolved in water, reproduced the taste and effects of the natural mineral waters of Bohemia. This first success was joined in 1907 by a second product, Ipana toothpaste, the first dentifrice to include a disinfectant to prevent bleeding gums. Because few remedies actually worked as promised, the toothpaste soon became very popular.

The increasing demand for Sal Hepatica and Ipana turned Bristol-Myers from a regional company into a national, and then an international, company. Although it also produced some pharmaceuticals, Bristol-Myers

See also:
Business Ethics; Health Care Services Industry; Patent.

dropped them during the Great Depression and devoted its marketing efforts entirely to Sal Hepatica, Ipana, and other consumer products like toiletries, antiseptics, and cough syrups. By 1924, gross profits topped $1 million and the company's products were on sale in 26 countries. Bristol-Myers was listed on the New York Stock Exchange in 1929.

The ER Squibb Company

Dr. Edward Robinson Squibb founded his company, ER Squibb in Brooklyn, New York, in 1856. Squibb was a lifelong crusader for safe, reliable pharmaceuticals. He formed Squibb Pharmaceuticals to produce and sell effective medicines directly to doctors. His campaign for laws governing the production of consistently pure medicines eventually contributed to the passage of the Pure Food and Drug Act by Congress in 1906, six years after his death. By then, Charles and Edward Squibb had sold the company to new owners, who had incorporated it in 1905.

With the outbreak of World War II, demand for reliable pharmaceuticals, especially antibiotics, increased enormously. In 1944 Squibb opened the world's largest penicillin production plant in New Brunswick, New Jersey. A year earlier Bristol-Myers had acquired Cheplin Laboratories, a Syracuse, New York, manufacturer of acidophilus milk (which required fermentation techniques similar to those used in the production of penicillin), and the company returned to the ethical pharmaceutical business. Throughout the war, both companies were key suppliers of penicillin to the United States War Production Board.

The Modern Pharmaceutical Company

By the end of the war both companies clearly saw that the manufacture of penicillin and other antibiotics was a huge opportunity. Both companies began to diversify.

Bristol-Myers began a program of acquiring well-managed smaller companies. One of its first acquisitions, in 1959, was Clairol, a company founded by the husband-and-wife team of Lawrence M. Gelb and Joan Gelb (Joan Gelb's professional name was Joan Clair). While on vacation in Europe, the Gelbs had purchased the rights to a French hair dye and turned it into an entire industry. Previously, virtually all hair coloring products were distributed to beauty parlors, but

In 2000 protesters gather outside Bristol-Myers Squibb headquarters in New York, objecting to what they feel are unfairly high drug prices.

In 1999 in Washington, D.C., Bristol-Myers president Charles Heimbold Jr. announces that the company will donate $100 million to the fight against AIDS in Africa. Looking on is Grace Mngumi, of Friends for Life, a group that provides counseling and medical care to people in Africa with AIDS.

the release of Miss Clairol launched the huge home-coloring market. Along with Clairol came the Gelbs' eldest son, Richard, who later became CEO of Bristol-Myers. After Clairol, Bristol-Myers acquired companies like Mead Johnson, a manufacturer of the infant formula Enfamil and other nutritional products, and Zimmer, a maker of crutches and artificial knees and hips.

During the 1950s and 1960s, Squibb also began diversifying. It used mergers and created subsidiaries to move into agricultural products, infant food, and cosmetics.

Both companies followed similar paths during the 1970s and 1980s, with breakthroughs in the treatment of cancer and high blood pressure. In 1975, Squibb researchers created Capoten—the first in a new class of antihypertensive agents called acetylcholinesterase inhibitors, which revolutionized the treatment of high blood pressure. Bristol-Myers became a pioneer in the area of chemotherapy, as well as creating the over-the-counter headache medicines Excedrin and Bufferin.

The 1989 merger of Bristol-Myers and Squibb was called a synergistic merger because the new company was much larger than the sum of its parts; the merger expanded markets for the products of both companies and gave them resources they could not command by themselves. In 1991, the National Cancer Institute awarded Bristol-Myers Squibb the contract to commercially develop the cancer-fighting compound paclitaxel. The resulting drug, Taxol, has been very effective in the treatment of advanced ovarian cancer and breast cancer. Another Bristol-Myers Squibb drug, Pravachol, has been proven to reduce the risk of first heart attacks.

Bristol-Myers Squibb is also one of the largest companies manufacturing drugs used in the treatment of AIDS. The company has come under fire from AIDS activists. For many years Bristol-Myers Squibb refused to lower its prices or release its manufacturing patents on AIDS drugs so they could be sold more cheaply in Africa and Asia, where few can afford the expensive treatments. Bristol-Myers Squibb, along with other pharmaceutical companies that make AIDS medicines, points out that the drugs are extremely expensive to develop, and it needs to make a profit. In March 2001 Bristol-Myers Squibb did agree to drop the price of its nucleoside reverse transcriptase inhibitors Videx (didanosine) and Zerit (stavudine) below cost, but the criticism of the company from activist groups like Médecins sans Frontiéres (Doctors without Borders) continues.

Further Reading

Kornberg, Arthur. *The Golden Helix: Inside Biotech Ventures.* Sausalito, Calif.: University Science Books, 1995.

Spilker, Bert. *Multinational Pharmaceutical Companies: Principles and Practices.* 2nd ed. New York: Raven Press, 1994.

Werth, Barry. *The Billion-Dollar Molecule: One Company's Quest for the Perfect Drug.* New York: Simon & Schuster, 1995.

—Lisa Magloff

See also:
Competition; Privatization; Socialism; Tourism Industry; Transportation Industry.

British Airways

British Airways is the world's largest international airline, transporting more than 30 million international passengers yearly. International travel accounts for the bulk of its business. Although several American airlines annually carry more passengers, none can match British Airways' global reach, with flights to nearly 270 destinations in 97 countries.

The airline industry is exposed to many and unpredictable influences. Fluctuations in fuel prices can destroy profits, as can sudden downturns in air travel triggered by economic hard times or military conflicts and terrorist attacks. Nonetheless, British Airways has turned a profit in most years since becoming a shareholder-owned public company in 1987.

This record of profitability is remarkable. British Airways used to be an entirely different kind of public company—one owned and managed by the British government. As a state-owned company, British Airways was not run to make a profit; instead it focused on fostering British air superiority and propping up the British industrial sector. Thus protected from market competition, it operated inefficiently. Its transition to the growing, profitable airline it has since become was a long and not entirely smooth process.

The first commercial flights in Great Britain took off in 1919, flown by a number of very small private firms that almost immediately failed. By 1924, the British government—concerned that airplane technology would never advance, given the industry's shaky financial status—consolidated four private carriers into the heavily subsidized Imperial Air, which concentrated on flying to British colonies in the Middle East, Africa, and India. In 1936 three independent British airlines merged their operations to create British Airways, which the government also began to subsidize, hoping to develop more routes into Europe. In 1939, the British government combined Imperial Air and British Airways into the state-owned British Overseas Airways Corp. (BOAC), with the objective of advancing British air technology. Following World War II, the government split BOAC into three companies—BOAC, British European Airways (BEA), and the short-lived British South American Airways—and barred any other airline from operating in Great Britain.

That policy was eventually abandoned, and by the 1960s several independent airlines were competing with BEA. Both BOAC and BEA were hamstrung by state policies requiring them to buy airplanes and supplies from more expensive British producers, and losses at both airlines led the government to merge them in 1974 as British Airways.

The merger, combined with higher fuel prices and an economic downturn, created immense problems for British Airways. In 1978 the company had 57,000 employees, who were

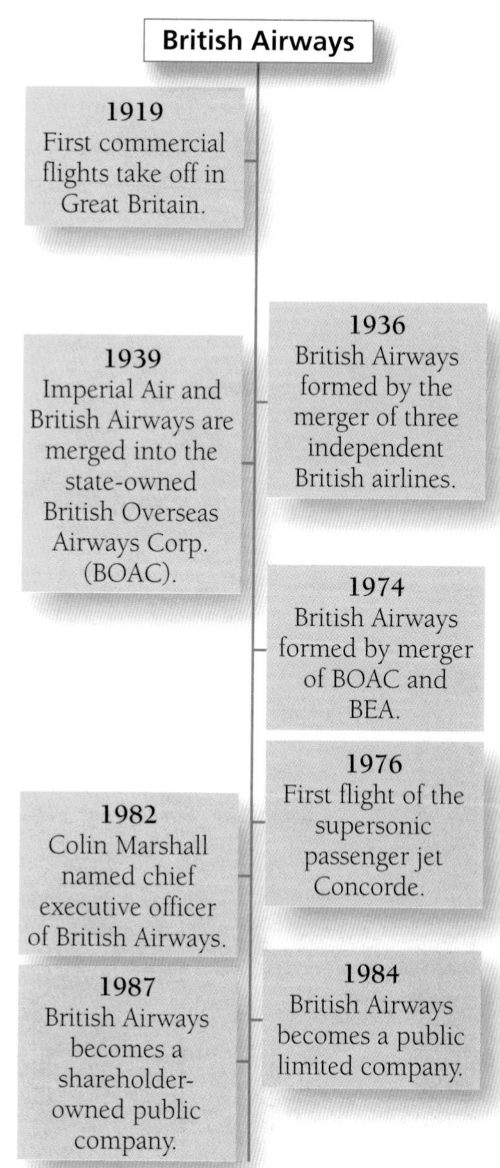

on average only 60 percent as productive as employees at other airlines. In 1977–78, strikes and labor actions cost the company 59,000 working days (a working day is one day of work by one worker). At the same time, the United States had embarked on a program of airline deregulation, raising the specter of low-cost foreign competition. British Airways executives were ill-equipped to respond to this challenge, in part because the company's top management would change whenever the political landscape shifted. A significant transformation was needed.

Change seemed certain in 1979, when England's Conservative Party was elected to power and announced plans to privatize many of Britain's industries, British Airways in particular. Privatization did not actually happen for another eight years. The government meanwhile had injected some £10 million into the company annually since the mid-1970s. Nonetheless, a sharp downturn in air travel in the early 1980s hit the overstaffed British Airways especially hard: In 1982, British Airways lost £144 million before taxes and was more than £1 billion in debt. The airline was in no shape to be sold.

The task of restoring British Airways to solvency fell to John King, who instituted a major restructuring after he became chairman of the board in February 1981. One obvious target was labor costs; King reduced the workforce from 52,300 employees in September 1981 to 37,500 in March 1983, mainly through voluntary layoffs and by offering severance packages. Although the massive job cuts did lead to some labor disputes, on the whole the reductions went smoothly, largely because of the generous severance packages and the company's well-publicized financial problems. King also reduced the number of planes, largely scrapped the costly buy-British policy (although that met with considerable political resistance), and instituted a policy of fleet standardization. In 1982, King brought on Gordon Dunlop as the airline's first-ever chief financial officer.

At London Airport in 1952, passengers board the inaugural flight of the Haviland Comet Jet. British Overseas Airways Corporation was the first airline to provide regular jet service.

First inaugurated in 1976, British Airways announced termination of its commercial supersonic service in 2003.

Also in 1982, Colin Marshall joined British Airways as chief executive officer. Like King, Marshall brought a background in business, not aviation. Marshall decided that British Airways needed to focus on customer service; he later said that most British Airways employees came from the military or the civil service, and they saw their job as simply to get airplanes safely into the sky and bring them back down again, not to satisfy customers. British Airways had long been organized into geographical divisions; Marshall reorganized it into marketing and operations divisions, giving the company more flexibility and eliminating redundancies.

Marshall also focused sharply on marketing—redecorating British Airways planes and launching major advertising campaigns. In addition, British Airways focused its marketing on certain kinds of tickets: To fill airplanes, cheap fares were offered for tourists during the late winter and early spring months. The money-losing Concorde jet, which flew faster than the speed of sound, was turned into a profit-maker by combining Concorde flights with superluxury travel packages to places like New York City.

In 1984 British Airways became a public limited company, with all its shares held by the British government. It was the first step toward becoming a truly independent company. Three years later, the shares of British Airways were tendered on the London stock exchange and the privatization was complete.

In conjunction with Air France, in 1976 British Airways made aeronautical history with the inauguration of passenger service on the Concorde, a supersonic jet. In 1979 a British Airways Concorde flight traveled from London to New York in just under three hours. In July 2000 an Air France Concorde flight crashed outside Paris due to engine failure; all 109 people on board plus four on the ground were killed. Although Concorde flights to New York resumed late in 2001, early in 2003 British Airways and Air France announced that Concorde service would end in 2003.

Further Reading

Campbell-Smith, Duncan. *The British Airways Story: Struggle for Take-off.* London: Coronet Books, 1986.

Corke, Alison. *British Airways: The Path to Profitability.* New York: St. Martin's Press, 1986.

Reed, Arthur. *Airline: The Inside Story of British Airways.* London: BBC Books, 1990.

Shibata, Kyohei. *Privatisation of British Airways: Its Management and Politics, 1982–1987.* Florence: European University Institute, 1994.

—*Mary Sisson*

Budget

A budget is a plan detailing projected income and expenses for a specific period. Such documents are used by businesses, governments, and personal households to set financial goals and determine steps by which to achieve them.

To understand the purpose and importance of budgeting, think of an Olympian trying to break the world record in the long jump. To make the attempt, the athlete must know the record in advance and use it as a benchmark against his own performance. Without this benchmark, the Olympian would not know how much time to put into training or how close he is to achieving the world record. Like an Olympian, individuals and businesses are more likely to achieve a goal that is clear and concrete. A budget sets a path for achieving that goal.

Corporate Budgeting

Successful companies use budgets for every area of the business. They use budgets for every dollar they expect to earn or spend, for the amount of inventory they expect to hold, for the number of products they expect customers to return, and even for the number of products they expect to be

See also:
Accounting and Bookkeeping; Balance Sheet; Finance, Business; Finance, Personal; Income Statement.

Income Statement
(in thousand dollars)

Revenues	*Prior year*	*Current budget*	*Responsible manager*
Northern sales	5.5	6.1	Northern regional sales manager
Southern sales	1.2	3.0	Southern regional sales manager
Eastern sales	5.8	5.5	Eastern regional sales manager
Western sales	9.7	10.0	Western regional sales manager
Total returns	–1.7	–1.5	Quality control manager
Total sales	20.5	24.6	
Expenses	*Prior year*	*Current budget*	*Responsible manager*
Cost of goods sold	–6.5	–7.0	Purchasing manager
Transportation costs	–1.2	–1.1	Transportation manager
Inventory loss	–.9	–.5	Operations manager
Salary expense	–5.2	–4.5	Human resource manager
Bonus expense	–1.2	–3.0	Human resource manager
Depreciation (M&E)	–1.5	–1.7	Operations manager
Depreciation (Plants)	–1.2	–3.0	Plant manager
Office supplies	–.4	–.2	Office manager
Insurance expense	–.1	–.1	Operations manager
Other expenses	–1.1	–.7	Operations manager
Total expenses	–19.3	–21.8	
EBIT	1.2	2.8	
Interest expense	–8	–1.3	Treasury manager
Taxes	–.2	–.2	Finance manager
Net income	.2	1.3	Chief executive officer

EBIT = Earnings Before Interest and Taxes.

A sample corporate income statement.

Balance Sheet
(in thousand dollars)

Assets	*Prior year*	*Current budget*	*Responsible manager*
Cash	2.1	3.5	Treasury manager
Inventory	4.8	2.4	Operations manager
Accounts receivable	3.5	2.0	Finance/treasury manager
Land, Plants	13.5	15.5	Plant/finance manager
Machinery, Equipment	7.2	10.0	Operations manager
Liabilities	*Prior year*	*Current budget*	*Responsible manager*
Accounts payable	1.2	1.5	Finance/treasury manager
Salaries payable	.3	.5	Human resource manager
Notes payable	9.5	7.5	Finance/treasury manager
Owner's equity	*Prior year*	*Current budget*	*Responsible manager*
Capital	15.0	15.0	Treasury manager
Retained earnings	5.1	8.9	NA

A sample corporate balance sheet.

stolen. In large companies, many managers control parts of each category. For example, the quality control manager works to achieve a low level of customer returns by ensuring that the company's products are acceptable. The higher the quality, the fewer returns and the more likely the product return category will be on budget. If the quality control manager's compensation is based on the actual return performance versus the budgeted or projected performance, the manager will try very hard to improve quality for each product. Improving the quality of its products is the company's goal: Determining a method by which to measure that quality makes the goal more obtainable.

Similarly, assume a particular salesperson is responsible for selling the company's product in a specific region. To achieve profitability, the company must sell 500 units in that region. Knowing this, the salesperson can put steps into place to achieve the goal. Without this benchmark, or budget, the salesperson's goal might be set randomly, either too low or unrealistically high.

The examples of the quality control manager and sales manager demonstrate some of the various budgeting strategies that can be used by a corporation. Budgets can be set on each section of the income statement, as well as on each section of the balance sheet and other financial statements. Each manager directs a team to work toward the planned budget daily. The manager must educate team members about what must be done to achieve budgetary goals in a given time. Team members must alert the manager about their performance, so the manager can make adjustments if necessary.

For example, if halfway through the period, a sales manager notices that her team has sales of only $2 million, knowing the budgeted goal is $5.5 million, the manager would need to implement new strategies to help the team achieve its goal. One solution could be to hire additional people to sell the product more aggressively. Another solution could be to offer prizes to the best salespeople in the second half of the period. Managers must know the budget variances at certain intervals during the period to give them more opportunities to realize their goals.

Personal Budgeting

Most individuals have one or more financial goals. A person might want to save for a house, a car, college, or retirement. A budget can help provide a solid understanding of what can be achieved. Usually, an individual knows what his or her income, or earnings, will be over a specified period. Even if an individual is paid per hour, the number of hours to be worked is usually known. Some expenses—rent, food, and utilities—are predictable; others are variable—money spent on entertainment or recreation, clothing, and medical services.

Consider the following budget for the Smith family. The Smiths earn an annual income of $100,000. The Smiths want to buy a house in one year but need $25,000 as a down payment. The Smiths have only $1,000 in the bank at the beginning of the year. The Smiths put together an annual budget to help them achieve their goal. At the end of the period, the Smiths also record the actual amount in each budget category.

The Smiths developed a budget to save $24,300 (including expected salary and subtracting all expected expenses for the year). Therefore, the Smiths expected that by the end of the year they would be able to buy their house ($1,000 already in savings + $24,300 to be saved this year = $25,300). However, looking at the actual results at the end of the year, the Smiths had saved only $18,500. They did not meet their goal and, therefore, were unable to buy a home.

The budget information at the beginning of the year is very valuable. If the Smiths were serious about buying a house at the end of the year, they certainly would not have taken an extra vacation or eaten out as much. By controlling these two expenses throughout the year, the Smiths would have had no problem achieving their goal of saving $25,000. If they wanted to save even more, they could have done many things to lower expenses, such as shop less or move to a less expensive apartment. This shows how critical and valuable creating budgets and taking the time to monitor variances are for individuals as well as for corporations.

Setting Budgets

The most difficult part of the budget process is the actual setting of the budget: Once a budget is set, the actions to be taken are fairly straightforward. Typically, managers and individuals use historical data to set the current budget. For example, if the average sales over the last few years were $2 million, the budget should

Smith Family Budget

Budget item	*Budget*	*Actual*	*Reason for variance*
Salary	$100,000	$103,000	Additional bonus
Living expenses			
Taxes	–$35,000	–$36,500	Higher salary
Rent	–$19,000	–$19,000	
Utilities (phone, heat)	–$2,800	–$2,900	Cold winter, more heat needed
Car	–$3,600	–$3,600	
Insurance	–$2,000	–$2,000	
Gas for car	–$800	–$500	Drove car less than expected
Drug store expenses	–$3,000	–$3,000	
Grocery expenses	–$2,000	–$2,000	
Entertainment expenses			
Restaurant expenses	–$500	–$3,500	Ate out more this year
Vacations	–$3,000	–$7,000	Took one extra vacation
Shopping	–$4,000	–$4,500	Bought a new wardrobe
Savings	$24,300	$18,500	

A sample family budget.

Making a family budget involves reviewing expenses and setting future goals.

estimate sales at close to $2 million. Next, the manager typically considers the latest developments and adjusts estimates. For example, if the company expects to hire more salespeople, the manager would expect sales to increase this year. Also, if customers tell the manager they expect to buy more this year, the manager will raise the budget by an appropriate amount.

Above all, however, the budget should be realistic. Failing to meet the budget could lead to major problems (for instance, a low salary for the manager or no house for the individual). Budgeting is an important activity, not only for a corporation, but also for families and individuals. Goals help people achieve success, and budgets help set those goals.

Further Reading

Burkett, Larry. *The Family Financial Workbook: A Practical Guide to Budgeting*. New York: Moody Press, 2002.

Rachlin, Robert. *Handbook of Budgeting*. New York: John Wiley & Sons, 1999.

———. *Total Business Budgeting*. New York: John Wiley & Sons, 1999.

Shim, Jae K., and Joel G. Siegel. *Budget Basics and Beyond: A Step-By-Step Guide for Nonfinancial Managers*. New York: Prentice Hall, 1994.

Welsch, Glenn A., Ronald W. Hilton, and Paul N. Gordon. *Budgeting: Profit Planning and Control*. 5th ed. New York: Prentice-Hall, 1988.

—Andréa Korb and David Korb

Building Trades

More than six million people work in the building trades, constructing and maintaining homes, factories, office buildings, roads, canals, and water and sewer pipes. Building is one of the oldest occupations, and in some respects the trades have not changed all that much from the days of the medieval craft guilds. Despite modern construction machinery, the building trades are generally still quite physically demanding, and they are among the most dangerous. Most construction work is custom work, thus mass-production techniques can only rarely be applied, so workers in the building trades must be quite skilled and usually have a high degree of autonomy.

Kinds of Employment

The building trades are generally broken into three segments: general contractors, heavy contractors, and specialty contractors. General contractors take overall responsibility for constructing buildings, which can range from single-family dwellings to schools to large office buildings. Usually a general contractor specializes in a specific kind of building. Heavy contractors work on large, usually government-funded, infrastructure projects like roads, bridges, or sewer systems. Specialty contractors perform specific tasks and are skilled craftsmen—plumbers, electricians, ironworkers, carpenters, and the like. Specialty contractors can work for general or heavy contractors, or they can run their own businesses.

Individual skills are highly valued in the building trades because much of the work is custom. Although some housing developments are built so that the houses are all quite uniform, allowing for houses to be prefabricated, for the trades as a whole, such uniformity is quite rare. Large office buildings, for example, are almost always designed so that they stand out from the buildings around them. A new road or bridge has to be built into the landscape where it is located. Workers renovating old buildings often find the unexpected when they tear into walls. A building trades worker has to be skilled enough to handle new and different building situations.

Individual worker's skill colors many aspects of the building trades. Workers in the

See also:
Human Capital; Labor Union; Occupational Safety and Health Administration; Professional Associations; Unemployment.

A carpenter frames out a roof in Phoenix, Arizona.

Building Trades Industry: Establishments, Employees, and Payroll in the Construction Industry 1999

Industry	*Establishments*	*Employees (in thousands)*	*Annual payroll (in millions of dollars)*
Building, developing, and general contracting			
Land subdivision and land development	12,383	68.0	2,814.5
Single-family housing construction	151,952	677.1	20,956.6
Multifamily housing construction	8,226	64.5	2,269.2
Manufacturing and industrial building construction	6,998	166.0	6,461.9
Commercial and institutional building construction	36,796	562.5	23,381.6
Total	216,355	1,538.1	55,883.8
Heavy construction			
Highway and street construction	11,006	248.8	11,707.0
Bridge and tunnel construction	905	35.6	1,762.5
Water, sewer, and pipeline construction	7,597	163.8	6,728.8
Power and communication transmission line construction	3,436	85.3	3,187.0
Industrial nonbuilding structure construction	696	98.6	3,844.7
All other heavy construction	15,916	216.4	8,578.0
Total	39,556	848.4	35,807.9
Carpentry and floor contractors			
Carpentry contractors	44,449	256.3	6,935.4
Floor laying and other floor contractors	13,352	71.5	2,169.1
Total	57,801	327.8	9,104.4
Special trade contractors			
Plumbing, heating, and air conditioning contractors	89,125	862.0	31,044.9
Painting and wall covering contractors	39,767	212.1	5,684.3
Electrical contractors	66,220	742.5	28,361.5
Masonry and stone contractors	24,532	182.7	5,208.9
Drywall, plastering, acoustical, and insulation contractors	21,515	312.7	9,454.2
Tile, marble, terrazzo, and mosaic contractors	6,657	43.5	1,332.2
Roofing, siding, and sheet metal contractors	30,767	257.6	7,614.4
Concrete contractors	29,870	269.2	8,718.1
Water well drilling contractors	3,789	20.5	636.8
Total	312,242	2,902.8	98,055.3
Other special trade contractors			
Structural steel erection contractors	4,945	86.6	3,199.8
Glass and glazing contractors	5,450	42.3	1,409.8
Excavation contractors	25,060	133.2	4,625.7
Wrecking and demolition contractors	1,519	19.4	703.0
Building equipment and other machinery installation contractors	4,374	73.4	3,472.6
All other special trade contractors	31,239	229.6	6,824.9
Total	72,587	584.5	20,235.7
Total, all construction	698,541	6,201.6	219,087.1

Note: Subtotals may not match totals exactly due to rounding.
Source: U.S. Census Bureau, *County Business Patterns*, annual.

building trades generally identify with their specialty rather than their employer. A plumber, for example, might work for several different contractors in a year, as well as running his own business on the side. Because the quality of tools can affect the quality of the finished work, skilled trade workers often own their own tools, which they bring to a work site. As a plumber probably knows a lot more about plumbing than the contractor who hired him, he is usually left alone to do the work and is only lightly supervised.

Another result of such specialization is that prospects for promotion within a large contracting firm are limited. Positions above the level of supervising other workers on a job site tend to be held by engineers, who can provide a structural overview of a project. Consequently many workers in the building trades start their own businesses—about 1.5 million trade workers are self-employed.

The cost of starting such a business is low: Starting a one-person contracting firm requires skills and tools, both of which the owner of the business probably already has. Such a business can easily be run out of a home. If the owner needs more workers for a particular project, he almost certainly knows people in the building trades to call and hire. As a result, thousands of contracting firms, most of which have only a few workers, are in existence. The resulting competition leads to a high rate of business turnover.

Even at the larger, more stable contracting firms, employment in the building trades tends to be unpredictable. The construction industry follows its own business cycle, which often does not synchronize with the rest of the economy. For example, low home-mortgage rates during 2000 and 2001 resulted in a high number of new homes being built—even as the economy began to slow.

Work in the building trades can be erratic even in boom times. Because bad weather can slow a construction project or make the work unsafe, relatively little building is done in the winter, and many trade workers are unemployed in that season. Even in the summer, an unexpected rainstorm can stop a project for as long as the storm lasts. Workers in the business trades are accustomed to periodic layoffs and last-minute changes in their work schedules.

In any weather, work in the building trades is more dangerous than other kinds of work. Construction employs less than 5 percent of the total U.S. workforce, but construction fatalities account for fully 20 percent of all workplace fatalities in the United States. Injury rates are likewise high, especially in trades like roofing.

Unions and Building Trades

Given the dangers inherent in the work and the general alienation from employers, workers in the building trades have long organized to protect their interests. In the United States groups representing the building trades date back to the 1790s.

Roughly 20 percent of the workforce in the building trades is unionized, but those that are nonunion are often members of employee associations like the National Association of Homebuilders. These organizations provide workers with many services like health and disability insurance that might be provided by labor unions in other

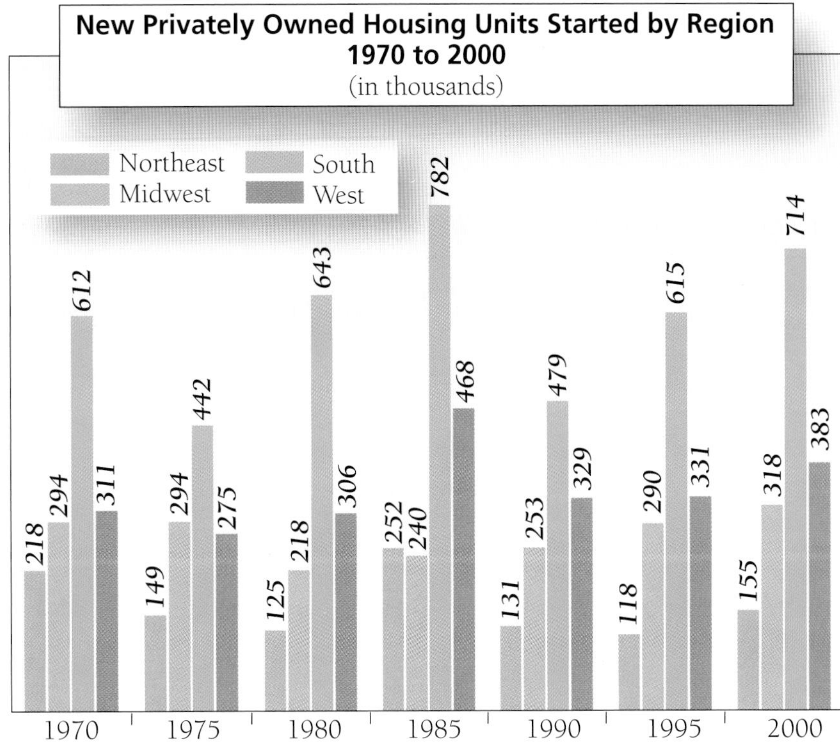

Source: Bureau of the Census, *Current Construction Reports*, Series C20, *Housing Starts*, Washington, D.C., 2001.

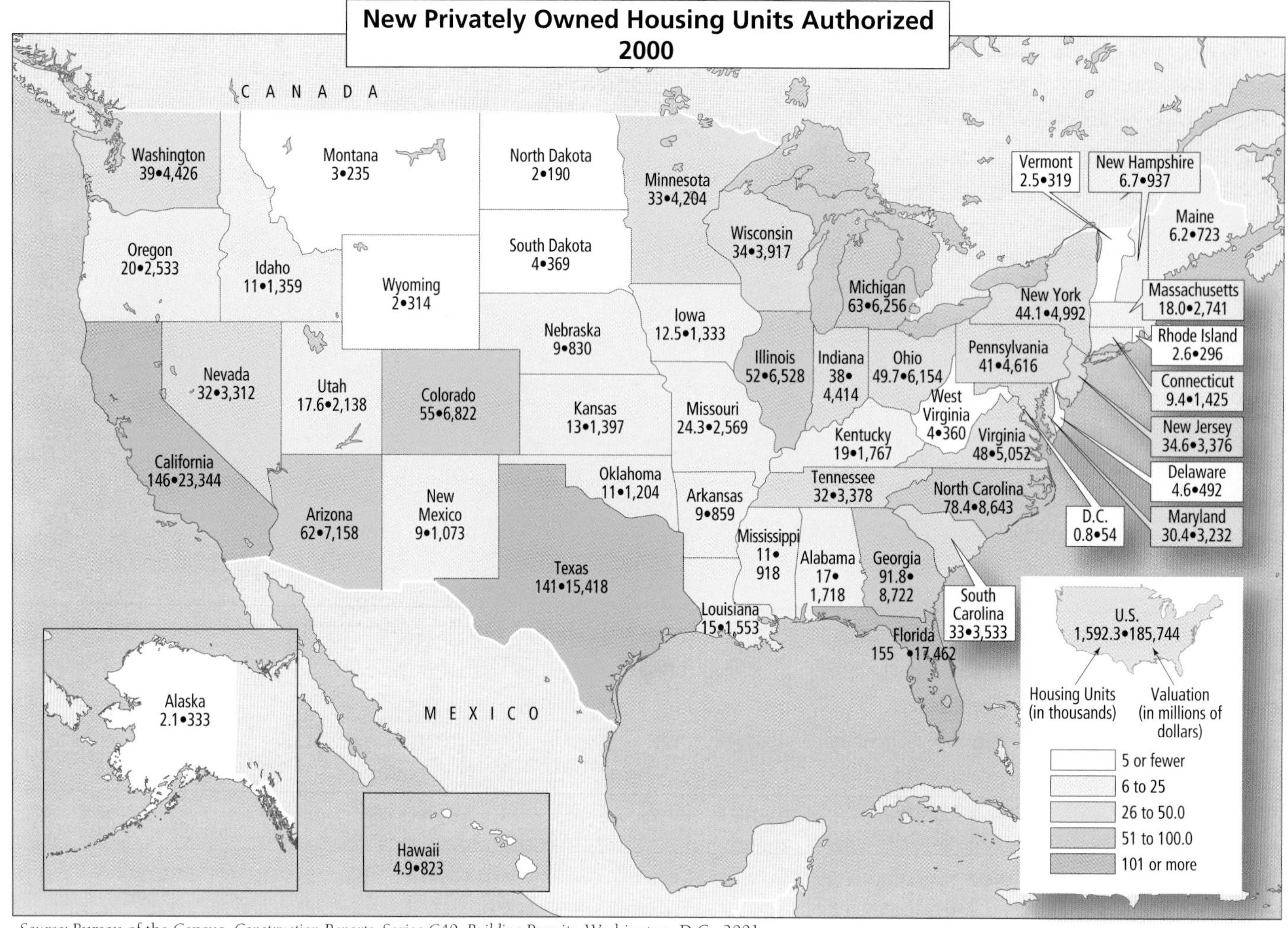

Source: Bureau of the Census, *Construction Reports,* Series C40, *Building Permits,* Washington, D.C., 2001.

Careers in the Building Trades

The building trades, with their erratic work schedules and unreliable employment, might seem like careers to avoid. However, some aspects of the work—for example, the sense of autonomy—appeal strongly to many. People in the building trades tend to work alone or in small teams, and while they may be given a particular assignment, they usually decide how best to perform it themselves. In a survey of workplace supervision, 62 percent of workers in the building trades said that they alone decide how they do their work, and fewer than 8 percent said that they are told how to do their jobs by a supervisor.

Another appealing element is the pay skilled workers receive. Work can be erratic, but skilled workers are paid well enough to tide them over periods of unemployment, and highly skilled workers are rarely unemployed long. Indeed, while unemployment in the building trades is often reported as higher than in most fields, high reported rates—which capture the layoffs that accompany the completion of specific projects—can coincide with serious worker shortages. Finally, trade workers generally take considerable pride in their skills. They also often gain great satisfaction from the projects they build, which can vary from a family's new home to a skyscraper.

The building trades generally do not require much in the way of formal education; however, trade workers have extensive skills that can take years of training to master. An electrician or plumber may have to complete an on-the-job apprenticeship that can be as long as five years. In addition, trade workers rarely go outside their specialty—a skilled carpenter, for example, will not try to wire a building for electricity.

professions. Likewise, although nonunion workers generally receive lower wages than union workers, their wages tend to be based on what union workers are getting.

As a result, the role of unions in the building trades is rather unusual. Unions are very common in certain fields of construction and quite rare in others. Generally speaking, unions dominate large and medium construction projects—the building of large office and residential complexes as well as infrastructure construction. The building and repair of single-family homes, however, is usually done with non-union labor.

Large construction projects require very specialized workers, and unions in the building trades have a significant role in training and certifying such workers. To be, say, a union electrician, a worker must complete a formal training program, including a lengthy apprenticeship. Because they participate in a uniform training process, union workers tend to have a very consistent level of skill. In addition, union workers in the building trades tend to be older and have more experience than nonunion workers, and they have a reputation for doing better-quality work in less time, which for many employers justifies the higher wage rate.

Discrimination and Building Trades

Unions can also serve to keep new workers out of a profession, and for many years the building trades were notorious for their exclusion of women and minorities. Such exclusion was especially galling because building-trade jobs generally pay well, making them desirable professions for people who want to make more money but lack a college degree.

Part of the exclusion was simple discrimination; in addition, the building trades tended and still tend to be almost clubby professions, with employers often relying on word-of-mouth from workers they already know to find new workers, and individuals sometimes getting a start by working as an assistant to a friend or relative in the business. These informal ways of getting employment can ensure that jobs in the building trades are effectively reserved for members of certain ethnicities and even certain families.

Beginning in the late 1970s, federal, state, and local governments began to demand "set-asides," requirements that a general or heavy contractor awarded a government contract agree to give a certain percentage of the business to minority- or women-owned subcontractors. Although such set-aside programs have been controversial and some have been dismantled, the number of Hispanic- and women-owned construction firms has increased dramatically. The number of black-owned firms has also risen.

From the early 1980s to the mid-1990s, the percentage of Hispanics in the building trades doubled to 11 percent (slightly more than the percentage of Hispanics in the overall population). The percentage of blacks increased only 15 percent, to almost 10 percent of trade workers, slightly less than the percentage of blacks in the overall population. The number of women in construction has also increased dramatically but remains low. Less than 4 percent of trade workers are women, and women make up a mere 2 percent of higher-paid trade workers like plumbers and electricians.

An ironworker on the job at a construction site in 2000.

Despite demographic changes among workers, the building trades themselves probably will remain a distinctive group of professions that operate more or less by their own rules. While the economy may change, building is likely to remain physical work that requires considerable skill and creativity.

Further Reading

Applebaum, Herbert. *Construction Workers, U.S.A.* Westport, Conn.: Greenwood Press, 1999.

Finkel, Gerald. *The Economics of the Construction Industry.* Armonk, N.Y.: M. E. Sharpe, 1997.

Lange, Julian E., and Daniel Quinn Mills, eds. *The Construction Industry: Balance Wheel of the Economy.* Lexington, Mass.: Lexington Books, 1979.

—*Mary Sisson*

See also:
IBM; Microsoft; Pricing; Sherman Antitrust Act.

Bundling

Bundling is a strategy of selling goods and services by offering them together in a single package. Bundling can vastly improve a company's bottom line, or it can alienate customers and spark antitrust investigations. Determining what kind of bundle to offer and how to offer it can be quite complex. While a business selling items singly must determine at which price to offer the items, a business selling bundles must also figure out what combination of items should be priced as a bundle.

Sometimes bundles are priced at a premium, as when a book dealer offers a complete set of first editions of *The Wizard of Oz*. More often, a bundle is offered at a discount to what the items would cost if purchased separately. Even with a discount, well-designed bundles can increase revenues and profits. For example, consider the "value meals" offered at fast-food restaurants like McDonald's. A value meal is a combination of a drink, fries, and a burger or a sandwich that costs slightly less than the three items would if they were purchased separately. Despite the discount, value meals increase revenues because many budget-minded customers who might otherwise buy just a burger—leaving out the fries and drink as an unnecessary expense—instead buy a value meal. Selling more fries and drinks is good for McDonald's because profits on those items are higher than profits on even an undiscounted burger.

Just like the value meal encourages the average McDonald's customer to buy more food, another popular kind of bundle—bundles of several options on a new car—encourages car buyers to purchase more options. As with the value meal, the discount is essential: A customer who might buy just two options will buy four if they are in a discounted bundle because the customer believes he is getting a deal. To the customer, the bundle is well worth buying—he is spending more, but he is getting more for his money. To the car manufacturer, the bundle is well worth offering because the average customer will spend more per car. In addition, offering standard bundles on car options can cut manufacturing costs because certain options are manufactured more economically when produced at the same time.

Another advantage of bundling is that it sometimes allows a company to raise the prices of the individual components. For example, a person who really wants call waiting on her home telephone but does

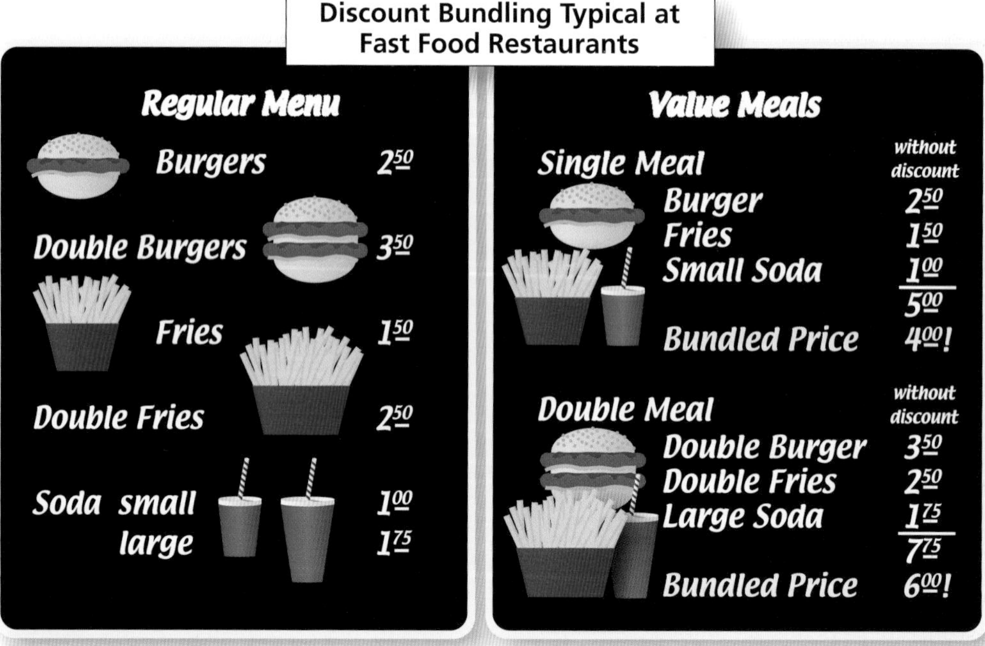

The basic economics of the bundling strategy can be seen in fast-food restaurants.

Auto dealerships commonly use bundling in selling new cars.

not want any of the other available services probably cannot afford to miss calls for a good reason. Thus, she is probably willing to pay more for call waiting as a stand-alone service. On the other hand, if she mildly wants call waiting but is not willing to pay a lot for it, she may also mildly want any number of other services and could easily be sold a bundle—especially when she sees the discount the bundle offers over buying two or three stand-alone services.

Bundling can also be used to sell supplies or services associated with the use of the device sold. Cellular phones are often sold at a very low price if customers also purchase a contract for a year of phone service. Likewise vendors of copy machines often sell servicing contracts and supplies of toner along with the machines. Such bundles are popular because consumers tend to focus on the up-front, one-time costs of the item and give less thought to the future regular charges for the service or goods.

Bundling services with goods can ease the introduction of new technology as customers feel they will not be stuck by themselves trying to figure out how to work the device. For example, a company might sell a new inventory-tracking software system bundled with the services of consultants who can help install and run it.

Bundling does not always help make sales. When the telecommunications industry was largely deregulated in 1996, many observers thought that consumers would be eager to purchase bundles of telephone, Internet, and cable television service from a single provider. Consumers, however, did not see much advantage to such bundles and did not particularly mind using different providers.

Sometimes bundles are used to encourage a person to buy something he or she does not particularly want—a toiletries manufacturer who makes a popular shampoo and an unpopular body wash might bundle the two together to promote the body wash or at least get it out of inventory. If an unwanted service or good is bundled with something that people must buy, and the person cannot opt out of the bundle, that practice is called tying. For example,

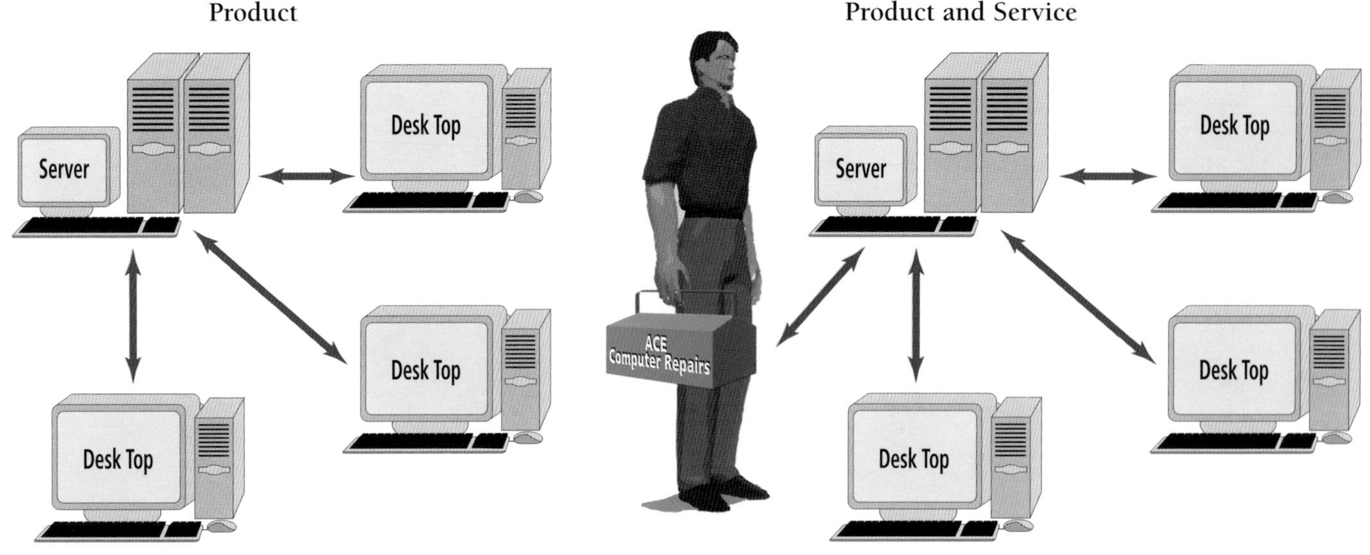

Local Area Network (LAN) equipment

LAN equipment plus installation and maintenance contract

Bundling services, like user support with computers, can be an effective way for customers to get both the technology they require and the help they need to use it.

until the practice was banned in the early 1960s, movie studios forced movie theaters to book groups of movies. If a theater wanted to show a hit film by a particular studio, it also had to pay for some flops from the same studio.

Tying tends to run afoul of antitrust laws because monopolies can use it to expand their monopoly into new areas. For example, in the early twentieth century IBM controlled most of the market for tabulating machines that ran on punch cards. The machines were complicated, and very few companies made them. The punch cards themselves, in contrast, were easy to make, and many companies could have made them. IBM, however, would not sell its machines to a company unless that company promised to buy the punch cards from IBM as well. IBM used tying to leverage its domination of the tabulating-machine industry into a domination of the punch-card industry until 1936 when the U.S. Supreme Court banned the practice.

The antitrust suit brought by the U.S. Department of Justice against Microsoft focused on tying. For years Microsoft bundled different kinds of software with its Windows operating systems, which were used on roughly 90 percent of desktop computers and often came installed with the computer—another type of bundling. The antitrust suit alleged that these were anticompetitive practices and argued that computer makers had no choice but to buy the additional software when they bought Windows and that Microsoft was attempting to leverage its operating-system monopoly into other kinds of software. Ultimately, the courts forced Microsoft to discontinue some of its most anticompetitive practices but allowed the bundling to continue. Bundling has helped Microsoft enter new software markets—further evidence of the power that can be tapped through this marketing and pricing strategy.

Further Reading

Armentano, Dominick T. *Antitrust and Monopoly: Anatomy of a Policy Failure.* 2d ed. Oakland, Calif.: The Independent Institute, 1990.

Carney, Dan, and Mike France. "The Microsoft Case: Tying It All Together." *Business Week,* December 3, 2001, 68.

Dolan, Robert J., and Hermann Simon. *Power Pricing: How Managing Price Transforms the Bottom Line.* New York: The Free Press, 1996.

—Mary Sisson

Burnett, Leo

1891–1971
Founder of Leo Burnett Company

See also:
Advertising, Business Practice; Advertising Industry; Brand Names; Trademark.

Advertising pioneer Leo Burnett operated out of the Midwest at a time when most of the successful advertising agencies were located in eastern cities. He had a double chin and wore rumpled suits when his competitors were fashionably dressed and smooth in manner. While other agencies emphasized market research that turned consumers into statistics, Burnett focused on turning buyers into believers.

These differences were perhaps the result of an atypical career path. Burnett was born in St. Johns, Michigan, in 1891 to Noble Burnett and Rose Clark. His father's dry-goods business offered the young man his first brush with advertising when he hand-lettered signs with sales and prices for display in the store window. Burnett's interest, however, was in writing, and he graduated from the University of Michigan with a degree in journalism.

Burnett worked for the *Peoria* (Ill.) *Journal* as a reporter but soon learned more money was to be had in writing advertisements for the Cadillac Motor Car Company. In 1919 Burnett joined the Homer Mckee Company, a local advertising agency in Indianapolis. Several years later he was hired by the New York firm of Erwin, Wasey and Company to head its advertising agency in Chicago. In 1935, in the middle of the Great Depression, he and several associates left Erwin, Wasey to start their own firm. Leaving his job when others had none and starting a business when others were failing was considered by many to be folly. At the time, a local newspaper writer suggested that Burnett would soon be selling apples on the street.

From the beginning, Burnett defined excellence in advertising as turning brand buyers into brand believers. One of the best examples was a client that began with Burnett in 1935, the Minnesota Valley Canning Company. The Burnett Agency created an ad campaign based not on statistics or prices but on the archetypal figure of a giant, green, benevolent man who oversaw and blessed the growing of vegetables in a magically fertile valley. The "Jolly Green Giant" campaign was so successful that Minnesota Valley Canning became the Jolly Green Giant Company. Consumers did not purchase just a can of beans, they came to believe in the brand and its logo.

In the 1950s Phillip Morris hired Burnett to increase the sales of a brand of filter cigarettes bought primarily by women. To change the image of these filter cigarettes so they would be more acceptable to male smokers, the Burnett agency focused the advertising on a rugged, virile, cowboy figure who came to be called the Marlboro Man.

The Burnett Agency continued to turn for-sale commodities into icons. For Star-Kist Tuna it created Charlie, the cartoon tuna with glasses who wisecracked about never

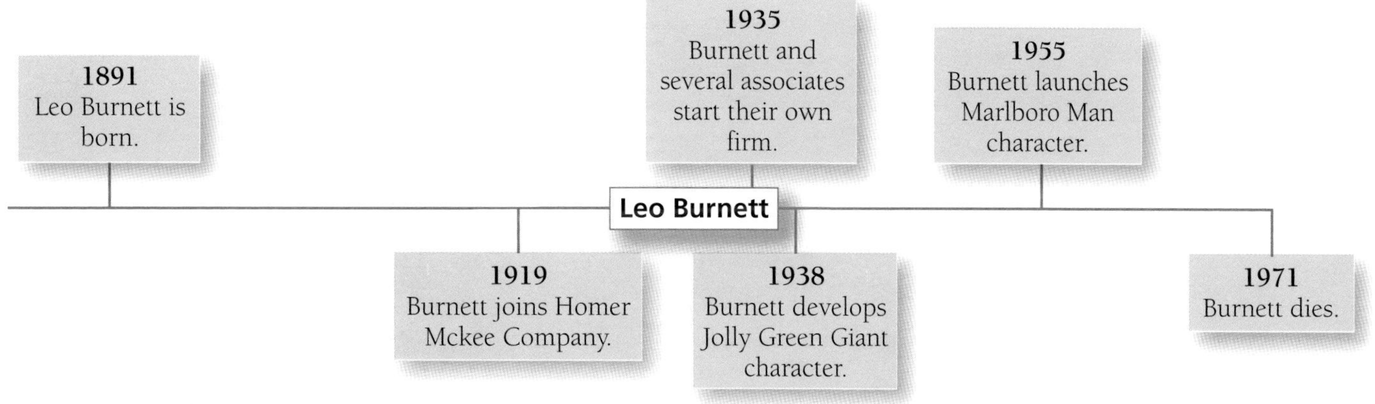

Ad man Leo Burnett, circa 1950.

being good enough to be chosen by the Star-Kist fishermen. Other Burnett-created advertising icons include Tony the Tiger (1951), the Pillsbury Doughboy (1965), and Morris the Cat (1968). These characters enjoyed very long lives as representatives of their brands, and their recognition factor allowed consumers to feel they were not just buying something so much as they were continuing a relationship.

These campaigns were also based on Burnett's belief that pictures were more important than words. This philosophy dovetailed well with the rise of television, which delivered images into millions of homes. Burnett knew that, though advertising claims made with words might be rejected by the critical thinking of a consumer, an image could bypass that inherent skepticism and connect directly with the target's subconscious. A picture could be more persuasive than an argument, partly because an image could not be refuted.

Burnett died in Lake Zurich, Illinois, in 1971, but the company he founded continues to be a leader in the advertising business. By the year 2000, Leo Burnett Worldwide had a global network of 282 operating units, employing 11,000 people. Its billings (a measurement of advertising agency success according to the cost of the advertising that clients purchase) of $8.5 billion ranked it eighth in the world.

The reception area of every Leo Burnett Agency has a bowl of fresh, red apples to remind everyone of the skepticism that greeted the company's founding. At Leo Burnett, a well-crafted picture can be worth a thousand words, as well as a share of the market.

Further Reading

Broadbent, Simon, ed. *The Leo Burnett Book of Advertising.* London: Business Books, 1984.

Burnett, Leo. *A Tribute to Leo Burnett: Through a Selection of the Inspiring Words that He Wrote or Spoke.* Chicago: Leo Burnett Co., 1971.

Fox, Stephen. *The Mirror Makers: A History of American Advertising and Its Creators.* Urbana: University of Illinois Press, 1997.

Higgins, Denis. *The Art of Writing Advertising: Conversations With William Bernbach, Leo Burnett, George Gribbin, David Ogilvy, and Rosser Reeves.* New York: McGraw-Hill/ Contemporary Books, 1986.

Jacobs, Brian, ed. *The Leo Burnett Worldwide Advertising and Media Fact Book.* Chicago: Triumph Books, 1994.

—Gary Baughn

Glossary

accounts receivable Debts owed to a business by its customers.

antitrust The process of encouraging business competition. See encyclopedia entry, Monopoly.

best practice Using companies or individuals who operate most efficiently as a business standard for comparison.

bond A certificate stating that a firm or government will pay the holder regular interest payments and a set sum upon a specific maturity date.

branding Creating an image for a person or product. See encyclopedia entry, Brand Names.

broadband A range of communication methods, including cellular phone, cable, and satellite, among others.

Chapter 11 reorganization A legal proceeding in which a business can continue to operate while it restructures its finances and pays its creditors.

commodity Any natural resource or good that is traded.

conglomerate A company that grows by merging with or buying businesses in several different industries.

copyright The exclusive ownership rights of authors, artists, or corporations to their works. See encyclopedia entry.

craft unionism The belief and practice that workers should be organized according to the specific job performed.

demographics The study of groups within a population, subdivided by age, gender, income, or other factors; related to marketing, the groups studied are buyers of specific products and services. See encyclopedia entry.

double-entry accounting The practice of recording each financial transaction in a debit account and a credit account to maintain the basic accounting equation: assets = liabilities + owner's equity.

e-commerce Conducting business transactions over the Internet.

equity (owner's equity) The amount invested in a business by the owners, as well as the cumulative profits or losses from business operations.

equity (stock) A portion of ownership in a corporation.

fixed costs Charges to a business that are not directly affected by the amount of goods or services sold.

industrial unionism The belief and practice that all workers in a particular industry, regardless of skill level, should be eligible for union membership.

insolvency A financial condition in which an individual is unable to pay his or her debts as they come due or a condition in which liabilities exceed assets.

inventory The supply of goods held by a business.

liquidity The ease with which assets can be converted into cash without a decline in value. See encyclopedia entry, Assets and Liabilities.

market share Percentage of all dollars spent on a product or service that a specific company earns for that product or service; the proportion of a particular market dominated by a specific company.

monopoly Type of market that involves only one seller. See encyclopedia entry.

note payable An IOU created when a business fails to pay a bill on time and signs a promissary note promising to pay the debt.

note receivable An IOU owed to a business for a purchase.

option The right to sell a stock, bond, or other financial instrument within a designated period at a set price.

patent Exclusive rights to a new product or invention for a set period. See encyclopedia entry.

profit The amount left over after the cost of doing business has been subtracted. See encyclopedia entry, Profit and Loss.

quota A predetermined limit on the amount of foreign goods that can enter a country.

residual value The value of an asset at the end of its expected usefulness.

reverse discrimination The argument that if certain individuals are favored in matters like employment and university admissions, others must necessarily be discriminated against.

security Stocks, bonds, and other financial instruments.

subsidy Financial assistance from government to a business.

sustainable agriculture A method of farming that attempts to minimize human impact on the environment.

tariff Tax on imported goods.

time-value of money The fact that money loses value over time. For example, one dollar of income today is more valuable than one dollar of income five years from now.

trade deficit When a nation buys more from abroad than it sells. See encyclopedia entry, Balance of Trade.

trademark A unique symbol or design associated with a product or service. See encyclopedia entry.

trade surplus When a nation sells more goods to other nations than it buys from other nations.

unearned revenue An accounting liability created when a customer pays in advance for a good or service.

variable costs Charges to a business that are directly related to the amount of goods or services sold.

Index

Page numbers in **boldface** type indicate complete articles. Page numbers in *italic* type indicate illustrations or other graphics.